More praise for *Booking Passage*

"Those of us with Irish ancestry will find this an appealing account of family, faith, destiny, and why so many Americans wish they were Irish, too." —Dan R. Barber, *Dallas Morning News*

"A master of the contemplative amble. . . . There is enough poetry in the writing of it, both in verse and in prose, that a reader cannot come away from it without knowing what Lynch is about. . . . Hearing Lynch's story . . . one can gain wisdom for one's own journey, Irish or not." —Marta Salij, *Detroit Free Press*

"A thoughtful rumination on what it means to be Irish-American. Part memoir, part cultural study, always exquisitely written, Lynch introduces fascinating insights into the strong pull Ireland has on America." —Len Cowgill, *BookSense Picks*

"In *Booking Passage: We Irish and Americans*, [Lynch] draws an enticing picture of his home away from home: the dreamlike environs of Moveen, County Clare. . . . The book's sentimentality cannot extinguish its lyricism and its appealing spiritual vigor." —Joseph O'Neill, *New York Times Book Review*

"He writes with grace, a questioning attitude and wry humor. . . . *Booking Passage* captured my imagination." —*Irish American News*

"Lynch's book is full of incident, touching and hilarious, and repays serious attention. It is a good read even for those who have not the least ancestral or national bias—for those who desire civilized entertainment along with brilliant narrative."

—Clarence Brown, *Seattle Times* and *Seattle Post*

"Compelling. . . . This is a deeply thought-out book filled with poetry, pathos, triumph and lots of Irish laughter."

—*Publishers Weekly*

"This book's essays will appeal particularly to an owner of a long-standing family home, an Irish American drawn to the old country, a Catholic in crisis from the church's scandals, and an appreciator of poetry. . . . Lynch's perspective is both rhapsodic and real . . . throughout he offers wit and wisdom. . . . At the feet of such a well-spoken writer, many a listener/reader would sit happily."

—Olive Mullet, *Grand Rapids Press*

"Lynch's book is especially strong where he passionately analyzes contemporary Ireland, with a sharp-eyed focus on the transformation of the Catholic Church's place in Irish life. . . . Lynch writes with perception and feeling about traditional Irish music . . . he is always interesting and authoritative on the subject of death."

—Terence Winch, *Wilson Quarterly*

Booking Passage was chosen by the Library of Michigan as a 2006 Michigan Notable Book.

"In *Booking Passage*, Thomas Lynch's 'romance with words,' realized as an altar boy responding in Latin, becomes a full-blown love affair in his prose about Ireland and fellow poets and what he thinks of the Church. His style has energy that takes my breath away it's so fresh and unexpected."   —Elmore Leonard

"With *Booking Passage: We Irish and Americans*, Tom Lynch proves yet again why he is one of the most important writers in the English language. Whether writing of the wonders of indoor plumbing added to his ancestral home in County Clare, or of a solemn funeral procession in the American desert southwest, or of a young man's quest for a job in Dublin, Mr. Lynch reveals time and again, in a voice riven with joy and sorrow and, above all, wisdom, what it means not just to be American or Irish, but human. I wish Tom Lynch wrote more books, because no matter what he writes—whether essays or poems—I am made better for it."

—Bret Lott, author of *A Song I Knew by Heart* and *Jewel*

"Thomas Lynch is one of our indispensable essayists, a master of skeptical realism and tragicomic relief. The true subject of this generous, rowdy book is Lynch's own wonderful mind, as it bobs and weaves, making connections between the personal and the tribal, history and the present moment, in language that is gorgeous and consistently apt."

—Phillip Lopate, author of *Getting Personal*
and *Waterfront: A Journey Around Manhattan*

"*Booking Passage* touches on Irish-American themes which are so fundamental that one wonders why they haven't been explored this revealingly until now. But, then, who else could match Thomas Lynch's perfect balance of American buoyancy and deflating (not to mention self-disparaging) Irish wit, tempering Irish doom with American optimism, romantic Irishness with American realism? The result is a book precisely true to the temperament and temperature of Irish-American relations, the annals of a master."

—Dennis O'Driscoll

BY THOMAS LYNCH

POETRY

Skating with Heather Grace

Grimalkin & Other Poems

Still Life in Milford

NONFICTION

The Undertaking—Life Studies from the Dismal Trade

Bodies in Motion and at Rest—On Metaphor and Mortality

Booking Passage

We Irish & Americans

THOMAS LYNCH

W. W. NORTON & COMPANY

NEW YORK · LONDON

For information about permission to reproduce selections from this book, write to
Permissions, W. W. Norton & Company, Inc., 500 Fifth Avenue, New York, NY 10110

Manufacturing by R. R. Donnelley Harrisonburg
Book design by Chris Welch Design
Production manager: Julia Druskin

Library of Congress Cataloging-in-Publication Data

Lynch, Thomas, 1948–
Booking passage : we Irish and Americans / Thomas Lynch.—1st ed.
p. cm.
Includes bibliographical references (p.   ).
ISBN 0-393-04206-5 (hardcover)
1. Clare (Ireland)—Social life and customs. 2. Lynch, Thomas, 1948– —Travel—Ireland.
3. Clare (Ireland)—Emigration and immigration. 4. Clare (Ireland)—Description and
travel. 5. Americans—Ireland. 6. Irish Americans. I. Title.
DA990.C59L96 2005
305.891'62073—dc22
2005004429

ISBN-13: 978-0-393-32857-8 pbk.
ISBN-10: 0-393-32857-0 pbk.

W. W. Norton & Company, Inc., 500 Fifth Avenue, New York, N.Y. 10110
www.wwnorton.com

W. W. Norton & Company Ltd., Castle House, 75/76 Wells Street, London W1T 3QT

1 2 3 4 5 6 7 8 9 0

This book is for

PATRICK LYNCH AND MICHAEL HEFFERNAN
Brethren, Boyos

and for

P.J., BREDA, AND LOUISE ROCHE
Friends for Life

I think, as far as the Irish people are concerned, it will be necessary to study the priests, the politicians, the publicans and the peasants. I omit hotel-keepers, the garage proprietors, the shop-keepers, the dairymen and the boarding house keepers, because in every country these types openly fly the flag of commercial piracy and even the most ignorant tourist will not fail to recognize them and to beware of them. However, if I discover, in my examination, any particular local eccentricity, I am going to set it down.

—from *A Tourist's Guide to Ireland,* by Liam O'Flaherty

What we call monsters are not so to God who sees in the immensity of his work the infinity of forms that he has comprised in it; and it is for us to believe that this figure that astonishes us is related and linked to some other figure of the same kind unknown to man. From his infinite wisdom there proceeds nothing but that is good and ordinary and regular; but we do not see its arrangement and relationship.

—from "Of a Monstrous Child," by Michel de Montaigne

I had a vision, or a nightmare, the other night. Dreamt I went to the Patents Office in Dublin Castle to try to patent being Irish. I had drawn up a very detailed specification. You see, I want this unique affectation protected by world right. I am afraid of my life that other people will find out being Irish pays and start invading our monopoly. I am not sure that certain sections of the population in America have not already infringed our immemorial rights in this regard. I did not get very far with the stupid officials I saw. They held that copyright did not subsist in being Irish and more or less suggested that it was open to any man to be Irish if he chose, and to behave in an Irish way.

—from "Bones of Contention" in the *Nationalist and Leinster Times,*
by George Knowall (aka Myles na Gopaleen,
aka Flann O'Brien, aka Brian O'Nolan)

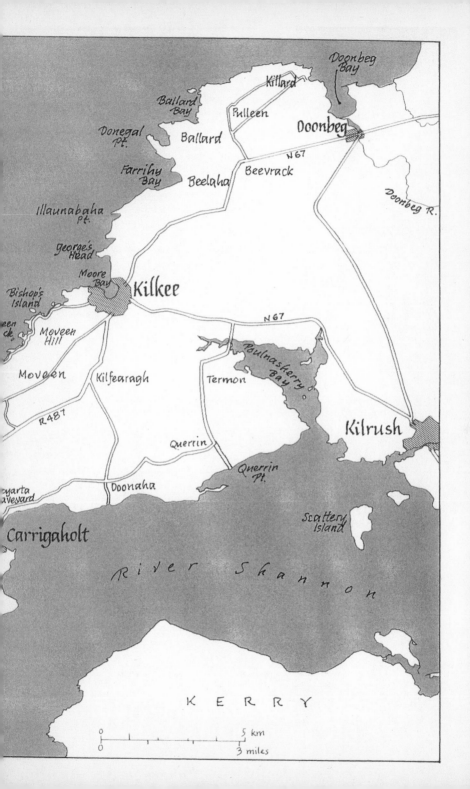

Contents

Fit & Start

I'M COMING THE coast road into Moveen. This part replays itself over and over to a standstill, until I'm hardly moving. Out in the ocean are islands I've never seen in the pictures I have of this place. I take this as a signal I'm dreaming.

It is early morning. I've been flying all night. The air is sparkling, dewy, and new. I've landed safely and am on the last leg of the journey.

Gulls diving everywhere are the souls of the dead, rising in the wind, hailing me by the working of their wings: Nora and Tommy, my mother and father, Mary Maloney and her brother Sean, sometimes Sam Curtin, Johnny Hickey, Peg and Siney Burns, the brothers Hedderman, Danny Gorman, Kant Lynch, that one-eyed man, the pink Collins sisters, Bridey and Mae, and their brother Patrick. Patrick was a lovely dancer.

Sometimes they set to dancing in the dream, the Caledonia, the thump of their boots on broad flagstones mixes with the music in the updrafts of air. Andrew McMahon and Patrick Murray. And John Joe, J. J. McMahon's ancient father. Haughs and Walshes, Deloughreys and O'Deas, and Paddy Mullany, a saintly class of a man, and lately Tom and Catherine Collins's boy, killed by a tractor gone astray—all of them circling and dancing and diving among the islands. The sea is rising now, silver blue, the gulls are dancing everywhere.

And everything is becoming new again and known. The Holy Well and Bishop's Island, the quarry and the rising, falling cliffs, then finally that curl in the road before Dunlicky, where the vista opens to the whole southwestern narrowing of land to its peninsular denouement at Loop Head. I stop and look and listen here, where in the year of "three eights," some cousins of mine were swept into the sea by a freak wave whilst they were collecting sea grass for the gardens or the dinner. There's a new stone here to mark the place and time where, twenty-some years ago, two boys from Cork drove off the cliffs on motorbikes. Nora wrote with word of the misadventure. "Drink," as she told it, "had been taken."

Sometimes in the dream my youngest son, Sean, is painting that picture of Murray's Island—the fourteen-acre stone that rises two hundred feet out of the ocean and has always looked to me from the landside like a great gray whale turning in the sea. Poor farmers, it is said, used to graze their sheep on this rock. They rowed out in curraghs to the sloping western side. Was I told that in a dream? Now it is mostly rookery. And Sean is stationed by a heap of rocks—all that is left of Dunlicky Castle. He has his canvas and his oils and his brushes. His sister, Heather, stands in the tall grass taking photos while his brothers, Mike and Tommy, are fishing the cliffs. Shoals of mackerel ruffle on the soft sea. Mary is back at the house making tea. Sitting above the mantel now, the painting was done when Sean was the age I was when I first came here, when this coast road first began to appear and reappear in the space between my waking and sleeping.

The road slopes downward to Moveen, past the fisherman's cottage gone to ruins at Goleen, where a stream slips under the road, down the rock ledges into the sea. Smoke curls from P. J. Roche's chimney, his mare and filly foal grazing in the field by Goleen. I make left at the bottom of the hill and back the narrow road past the fields and cattle and households of neighbors—Mahanys, Murrays, Keanes, McMahons, and Carmodys, Downses and Carmodys again. A mile from the sea, I'm at the gate I stood at all those years ago for the first time, home.

When I wake from all of this, the cry of gulls gives way to bird whistle. The roar of the sea is the morning's early traffic. The kettle gives way to the coffee machine. I go online to Clare FM and wait for the noontime news with Noel Fogarty. It's 7 A.M. in Milford, Michigan. There's news of the world, the country, and the county with the weather forecast and death notices. After news of the war and protests at Shannon, the gridlock in Ennis, and the chance of dry spells predicted for the evening, "Clare FM regrets to announce the following deaths." Noel's voice is proper and calm and among the sad details most recently: "Michael Murray, Moveen West, removal from Lillis Funeral Home, Kilkee, to St. Mary's Church, Carrigaholt, to Moyarta Cemetery. May they rest in peace."

The Lord have mercy on him, Michael was a quiet, decent man who farmed the westernmost acres of Moveen—high, dry pasturage and a herd of Friesians—then turned the spread over to his son, P. J., and built his retirement home by the road where he and Mary could live out their years. I'd often see him on my walks, painting the garden wall, working with his grandson in the yard, checking the fences around the cliffside fields. We'd have a little chat and go our ways. That was my last sight of him, last April, working his way down the land toward the sea to check on the yearlings grazing there—a Moveen man in his field, among his cattle, the sun divided by the evening clouds, the huge sea gone silver before him there on the western edge of his world.

My Mary and I send flowers and sympathies, through John and Martha Howard at Lillis's, to Michael's Mary and their family. We are, as is said there, "sorry for their troubles."

I COUNT, BY my passports current and expired, thirty-some crossings in thirty-some years between my home in Michigan and my home in Moveen. I owe to both places my view of the world, my sense of my self, whatever I know about life and times. In Michigan I am the local funeral director in a northwestern suburb of Detroit. In Moveen I am the every-so-often Yank who writes and walks and is related to the old woman, dead with years now, who lived here too. What once seemed different, distant worlds entirely, altogether other lives, now seem like different rooms of the one house, branches of the one family, one language spoken in a blend of local brogues.

THE RITUAL OF RETURN remains unchanged. I stop in Kilkee for bits and pieces, the latest paper, matches, bread and milk and tea. At the Central Stores, Marion gives me the latest news.

"Christina Clancy died at Christmastime, addressing cards at the kitchen table. She was so good. The funeral was huge."

"It was, I suppose."

"And young Gabriel McMahon in February, the poor man, of a cancer, and left a family."

"I saw that in the *Champion*. How very sad."

I consider my options at the roundabout at the bottom of O'Curry Street, then drive 'round the West End esplanade to the sign on the left marked, SCENIC ROUTE, which takes me uphill past the last row of new homes, out this coast road around the north edge of Moveen. It is always fresh and new to me—this treeless, edgy, thick-grassed landscape falling into the ocean, washed by the wind and rain and tides—and I am put in mind of the first time and the last time I was here. I'm giving out with bits of songs now, scraps of poems, lines from old sayings—talking to myself almost liturgically, as if though alone here I am not alone, though distant from home I am home all the same, as if my being here has meaning beyond the sureties. I mark changes in the near term and the far and arrive by turns at the gate of the home my people and I claim as our own, persuaded that we are all what Nora Lynch used to say we are—"just passing through life."

I'm passing through.

The Ethnography of Everyday Life

THE CENTER FOR the Ethnography of Everyday Life at the University of Michigan invited me to present at their recent conference, "Doing Documentary Work: Life, Letters and the Field."

Where I come from, upstream on the Huron from smart Ann Arbor, we rarely offload words like *ethnography* unless we are appearing before the zoning board of appeals or possibly trying to avoid jury duty. All the same, I thanked the organizers and said I would be happy, etc., honored, of course, and marked the dates and times in my diary.

To be on the safe side, I looked it up—*ethnography*—and it says, "The branch of anthropology that deals with the description of various racial and cultural groups of people." And *anthropology*— I looked that up too—is "the study of the origin, the behavior, and the physical, social and cultural development of human beings."

Anthology—"a gathering of literary pieces, a miscellany, an assortment or catalogue"—is on the same page as *anthropology*. It comes from the Greek, as students are told, for "gathering flowers." As the man in that movie about the big fat wedding says, everything comes from the Greek for something else.

Dictionaries are like that—you go in for a quick hit of ethnography and come out with flowers by the bunch. Two pages east and you've got *Antigone*, "the daughter of Oedipus and Jocasta, in Greek mythology, who performed funeral rites over her brother's body in defiance of the king" at Thebes. That ancient city's on the same page as *theater* and *theatre*, which have several definitions all derived from the Greek "to watch." Think of "the milieu of actors and playwrights." Think Mrs. Patrick Campbell. Think Sophocles.

At the Abbey Theatre in Dublin, just last week, a new version of *Antigone* called *The Burial at Thebes* opened to great reviews in the Irish papers. One commentator claimed that Creon the king was like President George W. Bush, caught in a conflict he'd a hand in making. How's that for ethnography and everyday? How's that for life, letters, and the field?

I avoided the quagmire of *milieu*, suspect as we are lately of anything French, but looked up *human* and *human beings* and got what you'd guess, but came across *humic*, which sent me to *humus*, which has to do with "a layer of soil that comes from the decay of leaves and other vegetation and which contains valuable plant food." It is a twin of the Latin word—because everything in our house came from Latin, except for the *Kyrie*—for soil, earth.

Which put me in mind of a book I'd been reading by Robert Pogue Harrison, *The Dominion of the Dead*, in which he speaks about our "humic density"—we human beings, shaped out of earth, fashioned out of dirt, because we are primally bound to the ground our shelters and buildings and monuments rise out of and our dead are buried in. Everything—architecture, history, religion—"rooted" in the humus of the home place and to the stories and corpses that are buried there.

Thus was I shown, in my first days in West Clare years ago, the house and haggard, hay barn and turf-shed, cow cabins and out-offices, gateposts, stone walls, fields and wells and ditches, forts and gaps, church and grave vault, names and dates in stone—all the works and days of hands that belonged to the people that belonged to me, all dead now, dead and gone back to the ground out of which arose these emblements of humic density.

The awareness of death that defines human nature is insepa-rable from—indeed it rises from—our awareness that we are not self-authored, that we follow in the footsteps of the dead. Everywhere one looks across the spectrum of human cul-tures one finds the foundational authority of the predeces-sor. . . . Whether we are conscious of it or not we do the will of the ancestors: our commandments come to us from their realm; their precedents are our law; we submit to their dic-tates, even when we rebel against them. Our diligence, hardi-hood, rectitude, and heroism, but also our folly, spite, rancor, and pathologies, are so many signatures of the dead on the contracts that seal our identities. We inherit their obsessions; assume their burdens; carry on their causes; promote their mentalities, ideologies, and very often their superstitions; and very often we die trying to vindicate their humiliations.

—*The Dominion of the Dead*, pages ix–x, Robert Pogue Harrison

Isn't that just like people? Ethnographically speaking? Or anthropologically? To think of the place where their ancients lived and worked, fought, believed, and are buried as sacred, central to their own identity.

So we're back to burials again—Antigone and Thebes. Creon and Bush. Do you suppose that humus is good for flowers?

Such is the trouble with the everyday—one thing leads to another. You start out with ethnography and end up with flowers, like the paperwhite narcissus my true love grows every Christmas from bulbs she buries in a kitchen pot, or the crocuses that press through the litter of old leaves, pine needles, melting snow, and warming soil every year in April up here at the lake. The everyday, predictable, measurable truth assumes a routine that we think we can study: how the seasons change, the moon runs through its phases, the sun rises earlier every day. "April showers," we say, "red sky at morning." Monday begets Tuesday, which in turn begets . . . well, you get it. We make our plans upon such reliable sciences. "Home by Friday, with the help of God," I tell my darling on the way out the door.

MAYBE YOU WANT to know what I said at the conference?

I said it looked like "a paradigm shift." (They were paying me a handsome honorarium.) I said it looked like a paradigm shift, from a sense of holy ground and grounding, to a kind of rootlessness—spiritually, ethnographically, anthropologically speaking, humanity-wise. At which point in the proceedings I removed from my bag and placed upon the table by the lectern from which I was holding forth, a golf-bag cremation urn. Molded, no doubt, out of some new-age resin or high-grade polymer, it stands about fourteen inches high and looks like everyone's idea of the big nut-brown leather bag with plump pockets and a plush towel and precious memories in which "Dad" or "Grandpa" or "Good Old [insert most recently deceased golf-buddy's nickname]" would have kept his good old golf clubs. The bottom of the golf-bag urn is fashioned to look like the greensward of a well-maintained fairway. So the whole thing looks like a slice of golf heaven. There is even a golf ball resting beside the base of the bag, waiting for the erstwhile golfer to chip it up for an easy putt. The thing is hollow, the better to accommodate the two hundred-some cubic centimeters, give or take, most cremated human beings will amount to.

I confess that the idea of the urn only came to me at the last moment, because I wanted to see the looks on their faces. It's a character flaw, based upon my own lack of scholastic pedigree. Except for an honorary doctorate in humanities from the university I never managed to graduate from—though the Dear knows I paid for many classes—I hold no degree. I'm not bachelor, master, or doctor of anything, and though I was "certified" in mortuary science by a regionally respected university, a battery of state and national board exams, and the completion of a requisite apprenticeship, I'm self-conscious about standing before a room full of serious students and scholars. It is this fear—surely every human has it—of being exposed as a fraud that makes one eager to supply a diversion. Thus the urn: if I could not *earn* their respect, I'd . . . well, never mind.

Still, I wanted to see the looks on their faces when I presented, as an article of documentary consequence, as an anthropological artifact, as a postmodern relic of a species that had accomplished pyramids, the Taj Mahal, and Newgrange, the ethnographically denatured and, by the way, chemically inert, plastic golf-bag-shaped cremation urn. It's one of a kind. It came from a catalogue. There's also one that looks like a pair of cowboy boots—a "companion" urn for "pardners"—and one that looks like a duck decoy for hunters or possibly naturalists: variations on the theme of molded plastics. So I wanted to tell them about the paradigm shift that it signified.

I came up burying Presbyterians and Catholics, devout and lapsed, born-again and backslidden Baptists, Orthodox Christians, an occasional Zen Buddhist, and variously observant Jews. For each of these sets, there were infinite subsets. We had right old Calvinists who only drank single malts and were all good Masons and were mad for the bagpipes, just as we had former Methodists who worked their way up the Reformation ladder after they married into money or made a little killing in the market. We had Polish Catholics and Italian ones, Irish and Hispanic and Byzantine, and Jews who were Jews in the way some Lutherans are Lutheran—for births and deaths and first marriages.

My late father, himself a funeral director, schooled me in the local orthodoxies and their protocols as I have schooled my sons and daughter who work with me. There was a kind of comfort, I suppose, in knowing exactly what would be done with you, one's ethnic and religious identities having established long ago the fashions and the fundamentals for one's leave-taking. And while the fashions might change, the fundamental ingredients for a funeral were the same—someone who has quit breathing forever, some others to whom it apparently matters, and someone else who stands between the quick and dead and says something like, "Behold, I show you a mystery."

"An act of sacred community theatre," Dr. Thomas Long, writer, thinker, and theologian, calls this "transporting" of the dead from this life to the next. "We move them to a further shore. Everyone has a part in this drama." The dead get to the grave or fire or tomb whilst the living get to the edge of a life they must learn to live without them. Ours is a species that deals with death (the idea of the thing) by dealing with our dead (the thing itself).

Late in the twentieth century, there was some trending toward the more homegrown doxologies. Everyone was into the available "choices." We started doing more cremations—it made good sense. Folks seemed less "grounded" than their grandparents, more "portable," "divisible," more "scattered" somehow. We got into balloon releases and homing pigeons done up as doves to signify the flight of the dead fellow's soul toward heaven. "Bridge Over Troubled Water" replaced "How Great Thou Art." And if Paul's Letter to the Romans or the Book of Job was replaced by Omar Khayyam or Emily Dickinson, what harm? "After great pain, a formal feeling comes," rings as true as any sacred text. A death in the family is, as Miss Emily describes it: "First—Chill—then Stupor—then the letting go."

Amidst all the high fashions and fashion blunders, the ritual wheel that worked the space between the living and the dead still got us where we needed to go. It made room for the good laugh, the good cry, and the power of faith brought to bear on the mystery of mortality. The dead were "processed" to their final dispositions with a pause sufficient to say that their lives and their deaths truly mattered to us. The broken circle within the community of folks who shared blood or geography or belief with the dead was closed again through this "acting out our parts," as Reverend Long calls it. Someone brought the casseroles, someone brought the prayers, someone brought a shovel or lit the fire, everyone was consoled by everyone else. The wheel that worked the space between the living and the dead ran smoothly.

Lately I've been thinking that the wheel is broken or gone a long way off the track or must be reinvented every day. The paradigm is shifting. What with distanced communities of faith and family, the script has changed from the essentially sacred to the essentially silly. We mistake the ridiculous for the sublime.

Take Batesville Casket Company, for example. They make caskets and urns and wholesale them to funeral homes all over the globe. Their latest catalogue, called "Accessories," includes suggested "visitation vignettes"—the stage arranged not around Cross or Crescent or Star of David but around one of Batesville's "life-symbols" caskets featuring interchangeable corner hardware. One "life-symbol" looks like a rainbow trout jumping from the corners of the hardwood casket, and for dearly departed gardeners, there is one with little plastic potted mums. There is the "sports dad" vignette done up like a garage with beer logos, team pennants, hoops, and hockey skates and, of course, a casket that looks a little like a jock locker gone horizontal. There's one for motorcyclists and the much-publicized "Big Mama's Kitchen," with its faux stove, kitchen table, and apple pie for the mourners to share with those who call. Instead of Methodists or Muslims, we are golfers now; gardeners, bikers, and dead bowlers. The bereaved are not so much family and friends or coreligionists as fellow hobbyists and enthusiasts. And I have become less the funeral director and more the memorial caddy of sorts, getting the dead out of the way and the living assembled within a theatre that is neither sacred nor secular but increasingly absurd—a triumph of accessories over essentials, of stuff over substance, gimmicks over the genuine. The dead are downsized or disappeared or turned into knickknacks in a kind of funereal karaoke.

Consider the case of Peter Payne, dead at forty-four of brain cancer. His wife arranged for his body to be cremated without witness or rubric, his ashes placed in the golf-bag urn, the urn to be placed on a table in one of our parlors with his "real life"—which is to say, "life-size" golf bag standing beside it for their son and daughter and circle of friends to come by for a look. And if nobody said, "Doesn't he look natural?" several commented on how much he looked like, well, his golf bag. The following day, the ensemble was taken to the church, where the minister, apparently willing to play along, had some things to say about "life being like a par-three hole with plenty of sand traps and water hazards"—to wit, all too short and full of trouble. And heaven was something like a "19th Hole," where, after "finishing the course," those who "played by the rules" and "kept an honest score" were given their "trophies." Then those in attendance were invited to join the family at the clubhouse of Mystic Creek Golf Course for lunch and a little commemorative boozing. There is already talk of a Peter Payne Memorial Golf Tournament next year. A scholarship fund has been established to send young golfers to PGA training camp. Some of his ashes will be scattered in the sand trap of the par-five hole on the back nine with the kidney-shaped green and the dogleg right. The rest will remain, forever and ever, perpetual filler for the golf-bag urn.

Whether this is indeed a paradigm shift, the end of an era, or, as Robert Pogue Harrison suggests, an "all too human failure to meet

the challenges of modernity," is anyone's guess. But we are
nonetheless required, as he insists, to choose "an allegiance—
either to the posthuman, the virtual, and the synthetic, or to the
earth, the real and the dead in their humic densities."

"So, which will it be?" I posed rhetorically to the audience (which
seemed oddly fixed upon the *objet de mort*). "The golf bag urn?"
(read posthuman, virtual, and synthetic) "or some humus—the
ground and graveyard, village, nation, place or faith—the nitty-
gritty real earth in which human roots link the present to the past
and future?"

They looked a little blankly at me, as if I'd held up five fingers
and asked them what the square root of Thursday was. There was
some shifting in seats, some clearing of throats. I thought I might
have numbed them with the genius of it or damaged them in some
nonspecific way.

I thought about wrapping up with a little joke about a widow
who brings her cheapskate husband's ashes home, pours them out
on the kitchen table, and begins to upbraid him for all those things
she asked for but he never gave her—the mink coat, the convert-
ible, etc.—but thought better of it and closed instead with an invitation to engage in a little Q & A on these and any other themes
they might like to pursue. A man in the second row, whose eyes
had widened when I produced the urn and who had not blinked
or closed his mouth since the thing appeared, raised his hand to
ask, "Is there anyone in there?"

"Why, no, no, of course not, no," I assured him.

There was a collective sigh, a sudden flash of not-quite-know-
ing smiles, and then the roar of uneasy silence, like a rush of air
returned to the room.

The director of the Center for the Ethnography of Everyday Life hurriedly rose to thank me for "a thought-provoking presentation," led the assembled in polite applause, and announced that the buffet luncheon was ready and waiting in a room across the hall. Except for a man who wanted to discuss his yet-to-be-patented "water-reduction method" of body disposition, there was no further intercourse between the assembly and me.

It's only now, months later, the conference come and gone, the kindly stipend paid and spent, that it occurs to me what I should have said.

What I should have said is that ethnography seems so perilous just now, no less the everyday; that "life and letters and the field" seem littered more than ever with the wounded and the dead, the raging and the sad. That ethnicity, formerly a cause for celebration, now seems an occasion for increasing caution. That ethnic identity—those ties by which we are bound to others of our kind by tribe and race, language and belief, geography and history, costume and custom and a hundred other measures—seems lately less a treasure, more a scourge.

WHEN I BEGAN this book, I had in mind something that would help my family reconnect to our little history as Irish Americans, something that would resonate with other hyphenated types who've come from every parish in the world. I wanted the names and the records kept—a text my grandchildren, not yet born, might dip into someday for their own reasons. Something like *Roots* for the freckled and redheaded set, the riverdancing and flash-tempered descendants of immigrants—the seven million "willing" Irish men and women who have crossed the Atlantic in the last four hundred years, seeking a future in this New World that had been denied to them in the Old. From the first Scots-Irish, tired of the tithes and rents in Ulster in the seventeenth century—Davy Crockett's people, westward pressing, sturdy and curious—to the hundreds of thousands of oppressed Catholics in the eighteenth century who would fight in our revolution and help to shape our nation, like the man with my name, from South Carolina, who signed the Declaration of Independence; to the million Famine Irish, sick with hunger, fever, and want in the nineteenth century, one of whom, my great-great-grandfather, came and returned, and another, my great-grandfather, came to stay; to the rising and falling tides of Irish who washed ashore here in the twentieth century, building our roads, working our Main Streets, filling our senates and legislatures, rectories, schools, and universities; to the sons and daughters of friends in Moveen who left home in the 1970s and 1980s and 1990s—Anne Murray and her sister Kay, a couple of the Carmodys, Downses and O'Sheas. They are still going out to America, although now they come and go as they please on 747s that every day fly over Moveen on their way to and from the airport at Shannon. Ultimatum has become an option. American Wakes have become bon-voyage parties as the young in West Clare become, like the young in Michigan, working tourists in a smaller world full of portable opportunities and multiple possibilities.

By the time Alex Haley's *Roots* was published in 1976, I'd been back and forth to Ireland three times. Haley's hunger for knowing and reconstructing and reconnecting with the past was one I'd got a whiff of in my early travels. When the TV series the book inspired was aired in January 1977, I watched with a hundred thirty million other Americans who, thanks to Haley's gifts, saw, in the struggles of his family, something related to their own. For white Americans, it humanized blacks in a way that federal laws, however just and long overdue, had failed to do. For African Americans, it ennobled their struggle in a hostile world by connecting them to a formerly untold past.

When the African held his infant son, Kunta Kinte, up to the firmament and spoke his name into the dark face of creation, I understood the power of naming and keeping track of things, why all holy books begin with a litany of "begats," and how much each of our personal stories owes to the stories of our families and clans, our kind and kin. Second only to the forced migration of the African slave trade, the tide of Famine and post-Famine Irish marked the largest single wave of immigration in U.S. history.

SO, I WANTED a book that honored those who stayed and those who went, to bridge some of the distance that always swells between people who "choose" a different path, or find some footing in a life with few choices. I wanted to understand the man who left, the better to understand the man who returned to Moveen, to understand the ones who went between and who would follow after.

I wanted something chatty and jaunty like a good night's talk. Something that would find its market among even a fraction of the forty-some-million Americans alive today who trace their place back to the thirty-two thousand-square-mile island in the sea at the westernmost edge of Europe.

My agent and publishers oughtn't to be faulted for thinking of a kind of travel memoir, something with a little something for everyone, something that would earn back its advance and then some. Something that would offset the losses on poetry. Truth told, it's what I was hoping for, too.

The brother (about whom more anon), ever the raconteur, suggested at the outset a regimen of weekly audiences with himself and tendered *Wednesdays with Patrick* as a working title. "Or maybe *Paddy*—you know, for the folksy crowd—like that Paddy whiskey, easy sipping with a little bite. And maybe Thursdays, Tom. Yes, *Thursdays with Paddy*. That's just the t'ing." And the truth is I'd have no problem with that. He's a great man in all ways with a skeptic's temperament, a heart of gold, and a "fierce big brainbox," as Martin Roche once said about J. J. McMahon, our neighbor in West Clare.

I wanted it all to be a gift, in thanksgiving for the gift that had been given me, of Ireland and the Irish, the sense of connection, and the family I found there and the house they all came from that was left to me.

SEPTEMBER 11 CHANGED all of that. The book I first imagined was no longer possible. Just as our sense of safety here, protected by oceans and the globe's largest arsenal of weapons and resources, was forever shaken, irreparably damaged by the horrors of that day, so too was the sense that ethnicity is always and only quaint and benign.

Lost too was the luxury of isolation and purposeful ignorance of the larger world of woes, a taste for which I'd acquired in my protected suburban youth and overindulged throughout my adulthood—fattening, as Americans especially do, on our certainty that it will all be taken care of by whoever's in charge.

I remember telling prospective tourists, fearful of what they'd heard about the "Troubles" in Ireland—the last century's longest-running war in Western Europe—not to worry about a thing. Belfast and Derry were distant concerns, small towns in a tiny province—"little more," I'd assure them, "than a bar fight in Escanaba or Munising." I'd acquired the Irish gift for strategic understatement, too.

The day that terrorists bombed embassies in Africa, was it?—killing dozens or hundreds, I couldn't say—I was shopping in Kilrush for kitchen things at Brews and Gleeson's, certain that the troubles really didn't concern me and that out by Dunlicky the mackerel would be plentiful and the walk to the sea would do me good, and nothing could be better than fresh fish and tea.

So maybe what I should have said is that ethnography, which formerly seemed a parlor game, seems more a dangerous science now, especially "the ethnography of everyday life," because life, everyday life, here in the opening decade of the new millennium, constantly obscures, daily nullifies, and relentlessly confounds the needful work of such inquiry. The subgroup we were about to study is suddenly removed or written off by the first drafts of a history that our all-day-everyday news cycle proclaims.

"A Decade After Massacres, Rwanda Outlaws Ethnicity," proclaims the headline in the *New York Times* on April 8, 2004. Marc Lacey reports from the capital, Kigali:

> This country, where ethnic tensions were whipped up into a frenzy of killing, is now trying to make ethnicity a thing of the past. There are no Hutu in the new Rwanda. There are no Tutsi either. The government, dominated by the minority Tutsi, has wiped out the distinction by decree.

Ethnicity has already been ripped out of schoolbooks and rubbed off government identity cards. Government documents no longer mention Hutu or Tutsi, and the country's newspapers and radio stations, tightly controlled by the government, steer clear of the labels as well.

It is not just considered bad form to discuss ethnicity in the new Rwanda. It can land one in jail. Added to the penal code is a crime of "divisionism," a nebulous offense that includes speaking too provocatively about ethnicity.

As elsewhere, there are the politically incorrect.

A Tutsi woman, who was raped in 1994 by so many Hutu militiamen in the village of Taba that she lost count, said she has difficulty interacting comfortably with Hutu.

"I don't trust them," said the woman, who, identified only as J. J., testified about her ordeal before the international tribunal in Rwanda.

Tutsi and *Hutu*—such neighborly words—equal in syllables and vowel sounds, trochees and pleasantly fricative "t's": who'd ever guess that they accounted for eight hundred thousand deaths in a hundred days a decade ago, most by machete, that the rest of the world largely ignored.

While marking another anniversary of the Rwandan genocide this year, we are avoiding naming what is happening in Sudan's Darfur region as "genocide." That particular noun requires verbs— by international convention, something remedial would have to be done—whereas *atrocity* or *ethnic cleansing* leaves us options. The systematic rape, pillage, and slaughter of tribal Africans by Arab

Janjaweed militia, armed by the Sudanese government, are, like the atrocities of the twentieth century—Armenians in Turkey, Jews of the Holocaust, Cambodians, Kurds, Bosnians, Nigerians, Bengalis—all lamentable mostly after the fact.

Asked whether the recent run of genocides might finally get it to "stick in people's minds" that we've responsibilities, Samantha Power, author of *A Problem from Hell,* replies, "I think we tell ourselves, though, that that was the product of peculiar circumstances. 'Oh, that's Africa, you know, the tribes, they do that.' 'It's the Balkans, this stuff happens in the Balkans.' There's a way that we *otherize* [my italics] circumstances that challenge our universal premises." (Atlantic Unbound Interviews, March 14, 2003)

How do we *otherize* our fellow humans? How do we mistake them for something other than our kind? In what ways has our ethnicity poisoned the well of our humanity? Why must our religions so miscalculate our gods? If there is only one God, as all Muslims, Christians, and Jews believe, then isn't the One we believe in one and the same? If there is no God, aren't we only off by one? And if there are many, aren't there plenty to go around? In the wake of that godawful September, after bombing the bejaysus out of Afghanistan, after bombing, invading, and occupying Iraq, a book about the forty shades of green I'd encountered driving around the Ring of Kerry seemed a little like a golf-bag urn—plastic, silly, curious, but idiotic. All I saw was forty shades of gray, and in each of them still forty more.

FROM THE POST-FAMINE cottage of my great-great-grandfather, to the Moveen my great-grandfather left in 1890, to the West Clare that Dorothea Lang photographed in the mid-1950s, to the Ireland I found in 1970, the greatest change in a hundred years was light—electric light. So says my neighbor J. J. McMahon, a scholarly and insightful man. It illuminated the dark hours, lengthened the evenings, shortened the winter's terrible hold. Folks read later, talked later, went out in the night, certain their lamps would see them home. Still, life remained circumscribed by the limited range of transportation and communication. The immediate universe for most small farmers extended no farther than town, church, and marketplace, distances managed by ass and cart, or horse and trap, on Raleigh bike, or on foot—shank's mare, as it was locally called. Communication was by gossip and bush telegraph, from kitchen to kitchen, with the postman up the road, with the men to and from the creamery, with the priest or teacher on their daily rounds, with women returning from market stalls. Talk was almost entirely parochial. The "wireless"—electric light's chatty cousin—brought news of the larger world in thrice-daily doses whilst newspapers were read aloud, entirely. Still, these were one-sided communiqués. There was no escape, no geographical cures, no way to get out of the local into the world. Folks had to live with one another. This made them more likely to bear fellow feelings, to understand, to empathize. However much familiarity bred contempt—and it bred its share—the neighbors shared a common life experience, the same perils, the same hopes for their children, the same borders and limitations. They formed, if only by default, a community.

In the kitchens, shops, and snugs of those remote parishes, the visitor or stranger or traveler was, much like the bards of old, a bearer of tidings unheard before, like correspondence from a distant country, or a missionary or a circus come to town. The new voice at the fire relieved the tedium of the everyday, the usual suspects in the house, the same dull redundancy of the Tuesday that followed Monday, which in its turn followed Sunday, where the priest gave the same sermon he had last year at about the same time.

I was such a Playboy of the Western World, in the months of my first visit to West Clare. Deposed for hours on a variety of topics (music, money, presidential politics), and my opinion sought on all manner of things (the war in Vietnam, who shot Kennedy, the future of Ireland), I thought I must be a very interesting specimen indeed. It was years before I understood that, during those blustery winter evenings in Moveen, I provided only some little relief from habit and routine, what Samuel Beckett had identified years before as "the cancer of time." I was not so interesting as I was something, anything, other than the known thing.

But today, the easier communications become, the easier it becomes not to communicate. The more rapidly we travel to the ends of the earth, the more readily we avoid our nearest neighbors. The more communing we do, the more elusive a sense of community seems. We are each encouraged to make individual choices, to seek personal saviors, singular experiences, our own particular truth. We make enemies of strangers and strangers of friends and wonder why we feel alone in the world.

Americans seem terribly perplexed at all the hatred of us in the world. Where, we wonder, are all those happy Iraqis who were supposed to greet us with smiles and flowers after we had liberated them? Where have all the flowers gone? Anthology? Antigone?

In his unstintingly titled *How the Irish Saved Civilization,* historian Thomas Cahill comments on page 6 on the tendency of one "civilization" to miss the point of an "other":

To an educated Englishman of the last century, for instance, the Irish were by their very nature incapable of civilization. "The Irish," proclaimed Benjamin Disraeli, Queen Victoria's beloved prime minister, "hate our order, our civilization, our enterprising industry, our pure religion [Disraeli's father had abandoned Judaism for the Church of England]. This wild, reckless, indolent, uncertain and superstitious race have no sympathy with the English character. Their ideal of human felicity is an alternation of clannish broils and coarse idolatry [i.e. Catholicism]. Their history describes an unbroken circle of bigotry [!] and blood." The venomous racism and knuckle-headed prejudice of this characterization may be evident to us, but in the days of "dear old Dizzy," as the queen called the man who had presented her with India, it simply passed for indisputable truth.

If this sounds a little like the conventional wisdom of the day, the policy and approved text on our "enemies in the war on terror," then perhaps we should be on the lookout for "venomous racism and knuckleheaded prejudice" of our own.

Cahill goes on to make his case of how Irish monks and scribes kept the candles burning and the texts illumined through the Dark Ages and recivilized and re-Christianized Europe from west to east in what he calls a "hinge" of history. Cahill's "hinges of history"— he has since done for the Jews and the Greeks what he did for the Irish—sound more than a little like what the German existentialist Karl Jaspers called the "Axial Age," from 800 to 200 BC, when most of religious thought was formed, an age marked by violence and upheaval.

Maybe it is time we looked to Ireland again for some clues to the nature of our ethnic imbroglios, our *jihads* and holy wars, and to how we might learn to live peaceably in the world with our "others." Surely the Shiite and Sunni of Iraq have something to learn from the Catholics and Protestants of Belfast and from the citizens of the Republic of Ireland. For here is a nation with a history of invasion, occupation, oppression, tribal warfare, religious fervor, ethnic cleansing, sectarian violence, and the tyrannies of churchmen, statesmen, thugs, and hoodlums. And yet it thrives on a shaky peace, religious convictions, rich cultural resources, and the hope of its citizens. It is a kind of miracle of civilization—where the better angels of the species have bested the bad. Such things could be contagious.

ON AUGUST 28, 1931, W. B. Yeats wrote "Remorse for Intemperate Speech," a line from which this book borrows for one of its chapters and organizing principles. "Out of Ireland have we come./Great hatred, little room,/Maimed us at the start." Yeats had witnessed and worked at the birth of a new Irish nation, had served as a Free State senator, and, after winning the Nobel Prize for literature, was at sixty-five the country's public man of letters. An Anglo-Irishman who had ditched his people's High Church Christianity in favor of swamis and Theosophists and his wife's dabbling in the occult, he was likewise deeply immersed in the fledgling nation's Celtic twilight, and torn between the right-wing politics of between-wars Europe and the romantic, mystic past of Ireland. His poem confesses and laments that reason and breeding, imagination and good intention are trumped by what he called "a fanatic heart." The remorse is real. Surely the age in which we live requires such self-examination. In a world made smaller by its benign and malevolent technologies, out of whatever country we have come, great hatred, little room, maims us at the start. Regardless of our heritage, we carry from our mothers' wombs our own fanatic hearts.

IF THE BOOK I first had in mind was made more difficult by the ethnography of everyday life hereabouts, something Yeats wrote in a letter to Maud Gonne affords a kind of guidance. "Today I have one settled conviction 'Create, draw a firm strong line & hate nothing whatever not even (the devil) if he be your most cherished belief—Satan himself'. I hate many things but I do my best, & once some fifteen years ago, for I think one whole hour, I was free from hate. Like Faust I said 'stay moment' but in vain. I think it was the only happiness I have ever known."

The bookish habits of Michel de Montaigne ought likewise to be imitated. (Already I've become more tolerant!) The *essai*, as the six-teenth-century Frenchman named it, is less a certainty and more a search, an attempt at sense-making, a setting forth, as if in a boat of words, to see if language will keep the thought afloat; a testing of the air for what rings true, an effort at illuminating grays.

We are told he retired to his library at a certain age and made his way among its books, endeavoring to understand his species by examining himself. "Each man bears the whole of man's estate," he wrote, and figured humanity could be understood by the scrutiny of a single human. As it was easiest, he chose himself and began to look. He was among the first ethnographers of the everyday. Whereas Augustine gave us his *Confessions,* in Montaigne we get, as his present-day disciple Phillip Lopate says gorgeously, "more of the cat examining its fur." We get his table fare and toilet habits, his favorite poets and his favorite books, what he thought about the sexes, his take on the weather. From the tiniest of details, he essays the real, the human, and the true.

THIS BOOK WAS begun in my home in Moveen, in the easy early months of 2001. It was shaped between funerals and family duties over the next two years in Milford and was finished over the late winter and early spring of 2004 in northern Michigan, at a home we have on Mullett Lake, a half-hour south of the Straits of Mackinac. In each location, the "cancer of time," the duties and routine of the everyday follow something like Montaigne's regimen. I wake early, make the coffee, read the e-mail and the *New York Times* online, check the *Irish Times* and Clare FM, cook up some Odlums Pinhead Oatmeal. "Aptly named," my loved ones sometimes say. At 7:30, I listen to *The Writer's Almanac* with Garrison Keillor on the radio, a kind of writerly morning office or book of days during which he says what happened on the date, lists the birthdays, reads a poem.

Our calendars, once full of feasts of virgins, martyrs, and confessors, now are crowded with unholy days. The day they struck our shining cities; the day we leveled theirs; the day they killed our innocents; the day we did the same to theirs. So to have a poem and some better news, every day, is no bad thing.

Yesterday was the day they put Galileo on trial for claiming that the earth revolved around the sun. "You can think it," the pope told him, "just don't say so out loud." "*E pur si muove . . .* ," the astronomer whispered, alas to no one in earshot.

And today is the birthday of Thomas Jefferson, born in 1743 in

Virginia, we are told, and "though he had grown up with slaves, and later kept them himself, his first legislative act was a failed attempt to emancipate the slaves under his jurisdiction. He later said, 'The whole commerce between master and slave is a perpetual exercise . . . in tyranny. . . . The man must be a prodigy who can retain his . . . morals undepraved by such circumstances.'"

And it's the birthday of Samuel Beckett, your "cancer of time" man, born on Good Friday in 1906 in a suburb of Dublin, who said of his childhood, "I had little talent for happiness." In 1928, he left for Paris to become James Joyce's acolyte. In 1937, he was stabbed in the chest by a pimp named Prudent. He visited his assailant in prison and when he asked the man why he had attacked him, Prudent replied, "*Je ne sais pas, monsieur.*" "I do not know, sir," became a prominent refrain in *Waiting for Godot,* his most famous play—in which, most famously, nothing happens.

We do not know. Such is the dilemma of the everyday. We rummage among books and newspapers, watch the fire go to ash, pace the room, walk out into the day that's in it, watch the snow give way to humus. The loons return. The first insuppressible flowers bloom. We find in our theatres and times, like Vladimir and Estragon, that life is waiting, killing time, holding to the momentary hope that whatever's supposed to happen next is scheduled to occur—wars end, the last thin shelf of ice melts, and the lake is clear and blue, like the ocean we are always dreaming of crossing, we get it right, we make it home—if not today, then possibly tomorrow.

TL

April 13, 2004

Mullett Lake

Milford

Moveen West

Booking
Passage

We Irish & Americans

The Brother

EVERY SO OFTEN the brother calls, ranting about having to get on a plane, fly over to Shannon, drive out to West Clare, and cut a finger off.

I blame myself for this.

"Not the finger again, Pat," is what I say.

He says he wants to leave it in Moyarta—the graveyard on the Shannon estuary where our people are buried in the ancient parish of Carrigaholt. He wants to leave his severed finger there—a part of himself—against the loneliness: the low-grade, ever-present ache he feels, like a phantom limb, whenever he's away from there too long. Will I come with him? He wants to know.

I blame myself for this. I know how it happens. I know it is only going to get worse. Lately he's been saying maybe better a thumb.

"Better yet two thumbs, Tom! That's it, both thumbs—one for the future and one for the past—there in Moyarta, that's just the thing. One for all that was and all that yet will be. . . ." He's waxing eloquent and breathing deeply.

"Never mind the thumbs, Pat," I tell him, but he knows it makes a kind of sense to me.

There's something about the impulse to prune and plant body parts on the westernmost peninsula of a distant county in a far country that goes a step beyond your standard tourist class. The brother is nothing if not a great man for the grim reaping and the grand gesture.

Maybe you're thinking the devil of drink, but neither of us has had a drop in years.

Big Pat swore off it decades ago, as a youth at university. He'd been given a football scholarship to the University of Dayton. He was a tight end and a good one. At six foot five and sixteen stone, he was fit and fast and difficult to tackle. Between games and his studies he would drink in the local bars, where invariably some lesser specimen would drink enough local lager to feel the equal of him. Pat found himself the target of too many drunken Napoleons—little men determined to have a go at the Big so as to make themselves feel, well, *enlarged*. He had bottles bashed over his head, sucker punches thrown, aspersions cast from every corner by wee strangers looking for a fight. After breaking a man's nose and spending a night in the lockup, Pat swore off the drink for the safety of all and everyone concerned. So he comes by his theory of thumbs quite soberly and knows that I know what he means to say.

IRELAND HAPPENED to Big Pat in 1992 the way it happened to me in 1970, as a whole-body, blood-borne, core-experience; an echo thumping in the cardiovascular pulse of things, in every vessel of the being and the being's parts, all the way down to the extremities, to the thumbs. The case he got, like mine, is chronic, acute, and likely terminal. The symptoms are occasionally contagious. He became not only acquainted with but utterly submerged in his Irish heritage—a legacy of Lynches and O'Haras, Graces and McBradys, Ryans and Currys, and the mighty people he married into—shanty and lace-curtain tributaries of a bloodline that all return to Ireland for their source.

Of course, there are more orderly ways to do it.

You can dress up one day a year in the shamrock tie and green socks, haul out the beer-stained jacket, get a little tipsy cursing the Brits and the black luck of the draw into the wee hours from which you'll wake headachy and dry-mouthed the next morning and return to the ordinary American life—the annual mid-March Oiyrish.

Once, as luck would have it, I found myself in Manhattan for the St. Paddy's Day Parade. I stepped out from my hotel into 44th Street near Fifth Avenue thinking it was a day like any other. It was not. Maureen O'Hara was the Grand Marshal. There were cops and crazies everywhere. Cardinal O'Connor, may he R.I.P., said Mass in St. Patrick's, and I had to cancel a meeting with editors downtown. The sheer tidal force of Irishry, or of Irish impersonators—one hundred fifty thousand of them—all heading fortysome blocks uptown made perambulation against the grain of the parade impossible.

For most people, this Marchy excess is enough: the pipers and claddagh blather, the cartoon and caricature of what it means to be Irish and American. The next morning everyone returns to business as usual.

Or you might, after years of threatening to make the trip, get together with some other couples from the ushers' club and take the standard ten-day tour, bouncing in the bus from the Lakes of Killarney to the Blarney Stone with a stop at the Waterford factory, a sing-along in Temple Bar; you'll get some holy water and retail relics at the Knock Shrine and some oysters in Galway, where you'll buy one of those caps all the farmers are wearing this year, and spend a couple hours in the duty-free, buying up smoked salmon and turf figurines, Jameson whiskey and Belleek before you fly home with the usual stories of seeing Bill Clinton or Bono in a bar in Wicklow or the man with the big mitts and droopy earlobes you met in a chipper in Clogheen who was the image of your dearly departed mother's late uncle Seamus, or the festival you drove through in Miltown Malbay—fiddlers and pipers and tinwhistlers everywhere—the music, you will say, my God, the music!

Enough for most people is enough. Some photo-ops, some faith-and-begorras, maybe a stone from the home place, a sod of turf smuggled home in the suitcase, some perfect memories of broguey hospitalities and boozy light—something to say we are Irish in the way that others are Italian or Korean or former Yugoslavian: hyphenated, removed by generations or centuries, gone but not entirely forgotten, proud of your heritage—your Irish-Americanity.

Enough for most people is enough. But Pat was thrown into the deep end of the pool.

He landed in Shannon for the very first time on the Sunday morning of the 29th of March, 1992. A few hours later, instead of hoisting pints or singing along, or remarking on the forty shades of green, he was helping me lift the greeny, jaundiced, fairly withered body of Nora Lynch tenderly out of the bed she died in, out of the house she'd lived all her life in, out through the back door of her tiny cottage, into the coffin propped in the yard, on sawhorses assembled for this sad duty.

While most Americans spend their first fortnight tour rollicking through bars and countryside, searching none too intently for ruins or lost relations, Pat was driven straightaway to the home that our great-grandfather had come out of a century before, and taken into the room in which that ancient had been born. For Pat it was no banquet at Bunratty Castle, no bus ride to the Cliffs of Moher, no golf at the famous links at Lahinch, no saints or scholars or leprechauns. It was, rather, to the wake of Nora Lynch, late of Moveen West, Kilkee, County Clare—her tiny, tidy corpse laid out in a nunnish blue suit in a bed littered with Mass cards, candlesticks, and crucifix assembled on the bedside table, her bony hands wrapped in a rosary, her chin propped shut with a daily missal, folks from the townland making their visits; "sorry for your troubles," "the poor cratur, Godhelpus," "an honest woman the Lord've mercy on her," "faith, she was, she was, sure faith"; the rooms buzzing with hushed talk and the clatter of tableware, the hum of a rosary being said in the room, the Lenten Sunday light pouring through the deep windows. Big Pat stood between an inkling of the long dead and the body of the lately dead and felt the press of family history, like the sea thrown finally against the shore, tidal and undulant and immediate. He sighed. He inhaled the air, sweet with damp-mold and early putrefaction, tinged with tobacco and turf smoke, hot grease and tea, and knew that though he'd never been in this place before, among these stones and puddles and local brogues, he was, in ways he could neither articulate nor deny, *home*.

He and his Mary, and me and mine, had booked our tickets two mornings before when the sadly anticipated word had come of Nora Lynch's death at half-twelve in Moveen, half-past seven of that Friday morning in Michigan, March 27, 1992, four months into her ninetieth year, one month after she'd been taken to hospital in Ennis, six weeks after our father had died in the middle of the February of that awful year.

We had buried our father like the chieftain he was, then turned to the duties of the great man's estate when word came from across the ocean that Nora had taken a turn for the worse. Two days of diagnostics had returned the sad truth of pancreatic cancer. The doctors were anxious to have her moved. In dozens of visits to Moveen since 1970, I had become Nora's next of kin—a cousin twice removed, but still the first of her people ever to return to Ireland since her father's brother, my great-grandfather, had left at the end of the nineteenth century. Neither her sisters nor her sisters' children had ever returned. Her dead brothers had left no children. Nora Lynch was the last—the withered and spinsterly end of the line until, as she often said, I came. Two decades of letters and phone calls and transatlantic flights had tightened the ties that bind family connections between Michigan and Moveen. So when it looked like Nora was dying, they called me.

I LANDED in Ireland on Ash Wednesday morning, March 4 that year, and drove from Shannon to the cathedral in Ennis, joining a handful of coreligionists for the tribal smudge and mumbled reminder that "you are dust and unto dust...," et cetera, et cetera. Then out the road to the County Hospital, a yellow stucco building trimmed in white, behind a wall on the north end of town at a corner on the Galway road. I remember the eight-bed ward of sickly men and women and Nora in the far corner looking jaundiced and tiny and suddenly old under crisp white linens. Four months before, we'd all celebrated her eighty-ninth birthday in Mary Hickie's Bayview Hotel in Kilkee with cakes and tea and drinks all around. P. J. and Breda and Louise and Mary and me— there in Kilkee—all singing, "Happy Birthday," and Nora not knowing what to do. She'd never had a birthday party before.

And here she was now, a season later, the mightiness gone out of her, wasting away in the corner of a county ward, dying, according to the doctors, of cancer. And I remember wanting to have the necessary conversation with her—to say out loud what we both knew but did not want to speak, that she was not going to be getting any better.

"The doctors tell me they think you're dying."

"We're all dying, Tom. I just want to get home."

"Home is where we'll go then, Nora."

I asked the doctors for a day or two to organize some care for her in Moveen. I spoke to Dr. Cox, who promised palliative care. I spoke to Catherine O'Callaghan, the county nurse, who promised to come by in the mornings. I spoke to Breda and P. J. Roche, her renters and defenders, who promised to oversee the household details, and I spoke with Anne Murray, a young unmarried neighbor, herself a farmer and forever my hero, who said she would stay the nights with Nora. I got a portable commode, a wheelchair, sheets and towels, fresh tea, bland foods, the *Clare Champion*. I called the priest to arrange a sacramental visit. I called home to see how the children were doing. I'd left my Mary with four teenagers in various stages of revolt. I promised to be home as soon as I could. "Do what you need to do," she said.

Once Nora was home from the hospital, the borders around her days became more defined by familiarity, gratitude, cancer, and contentment. She moved between bedroom and kitchen, sitting hours by the fire, half-sleeping in bed, whilst neighbors and professionals made their visits. Old friends came by to trade remembrances, old grudges were forgiven or set aside, old grievances forgotten or reconciled. After a sustainable pattern of care had been established in the house, I said my goodbyes to Nora on March 13, my dead father's birthday, and returned to my wife and children in Michigan to wait out the weeks or months it would be.

We deal with love by dealing with the ones we love, with sickness by dealing with the sick, and with death by dealing with the dead.

And after Nora died, it was the brother Pat who came to help me conduct her from one stone-walled incarnation to the next. We carried her out of her cottage to the coffin in the yard and processed down to the old church in Carrigaholt where Fr. Culligan, removed from his tea and paperwork, welcomed her with a decade of the rosary. The next morning Pat sang at Mass and followed us to Moyarta, where the Moveen lads had opened the old vault, built in 1889 by Nora's grandfather, our great-great-grandfather, Patrick Lynch. In the century since, it has housed the family dead, their accumulating bones commingled there in an orange plastic fertilizer bag at the side of the grave. And after the piper and tinwhistler played, and after Fr. Culligan had prayed, and after we lowered her coffin into the ground, we replaced the bag of our ancestors' bones, Nora Lynch's people and our own, three generations of kinsmen and women, and rolled the great flagstone back into place. Our Marys repaired to the Long Dock Bar, where food and drink had been prepared. And we stood and looked—the brother Pat and me—from that high place—the graveyard at Moyarta—out past the castle at the end of the pier, out over the great mouth of the Shannon whence our great-grandfather had embarked a century before, and landed in Michigan and never returned, out past the narrowing townlands of the peninsula, Cross and Kilbaha and Kilcloher, out past Loop Head and the lighthouse at the western end where, as the locals say, the next parish is America.

IT WAS THEN I saw Pat's thumbs begin to twitch, and the great mass of his shoulders begin to shake and wads of water commence to dropping from his eyeballs and the cheeks of him redden and a great heave of a sigh make forth from his gob and the hinge of his knees begin to buckle so that he dropped in a kind of damaged genuflection there at the foot of the family tomb into which poor Nora's corpse had just been lowered.

"Oh God," he half-sobbed through the shambles of his emotions, "to think of it, Tom, the truth and beauty of it."

And I thought it a queer thing to say, but admirable that he should be so overtaken with the grief at the death of a distant cousin whom he'd only met on a couple of occasions over the past twenty years when she'd made her visits to America. What is more, I remarked to myself, given that the brother and I were both occupationally inclined to get through these solemnities while maintaining an undertakerly reserve, I thought his emotings rather strange. Might it be the distance or the jet lag or maybe the sea air? It was his first time in Ireland, after all. It might all have overwhelmed him.

Truth told I was a little worried that my own bereavement didn't seem sufficiently keen compared to the way Pat had been leveled by his. All the same, I thought it my brotherly and accustomed duty to comfort the heart-sore with such condolence as I could bring to bear on such abject sadness.

"She'd a good life, a good death, and a great funeral, Pat. She's at peace now and there is comfort in that. It really was very good of you and Mary to come. My Mary and I are forever grateful."

He was still buckled, the thumbs twitching and the face of him fixed on the neighboring grave, and he was muttering something I made out to be about love and death because all he kept saying was, "In Love and in Death, together still." He was making an effort to point the finger of his left hand at the stone that marked the grave next to Nora's. I thought he might be quoting from the stone and examined the marker for "love" and "death." It was clean white marble, lettered plain, the name of *Callaghan* chiseled on it and not much else that was legible.

And then it came to me—his wife Mary's name is Callaghan.

"To think of it, Tom, here we are, four thousand miles from home, but *home* all the same at the grave of our great-great-grandparents; and the Lynches and Callaghans are buried together, right next to each other. In love and in death, they are together still. Who'd have ever imagined that?"

"Yes, yes, I see, of course. . . ."

"To think of it, Tom, all these years, all these miles. . . ."

"Yes, the years, the miles. . . ."

"Who'd have believed it, Tom?"

I helped him to his feet, brushed the mud from his trousers, and said nothing of substance for fear it might hobble the big man

again. At the Long Dock he embraced his wife as a man does who
has seen the ghosts.

PAT GOT SMITTEN at a funeral Mass one Saturday at Holy
Name when Mary Callaghan, accompanied by her father on the
organ, sang the "*In Paradisum*" as the sad entourage processed into
church. First cross bearer and acolytes, then Fr. Harrington, then
my father and Pat wheeling the casket in, the mourners rising to
the entrance hymn. The brother stood at the foot of the altar holding the pall, transfixed by the voice of the angel come to earth in
the comely figure of Mary Callaghan. When it came time to cover
the casket with the pall as the priest read, "On the day of her baptism she put on Christ. In the day of Christ's coming may she be
clothed in glory," Pat was elsewhere in his mind, imagining the
paradise into which Miss Callaghan, what with her dark curls, blue
eyes, and fetching attributes, might conduct him. My father
thumped him ceremoniously on the shoulder to snap him back
into the moment at hand. At the Offertory, she sang the "Ave
Maria." Pat swooned at the back of church at the Latin for *Hail* and
Mary and *the fruit of wombs*. At communion, "Panis Angelicus";
and for the recessional she sang an Englished version of the "Ode
to Joy." It was all Pat could do to get the casket in the hearse, the
family in the limousine, the cars flagged, and the procession on its
way to Holy Sepulchre, so walloped was he by the music in her
mouth and the beauty of her being.

When Fr. Harrington, riding shotgun in the hearse with Pat,
wondered aloud, as he always did, had Pat met any fine young
Catholic woman to settle down with yet—for a young man with a
good job at the height of his sexual prowess untethered by the

bonds of holy matrimony and indentured to nothing but his own pleasures is a peril second only to a young woman of similar station to any parish priest—Pat answered that he had indeed, and only within the hour. The priest looked puzzled.

When Pat explained further that he had only moments ago come to understand the trials of Job, the suffering of souls in purgatory, and meaning no blasphemy, the Passion itself—to behold such beauty and not to hold it, to have it, to take it home and wake to it, to be in earshot and eyeshot of such a rare specimen of womanly grace and gorgeousness and not be able to hold the hand of her, kiss the mouth of her, run a finger down the cheekbone of her—this was a suffering he had never had before. Fr. Harrington, blushing a little now, one supposes, had the brother exactly where he wanted him, on the brink of surrender to the will of God, ready to be delivered from the occasion of sin by the sacraments of the Church.

"Could you help me, Father?" Pat implored him.

"Leave it to me, boy. And say your prayers."

So it was a priest who made Pat's match with Mary Callaghan. Well, actually a bishop now. But back in that day it was Fr. Bernard Harrington, parish priest at Holy Name, who organized the courtship and consortium between the brother and the famous beauty.

Pat was twenty-three or twenty-four, recently finished with mortuary school, newly licensed and working funerals with our father and enjoying the life of the single man.

Mary was nineteen, an underclasswoman at Marygrove College studying theatre and voice under the tutelage of nuns. She was the fourteenth of the eighteen offspring of John F. Callaghan, a church organist, and Mary O'Brien Callaghan, whose once-promising operatic career was sacrificed to her marriage and motherhood duties. Of this prolific couple it was said that they had great music but never quite got rhythm.

It was the priest, later Bishop Harrington, who made discreet inquiries about the young woman's plans and prospects; the priest who put it in the organist's mind that a funeral director in the family would be no bad thing, the inevitabilities being, well, inevitable; and the priest who mentioned to the mother, "Queen" Mary, that a match between her namesake and heir to her vocal legacy and a tall and handsome Irish Catholic man, the son of famously honest people, would produce grandchildren of such moral, spiritual, intellectual, and physical pedigree as to ever be a credit to the tribe and race and species and, needless to say, to her own good self. It was the priest who advanced my brother's cause with the girl in question, letting it slip, more or less in passing, that he owned, albeit subject to a modest mortgage, his own three-bedroom bungalow in a good neighborhood, stood to take over the family business, was possessed, it was said, of a grand if untrained tenor voice, and sang "Danny Boy" with such aplomb that many's the young person and the old were set to weeping when he gave out with it.

It was the priest furthermore who blighted her other suitors, by novena or rosary or some other priestly medicine. One by one they all disappeared: the one in law school, the one with the family fortune, the one who later became a senator. Even Mary's twin brother Joe's best friend, a man of impeccable Irish-American stock who courted her with poems and roses and curried favor with the mother, even he was passed over. He went off to Ohio broken-hearted, married a Lithuanian woman, and was seldom heard from in these parts again. It was the priest who did it. And the priest who organized the first date, counseled them through the predictable quibbles, and after three years of courtship, pressed the brother to pop the question.

And standing before the dearly beloved and the church full of family assembled there—the Lynch and the Callaghan parents, like Celtic chieftains and their queens, the bride's seventeen siblings with their spouses and children and significant others, the groom's eight siblings with theirs as well, and the O'Brien and O'Hara cousins and uncles and aunts and host of friends all dressed to the nines for the nuptials—it was the priest who proclaimed it a great day for the Irish indeed.

INDEED, FOR THE IRISH and Irish Americans, the only spectacle more likely to bring out a crowd than a blushing couple at the brink of their marriage bed is a fresh corpse at the edge of its grave. Mighty at weddings, we are mightier still at wakes and funerals, to which we are drawn like moths to flame, where the full nature of our characters and character flaws are allowed to play out in a theatre that has deep and maybe pagan roots.

As Hely Dutton, an agriculturalist in the service of the Dublin Society opined in 1808 in the final chapter of his *Statistical Survey of the County of Clare*:

> Wakes, quite different from what are so called in England, still continue to be the disgrace of the country. As it would be thought a great mark of disrespect not to attend at the house where the corpse lies, every person makes it a point, especially women, to shew themselves; and when they first enter

the house, they set up the most hideous but dry-eyed yell, called the Irish cry; this, however, lasts but a short time. The night is usually spent in singing, not mournful dirges, but merry songs, and in amusing themselves with different small plays, dancing, drinking, and often fighting, &c.

When Pat's Mary's mother "Queen" Mary died, late last year at age eighty-five, we dispatched a hearse and driver to Pittsburgh to pick up a bespoke, carved-top mahogany casket for her. She'd have hated the expense but approved the bother. Mary O'Brien Callaghan was, like all the Irish dead, one of a kind. The much-doted-over only child of "Big Paul" O'Brien—a short man who made a respectable fortune as a lumber merchant—she passed her girlhood in Oswego, New York, with piano lessons, voice recitals, and the lace-curtain privilege of moneyed Irish. In high school she met her leading man, Jack Callaghan, when they played the love interests in *HMS Pinafore*. While attending Syracuse University on a voice scholarship, she married him and over the next twenty-two years gave birth to eight daughters and ten sons. He played the organ at daily Masses, directed choirs, and taught music at a women's college and a Christian Brothers school. They kept body and soul and household together. On the occasion of their fiftieth anniversary, an interviewer commented, "Mrs. Callaghan, you must really love children!" She replied, "Actually I just really love Mr. Callaghan." That same love—selfless, faithful, fierce, and true—still shines in the eyes of her sixty grandchildren, forty-some great-grandchildren, and one great-great-grandchild.

She had seen the generations grow up around her.

It was her grandson Paddy who helped his father wheel her cas-

ket into church, her granddaughter Caitlin whose soprano met the
mourners at the door. It was her daughters who covered her with
the pall and her sons who walked beside the hearse the few blocks
to Greenwood Cemetery, then bore her body to the grave where
another grandson piped the sad, slow air.

"Some say this is supposed to be a celebration of Mary's life,"
the priest said, "and we'll get to that, but not right now. Right now
it hurts too much. We must first mourn her death." There was
weeping and sighing, the breath of them whitening in the chill
November air. Folks held hands and embraced one another.

The brother's thumbs were twitching.

THE THUMBS ARE safe for another season. Because we cannot
go to Moveen this March, because Pat got himself elected president of the Funeral Directors' Association, because I'm finishing a
book about the Irish and Irish Americans, because we are bound
by duty and detail to the life in southeastern Lower Michigan, we
head downtown to celebrate the high holy day in the standard
fashion. A local radio station has a St. Patrick's Day party they
broadcast from the lobby of the Fisher Theatre on West Grand
Boulevard in Detroit. Then we make for Corktown and the annual
Mass at Most Holy Trinity, where the blessed and elect, the great
and small, will gather to give thanks for the day that's in it.

There's a crowd at the Fisher, and Paul W. Smith, the drive-time
disc jockey, makes his way among the guests and celebrities and
local business types who are keen for a little free air time to hawk
their wares in their best put-on brogue.

Pat does "Danny Boy" and I recite a poem about a dream of
going home, because here we are in a city of immigrants and their

descendants from every parish on the globe and all of them wearing the green today, and hoisting Guinness and humming sweet ditties about the Irish. I see my mother's cousin, Eddie Coyle, and Mayor Kwame Kilpatrick, the self-described "first six-foot, six-inch Irish African American." We laugh and glad-hand and then get on our way for Corktown on the southwest side of the city.

Corktown is the oldest neighborhood in Detroit. It was settled in the 1830s by Irish who came west on the Erie Canal from the eastern slums and the West of Ireland. Most Holy Trinity was the first English-speaking parish in the city that was, in the middle of the nineteenth century, still mostly French. The factory and railway and civil-service jobs that grew with the city attracted plenty of the Famine Irish and after the Irish, the Maltese came, and after the Maltese, mostly Mexicans. In a city that has been blighted by white flight, segregation, and racism, Corktown remains a little broken jewel of stable integration and diversity. There are blacks and whites and Hispanics sharing the row houses, family businesses, churches, schools, and community halls. New townhouses, vetted by the historical society for architectural correctness, fill in the old lots cleared for parking when the Detroit Tigers played at the stadium at the corner of Michigan Avenue and Trumbell until 1999.

This morning it's a mix of city people and suburbanites who fill Most Holy Trinity to celebrate the 170th anniversary of the church's founding. Sister Marietta always saves a place for Big Pat down front with the politicos, heavy donors, and dignitaries. We are seated near the plaster statue of the saint Himself whose life and times in the fifth century still seems relevant for the new millennium. He was kidnapped in his teens by Irish marauders, taken to Antrim and kept as a slave, escaped to Gaul where he became a priest and returned to the country of his captors to convert them to Christianity. The snakes and shamrocks might have been added in by overly enthusiastic biographers.

The cardinal is here and his concelebrants, the governor and her smiling aides, the county executives and secretary of state, the president of the Ancient Order of Hibernians and the president of the "Ladies'" AOH and a detail of knights from the Knights of Columbus. And the "Maid of Erin" and her pretty attendant court sponsored by the United Irish Societies, and all of them piped in by a corps of pipers and drummers in full regalia.

Everyone is wearing some paper shamrocks or a green carnation or a bright green scarf or tie or a badge that says something like, "Kiss Me I'm Irish" or "Erin Go Bragh." And as the pipes and drums begin, we rise, all smiles, because it's a great day for the Irish and Irish eyes are smiling and Oh Danny Boy things are good in Glocca Morra and God is in heaven and here, now, if only for a moment, all's right with the world.

But of course it's not. The litany of the world's woes expands exponentially from the local to the regional to the global.

There's famine in Africa, plagues in Asia; quiet little homicides and suicides and genocides go on around the globe while wars and rumors of war are everywhere, everywhere. The pitiful species remains its own worst enemy.

Fr. Russ Kohler, the pastor of Holy Trinity since 1991, steps to the lectern to welcome everyone. After the requisite niceties, he makes mention of the two young police officers from the neighborhood shot to death in the line of duty last month.

"I personally knew 21-year-old Officer Matthew Bowens and instead of a marriage I officiated at his funeral. And I per-

sonally knew 26-year-old Officer Jennifer Fettig and officiated not at her wedding, but her funeral. Illegal drug distribution throughout Michigan renders our cities into virtual
free fall. Inept political maneuvering demoralizes police
departments. Using sworn officers for after-hours escorts to
rave parties renders the whole city one big market for drug
distribution and consumption."

The cardinal speaks about the War on Terror and the violence
of euthanasia, abortion, the need for repentance, the hunger for
justice, forgiveness, and peace in the world.

The governor is concerned about the loss of manufacturing
jobs from Michigan to Mexico, where workers are paid much less.
There's an influx of illegal immigrants taking low-wage jobs
around the state. She has brought a proclamation to honor the
parish for one hundred seventy years of service to the immigrant
and homeless, the helpless and those in need, many of whom are
from, well, Mexico. The parish runs a free legal clinic, a free medical clinic, an outreach to sailors through the Port of Detroit.

The third-graders from the school sing, "I believe that children
are our future." Their faces are black and brown and white and
every shade in between. They are from everywhere. Watching their
performance, the Maid of Erin weeps, the governor is beaming
and singing along, the cardinal is enraptured or possibly dozing in
a post-communion reverie.

The Taoiseach (prime minister of Ireland) is in Washington,
D.C., to give the president a bowl of shamrocks.

In Chicago they dye the river green.

There's music and marching in Melbourne and Moscow and
Montreal.

AND OUT ACROSS the world the roseate Irish everywhere are proclaiming what a good thing it is to be them, possessed as they are of this full register of free-range humanity: the warp-spasms and shape-changing of their ancient heroes, their feats and parox-ysms and flights of fancy, their treacheries and deceits, sure faith and abiding doubts—chumps and champions, egomanias and inferiority complexes, given to fits of pride and fits of guilt, able to wound with a word or mend with one, to bless or curse in impec-cable verse, prone to ornamental speech, long silences, fierce tirades, and tender talk. Maybe this is why the couple hundred mil-lion Americans who do not claim an Irish connection identify with the forty-five million who do—for the license it gives them, just for today, for a good laugh, a good cry, a dirge or a dance, to say the things most in need of saying, to ignore the world's heart-breaks, the Lenten disciplines, their own grievous mediocrities, the winter's last gasping hold on the soul, and to summon up visions of a home-place where the home fires are kept burning, where the light at the window is familiar, the face at the door a neighbor's or friend's, the sea not far beyond the next field over, the ghosts that populate our dreams all dear and welcome, their voices sweet with assurances, the soft day's rain but temperate, the household safe for the time being from the murderous world's worst perils; home among people at one with all immigrants, all pilgrims, all of the hungry and vanquished and evicted strangers in a strange place, at odds with the culture of triumphalists and blue bloods.

Who's to know?

As for the brother, as for me, after making the rounds at the union hall in which all had assembled for corned beef and cabbage, we made for the road home before rush hour hit, singing the verses of "The Hills of Moveen," counting our blessings as we had come to see them: that here we were, the sons of an undertaker who was the son of a parcel-post inspector who was the son of a janitor and prison guard who was the son of an ass and cart farmer from a small cottage on the edge of West Clare to which our own sons and daughters do often repair, for the sense that it gives them of who they are and where they've come from and where they might be going still.

Along the way were the cute fools puking out their excesses of spuds and green beer or leaning out of their car doors pissing their revelries into ditches, or being taken into custody by the police. We drove past them all, out beyond the old cityscape of slums and ruins and urban renewal, out past the western suburbs, with their strip malls and parking lots, bearing the day's contentment like viaticum, singing the old songs, that "Wild Mountain Thyme" what with its purple heather, Pat tapping the time with his thumbs on the dashboard, out toward Milford where the sun was declining, where the traffic was sure to be thinning, and the last light of the day would be reddening and the false spring oozing from the earth might hold a whiff of turf smoke, a scent of the sea, and our Marys would have a plate of chicken and peas, a sup of tea, our place by the fire ready and warm for us to nod off in the wingback chairs, the brother and me, dreaming of the ancients and our beloveds and those yet to be—Nora and Tommy and Mrs. Callaghan and all the generations that shared our names; the priests and the old lads in the stories, our dear parents, gone with years, and our wives and daughters and sons, God bless them, and the ones coming after us we'll never see, bound to the bunch of them by love and death.

The Same but Different

IT IS MID-JUNE, nearly solstice, and I am adding a room onto the house in West Clare. A small room only—12 by 12— enough for a bed and a bureau and a chair. P. J. Roche has put up the block walls and Des O'Shea is roofing it, after which the work inside might proceed apace—flagstones and plaster and decor. There'll be a window to the east looking out on the haggard and a glass door to the south looking down the land, over the Shannon to Kerry rising, hilly on the other side.

It is an old house and changing it is never easy.

Near as I can figure it's the fifth addition and will make the house nearly seven hundred square feet, adding this wee room to what is here now: an entrance hall, the kitchen, a bathroom and bedroom—my cottage in Moveen West—my inheritance.

I'm returning in a month's time with my wife and her sister and her sister's friend, Kitty, for a fortnight's stay; and while the company of women is a thing to be wished for, sleeping on the sofa whilst they occupy the house's one existing bedroom—my ancestral bedroom—is not a thing I am prepared to do.

Back in the century when this house was first built, we'd have all bedded down together maybe, for the sake of the collective body heat, along with the dog and the pig and the milch cow if we could manage it. But this is the twenty-first century and privacy is in its ascendancy.

So P. J. and I hatched this plan last year of adding a room at the east side of the house. He understands the business of stone and mortar, plaster and space, time and materials, people, place. He has reconfigured this interior before, nine years ago after Nora Lynch died.

We have settled on particulars. Gerry Lynch will help with the slates and Matty Ryan will wire things. Damien Carmody from across the road will paint. And Breda, P. J.'s wife, is the construction manager. She sorts the bills and keeps them at it. "There's no fear, Tom," she assures me. "It'll all be there when you're home in August." There are boards and blocks and bundles of slates in the shed from Williams's in Kilkee. We've been to Kilrush to order curtains and bedding from O'Halloran's and buckets of paint from Brew's. The place is a permanent work in progress.

MY GRANDFATHER'S grandfather, Patrick Lynch, was given this house as a wedding gift when he married Honora Curry in 1853. They were both twenty-six years old and were not among the more than a million who starved or the more than a million who left Ireland in the middle of the nineteenth century in what today would be called a Holocaust or Diaspora but in their times was called the Famine.

On the westernmost peninsula of this poor county, in the bleakest decade of the worst of Irish centuries, Pat and Honora pledged their troth and set up house here against all odds. Starvation, eviction, and emigration—the three-headed scourge of English racism by which English landlords sought to consolidate smaller holdings into larger ones—had cut Ireland's population by a quarter between 1841 and 1851. Tiny parcels of land and a subsistence diet of potatoes allowed eight Lynch households to survive in Moveen, according to the Tithe books of 1825. Of these eight, three were headed by Patricks, two by Daniels, and there was one each by Michael and Anthony and John. One of these men was my great-great-great grandfather. One of the Patricks or maybe a Dan—there's no way of knowing now for certain. Their holdings ranged from three acres to nearly thirty. Of the eleven hundred acres that make up Moveen West, they were tenants on about a tenth. They owned nothing and were "tenants at will"—which is to say, at the will of a gentrified landlord class who likely never got closer to Moveen than the seafront lodges of Kilkee three miles away, always a favorite of Limerick Protestants. Their labor—tillage and pasturage—was owned by the landlord. The Westropps owned most of these parts then— James and John and later Ralph. The peasants were allowed their potatoes and their cabins. Until, of course, the potato failed. Of the 164 persons made homeless by the bailiffs of John Westropp, Esq., in May of 1849, in Moveen, thirty were Lynches. All of Daniel Lynch's family and all of his son John's family were evicted. The widow Margaret Lynch was put out of her cabin and John Lynch the son of Martin was put off of his nine acres. Another John Lynch could not afford the seven pounds, ten shillings rent on his small plot. The roofs were torn from their houses, the walls knocked down, their few possessions put out in the road. The potato crop had been blighted for four out of the last five years. Some of the families were paid a pittance to assist with the demolition of their homes, which made their evictions, according to the landlord's agents, "voluntary." Along with the Lynches evicted that day were Gormans and McMahons, Mullanys and Downses—the poor cousins and sisters and brothers of those marginally better situated economically or geographically who were allowed to stay but were not allowed to take them in. It was, for the class of landlords who owned the land, a culling of the herd of laboring stock, to make the ones who were left more fit, more efficient laborers. For those evicted, it was akin to a death sentence. For those who stayed, it was an often-toxic mix of survivors' pride, survivors' guilt, survivors' shame. Like all atrocities, it damns those who did and those who didn't. Like every evil, its roots and reach are deep.

In proportion to its population, County Clare had the highest number of evictions in all of Ireland for the years 1849 through 1854. The dispossessed were sent into the overcrowded workhouse in Kilrush, or shipped out for Australia or America or died in a ditch of cholera or exposure. As John Killen writes in the introduction to *The Famine Decade,* "That a fertile country, the sister nation to the richest and most powerful country in the world, bound to that country by an Act of Union some forty-five years old, should suffer distress, starvation and death seems incomprehensible today. That foodstuffs were exported from Ireland to feed British colonies in India and the sub-continent, while great numbers of people in Ireland starved, beggars belief."

But the words George Bernard Shaw puts into the mouths of his characters in *Man and Superman* get at the truth of it:

> MALONE: My father died of starvation in Ireland in the Black '47. Maybe you heard of it?
> VIOLET: The famine?
> MALONE (with smoldering passion): No, the starvation. When a country is full of food, and exporting it, there can be no famine.

The words of Captain Arthur Kennedy, the Poor Law inspector for the Kilrush Union who meticulously documented the particulars of the horror in West Clare, are compelling still:

> The wretchedness, ignorance, and helplessness of the poor on the western coast of this Union prevent them seeking a shelter elsewhere; and to use their own phrase, they "don't know where to face"; they linger about the localities for weeks or months, burrowing behind the ditches, under a few broken rafters of their former dwelling, refusing to enter the workhouse till the parents are broken down and the children half starved, when they come into the workhouse to swell the mortality, one by one. Those who obtain a temporary shelter in adjoining cabins are not more fortunate. Fever and dysentery shortly make their appearance when those affected are put out by the roadside, as carelessly and ruthlessly as if they were animals; when frequently, after days and nights of exposure, they are sent in by relieving officers when in a hopeless state. These inhuman acts are induced by the popular terror of fever. I have frequently reported cases of this sort. The

misery attendant upon these wholesale and simultaneous evictions is frequently aggravated by hunting these ignorant, helpless creatures off the property, from which they may perhaps have never wandered five miles. It is not an unusual occurrence to see 40 or 50 houses leveled in one day, and orders given that no remaining tenant or occupier should give them even a night's shelter.

The evicted crowd into the back lanes and wretched hovels of the towns and villages, scattering disease and dismay in all directions. The character of some of these hovels defies description. I, not long since, found a widow whose three children were in fever, occupying the piggery of their former cabin, which lay beside them in ruins; however incredible it may appear, this place where they had lived for weeks, measured 5 feet by 4 feet, and of corresponding height. There are considerable numbers in this Union at present houseless, or still worse, living in places unfit for human habitation where disease will be constantly generated.

The mid-nineteenth-century voice of Captain Kennedy, like mid-twentieth-century voices of military men proximate to atrocity, seems caught between the manifest evil he witnesses and the duty to follow orders he has been given.

I would not presume to meddle with the rights of property, nor yet to argue the expediency or necessity of these "monster" clearances, both one and the other no doubt frequently exist; this, however, renders the efficient and systematic administration of the Poor Law no less difficult and embarrassing. I think it incumbent on me to state these facts for the

Commissioners' information, that they may be aware of some of the difficulties I have to deal with. —*Reports and Returns Relating to Evictions in the Kilrush Union: Captain Kennedy to the Commissioners*, July 5, 1848

IT WAS A starvation, a failure of politics more than crops that cleared the land of the poor, killed off thousands in the western-most parishes, and dispersed the young to wander the world in search of settlements that could support them.

Moveen, of course, was never the same.

By August of 1855, when Griffith's Valuation was done, only three households of Lynches remained in Moveen—Daniel Lynch, the widowed Mary Lynch, and the lately married Patrick Lynch. It was Mary who gave Patrick and Honora their start, putting in a word for her son with the landlord and making what remained of the deserted cabin habitable.

My guess is Honora came from an adjacent townland, nearer the Shannon—Kilfearagh maybe, or Lisheen where her famous granduncle Eugene O'Curry, the Irish language scholar, came from; or north of here, toward Doonbeg, where the Currys were plentiful in those days. Maybe her people and Pat's people were both from the ancient parish of Moyarta and it is likely they met at church in Carrigaholt or in one of the hedge schools.

Pat came out of the house above, on the hill where the land backs up to the sea, where James and Maureen Carmody live now with their daughter Rachel and their son, Niall. James would be descended from Pat's brother, Tom; and, of course, from Mary, the widowed mother. We'd all be cousins many times removed.

The newlyweds leased twenty-six acres from Ralph Westropp,

the English landlord. The house had, according to the records, "stone walls, a thatched roof, one room, one window and one door to the front." In the famous illustration of "Moveen after the Evictions," which appeared in the *Illustrated London News* on December 22, 1849, there are sixteen cottages of this kind, most of them roofless, their gables angled into the treeless hillocks of Moveen, their fires quenched, their people scattered to Liverpool and the Antipodes and the Americas. In 1855, the Griffith Valuation assigned the place a tax rate of ten shillings. The more windows and doors a house had, the more the tax. No doubt to accommodate their ten children, Pat added a bedroom to the south.

On October 3, 1889, Honora died. She was buried in the great vault at Moyarta, overlooking the Shannon and the estuarial village of Carrigaholt. Hers was a slow death from stomach cancer, giving time for her husband and his brother Tom to build the tomb, there near the road, with its cobblestone floor, tall gabled end, and huge flagstone cover that was inscribed with her particulars by Mick Troy, the stonecutter from Killballyowen, famous for his serifs and flourishes. The brother Tom lost an eye to the tomb's construction when a chunk of stone flew off of Pat's sad hammering. The work must have taken most of a month—to bring the round gray rocks up from the Shannon beach by the cartload for the floor, ledge rocks from the cliff's edge to line the deep interior and build the gable he would plaster over, and finally the massive ledger stone that would serve as tomb roof and permanent record. Grave work, in anticipation of his grief—the larger muscles' indenture to the heart—it was all he could do for the dying woman.

For months after his mother's death, my great-grandfather, looking out the west window of this house at the mouth of the

River Shannon and the sea beyond, must have considered the prospects for his future. As ever in rural Ireland there were no guarantees. The labor and poverty were crushing. Parnell and land reform were distant realities. Their lease on the land would support just one family. A sister Ellen had gone off to Australia. A brother Michael married in a hurry when he impregnated a neighbor girl and moved far away from the local gossip, first to Galway and then to a place in America named Jackson, Michigan. Another brother, Pat, passed the exam to become a teacher but the Kilkee School already had a teacher, so he was given an offer in The North. His mother, Honora, had forbidden his going there, fearful for his soul among Protestants, so Pat sailed off to Australia to find his sister Ellen in Sydney. He was said to be a wonderful singer. "But for Lynch, we'd all do," is what was said about him after he'd regaled his fellow passengers on the long journey. He was, it turned out, good at seafaring too, keeping logs and reading the stars and charts. The captain of the ship offered him work as a first mate and it is rumored that after a fortnight's visit with his sister in Sydney, he returned to the ship and spent the rest of his days at sea. No one in Moveen ever heard from him again. He famously never sent money home. Dan and John, two other brothers, had died young, which left Tom and Sinon and their sister Mary who was sickly and their widowed father still at home.

Tom Lynch booked passage for America. He was twenty-four. I'm guessing he sailed from Cappa Pier in Kilrush and went through Canada, working his way from Quebec to Montreal to Detroit and then by train out to Jackson. He settled in a boarding-house near his brother Michael and the wife, Kate, there in Jackson—a place their father, Pat, had been to briefly years before—where a huge state prison and the fledgling auto shops promised work. Maybe it was in memory of his dead mother, or maybe because there was a space on the forms, or maybe just because it was the American style, he identified himself in his new life in the new world as Thomas Curry Lynch. Or else it was to distinguish himself from the better-known and long-established Thomas B. Lynch, proprietor, with Cornelius Mahoney, of Jackson Steam Granite Works, "Manufacturers of Foreign and Domestic Monuments," situated on Greenwood Avenue, opposite the cemetery. Maybe to better his job prospects or his romantic ones, he shaved four years off his age in the same way. Among his new liberties was to identify himself as he saw fit. The stone in Jackson in St. John's Cemetery maintains his version of it. *Thomas C. Lynch,* it reads, *1870–1930.* Back at the Parish House in Carrigaholt, his baptism is recorded in 1866.

Before he was buried in Jackson, in consort with Ellen Ryan, the Canadian daughter of Irish parents, to whom he was married in 1897, Thomas Curry Lynch fathered a daughter, Gertrude, who became a teacher, and two sons: Thomas Patrick who would become the priest I'd be named for, and Edward Joseph who would become my grandfather.

According to the *Jackson City Directory,* Thomas Curry Lynch worked as a "fireman," a "helper," a "laborer," a "painter," a "foundry man," and as a "janitor" at I. M. Dach Underwear Company. In September 1922, he was hired as a guard for the Michigan State Prison in Jackson. The picture on his employee pass shows a bald man with a long, square face in a three-piece double-breasted suit and white shirt, collar pin and tie. He is looking straight into the camera's eye, neither smiling nor frowning;

his closed mouth is a narrow level line between a good nose and a
square chin—a sound man, as they say in Clare, able and airy and
dressed to the nines. He bought a small frame house at 600 Cooper
Street, a block south of St. John's Church, outlived his wife by nine
years, and died in September of 1930. He never lived to see his son
receive his Holy Orders in 1934 or die of influenza in 1936. He is
buried there in Jackson among the Morrisseys and Higginses and
others from the western parishes of Clare, between Ellen and his
youngest son. He rests in death, as in life, as Irish men have often
done, between the comforts and vexations of priest and the missus, far from the homes they left as youths.

SINON, THE BROTHER Tom had left at home, stayed on and
kept his widowed father. In 1895 he married Mary Cunningham
from Killimer, east of Kilrush, and they raised sons and daughters,
the youngest of whom, Tommy and Nora, born in 1901 and 1902,
waited in the land and tended to their aging parents and kept this
house.

The census of a hundred years ago records a house with stone
walls, a thatched roof, two rooms, two windows, and a door to the
front. Early in the twentieth century, another room was added to
the north and divided by partition into two small rooms. So there
was a room for the parents, a room for the girls, a room for the
boys, and a room for them all where the table and the fire were.
The farm, at long last, was a freehold, the first in the townland,
bought from the landlord in 1903 under the provisions of the
Land Purchase Act. Cow cabins and out-offices appeared, and a
row of whitethorns that Pat Lynch had planted years before to
shelter the east side of the house were now full grown. He bought

them as saplings in Kilrush when he'd gone there for a cattle fair. He paid "two and six": two shillings and sixpence, about thirty cents, and brought them home as a gift for Honora who had them set beside some native elder bushes. They still provide shelter and berries for birds.

This is how I found it when I first came here—sheltered by whitethorns and elders on the eastern side, stone walls, stone floors, thatched roof, an open hearth with the fire on the floor, a cast-iron crane and hooks and pots and pans and utensils. There were three windows and one door to the front, three windows and a door to the back, four lightbulbs, strung by wires, one in every room, the kitchen at the center, the bedroom to the south, and two smaller rooms, divided by a partition, to the north. There was a socket for the radio perched in the deep eastern window, a socket for the kettle and the hotplate, and a flickering votive light to the Sacred Heart. There were pictures of Kennedy and the pope, Jesus crowned with thorns, the Infant of Prague, St. Teresa, St. Martin de Porres, and a 1970 calendar from Nolan's Victuallers. There was a holy-water font at the western door. The mantel was a collection of odd-ments—a wind-up clock, a bottle of Dispirin, some antiseptic soap, boxes of stick matches from Maguire & Patterson, plastic Madonnas and a bag of sugar, a box of chimney-soot remover called Chimmo, and cards and letters, including mine. There was a flashlight, and a tall bottle of salt and a bag of flour. Otherwise the house remained unencumbered by appliance or modernity—unplumbed, unphoned, dampish and underheated, unbothered by convenience, connection, or technology. It resembled, in its dimensions, the shape of a medieval coffin or an upturned boat, afloat in a townland on a strip of land between the mouth of the Shannon and the North Atlantic. It seemed to have as much in common with the sixteenth century as the twentieth. Perpendicular to the house on the south side was a cow cabin divided into three stalls, each of which could house half a dozen cows. On the north side of the house, also perpendicular, was a shed divided into two cabins. Hens laid eggs in the eastern one. In the western one was turf.

Last week for the first time in more than thirty years, I could see it all—as the Aer Lingus jet made its descent from the northwest, over the Arans to the Shannon Estuary, the cloud banks opened over the ocean, clear and blue from maybe 5,000 feet, and I could see the whole coastline of the peninsula, from the great horseshoe strand at Kilkee out the west to Loop Head. The DC-9 angled over Bishop's Island, Murray's Island, and Dunlicky, the cliffs and castle ruins, and the twin masts atop Knocknagaroon that the pilots aim for in the fog. I could see the quarry at Goleen and the Holy Well and James and Maureen Carmody's house on the hill and Patrick and Nora Carmody's, Jerry Keane's and J. J. McMahon's, and Sonny and Maura Carmody's and the Walshes' and Murrays' and there, my own, this house and the haggard and the garden and outbuildings and the land and the National School and Carrigaholt Castle and banking eastward Scattery Island and the old workhouse in Kilrush and the ferry docks at Tarbert and then, in a matter of minutes, we landed.

I never saw it so clearly before. The first time I came here, it was just a patchwork of green emerging from the mist, the tall cliffs, ocean, river, houses, lands.

Nothing had prepared me for such beauty.

I was the first of my people to return.

My great-grandfather, Thomas Curry Lynch, never returned to

this house he was born in nor ever saw his family here again. My grandfather, Edward, proud to be Irish, nonetheless inherited the tribal scars of hunger and want, hardship and shame, and was prouder still to be American. He never made the trip. He worked in parcel post at the Main Post Office in Detroit, wore a green tie on St. Patrick's Day, frequented the bars on Fenkell Avenue until he swore off drink when my father went to war and spoke of Ireland as a poor old place that couldn't feed its own. And though he never had the brogue his parents brought with them, and never knew this place except by name, he included in his prayers over Sunday dinners a blessing on his cousins who lived here then, "Tommy and Nora," whom he had never met, "on the banks of the River Shannon," which he had never seen, and always added, "Don't forget."

> *Bless us, O Lord*
> *And these thy gifts*
> *Which we are about to receive*
> *From thy bounty*
> *Through Christ Our Lord.*
> *Amen.*
>
> *And don't forget your cousins*
> *Tommy and Nora Lynch*
> *On the banks of the River Shannon.*
> *Don't forget.*

The powerful medicine of words remains, as Cavafy wrote in his poem "Voices":

> *Ideal and beloved voices*
> *of those dead, or of those*

who are lost to us like the dead.
Sometimes they speak to us in our dreams;
sometimes in thought the mind hears them.

And with their sound for a moment return
other sounds from the first poetry of our life—
like distant music that dies off in the night.

And this is how my grandfather's voice returns to me now—
here in my fifties, and him dead now "with" forty years (in Moveen
life and time go "with" each other)—"like distant music that dies
off in the night," like "the first poetry of our life."

Bless us, O Lord.
Tommy and Nora.
Banks of the Shannon.
Don't forget. Don't forget.

He is standing at the head of the dining-room table in the
brown brick bungalow with the green canvas awning on the porch
overlooking Montavista Street two blocks north of St. Francis de
Sales on the corner of Fenkell Avenue in Detroit. It is any Sunday
in the 1950s and my father and mother and brothers, Dan and Pat
and Tim, are there and our baby sister, Mary Ellen, and Pop and
Gramma Lynch and Aunt Marilyn and Uncle Mike and we've
been to Mass that morning at St. Columban, where Fr. Kenny, a
native of Galway, held forth in his flush-faced brogue about being
"stingy with the Lord and the Lord'll be stingy with you," and
we've had breakfast after Mass with the O'Haras—our mother's
people—Nana, and Uncle Pat and Aunt Pat and Aunt Sally Jean

and Uncle Lou, and then we all piled in the car to drive from the suburbs into town to my father's parents' house for dinner. And my grandfather, Pop Lynch, is there at the head of the dining-room table, near enough the age that I am now, the windows behind him, the crystal chandelier, all of us posing as in a Rockwell print—with the table and turkey and family gathered round—and he is blessing us and the food and giving thanks and telling us finally, "Don't forget" these people none of us has ever met, "Tommy and Nora Lynch on the banks of the River Shannon. Don't forget."

This was part of the first poetry of my life—the raised speech of blessing and remembrance, names of people and places far away about whom and which we knew nothing but the sounds of the names, the syllables. It was the repetition, the ritual almost liturgi-cal tone of my grandfather's prayer that made the utterance mem-orable. Was it something he learned at his father's table—to pray for the family back in Ireland? It was his father, Thomas Lynch, who had left wherever the banks of the Shannon were and come to Jackson, Michigan, and painted new cellblocks in the prison there and striped Studebakers in an auto shop there. Was it that old bald man in the pictures with the grim missus in the high-necked blouse who first included in the grace before meals a remembrance of the people and the place he'd left behind and would never see again?

Bless us O Lord, Tommy and Nora. Banks of the Shannon.
Don't forget.

When I arrived in 1970, I found the place as he had left it, eighty years earlier, and the cousins we'd been praying for all my life. Tommy was holding back the barking dog in the yard. Nora was

making her way to the gate, smiling and waving, all focus and cal-
culation. They seemed to me like figures out of a Brueghel print:
weathered, plain-clothed, bright-eyed, beckoning. Words made
flesh—the childhood grace incarnate: *Tommy and Nora. Don't for-*
get. It was wintry and windy and gray, the first Tuesday morning of
the first February of the 1970s. I was twenty-one.

"Go on, boy, that's your people now," the taxi man who'd
brought me from Shannon said. I paid him and thanked him and
grabbed my bag.

I'VE BEEN COMING and going here ever since.

The oval welcome in my first passport—that first purple stamp
of permission—remains, in a drawer in a desk with later and like-
wise-expired versions. *3 February 1970. Permitted to land for 3*
months.

The man at the customs desk considered me, overdressed in my
black suit, a jet-lagged dandy with his grandfather's pocket watch,
red-eyed, wide-eyed, utterly agape. "Gobsmacked," I would later
learn to call this state.

"Anything to declare?" he asked, eyeing the suitcase and the
satchel.

"Declare? Nothing."

"Passport." I handed it over.

"The name's good," he said, and made an "X" on my luggage
with a piece of chalk. "You're welcome home."

I walked through customs into the Arrivals Hall of Shannon
Airport. At the Bank of Ireland window I traded my bankroll of
one hundred dollars for forty-one Irish punts and change—huge
banknotes, like multicolored hankies folded into my pocket. I
walked out into the air sufficiently uncertain of my whereabouts

that when a taxi man asked me did I need a lift, I told him yes and showed him the address.

"Kilkee—no bother—all aboard."

That first ride out to the west was a blur. I was a passenger on the wrong side of a car that was going way too fast on the wrong side of roads that were way too small through towns and country-side that were altogether foreign. Cattle and parts of ruined castles and vast tracts of green and towns with names I'd seen on maps: Sixmilebridge, Newmarket on Fergus, Clarecastle, then Ennis where the signpost said, KILKEE 35 MILES, then Kilrush, where another said, KILKEE 8.

"How long are you home for?" the driver asked. I'd never been so far from home before.

"I don't know," I told him. I didn't know. I didn't know what "home" meant to the Irish then, or what it would come to mean to me. I'd paid two hundred and nineteen dollars for a one-way ticket from Detroit to New York to Shannon. I had my future, my passport, my three months, no plans.

The ride from Shannon took about an hour.

What a disappointment I must have been—deposited there in the road outside the gate, the Yank, three generations late, dressed as if for a family photo, fumbling with a strange currency for the five-pound note I owed for the ride, bringing not the riches of the New World to the Old, but thirty-six pounds now and a little change, some duty-free tobacco and spirits, and the letter that Nora Lynch had sent that said it was all right for me to come. Blue ink on light blue lined paper, folded in a square, posted with a yellow stamp that bore a likeness of "Mahatma Gandhi 1869–1948" and a circular postmark: *CILL CHADIOHE CO AN CHLAIR,* which I later learned to English as "Kilkee, Co. Clare." The hand-writing was sturdy, angular, and stayed between the lines.

Moveen West
Kilkee
Jan 8. '70

Dear Thomas
We received your letter before Xmas. Glad to know you are coming to Ireland. At the moment the weather is very cold. January is always bad. I hope it clears up before you land. Write and say when you expect to come so we'd get ready for you. I hope all your family are well.

With Best Regards to All the Lynch's
Nora & Tom

Of course she hadn't a clue about us—"All the Lynch's," as she called us. Whatever illusions Americans have about the Irish—that they are permanently good-natured, all saints and scholars, tidy and essentially well-intentioned drunks, cheerful brawlers—all that faith-and-begorra blindness behind *The Quiet Man* and the Irish Spring commercials, what the Irish knew about Americans was no less illusory.

The taxi man told me a joke en route, about the "Paddy" he called him, from Kilmihil, who'd gone off to the States to seek his fortune, having heard that the money there grows on trees and the streets are "literally paved with it," et cetera, and "he's after stepping off the boat in Boston of a Sunday and making his way up the road when what does he see but a ten-dollar bill in the street, plain as day. And your man, you know, is gobsmacked by the sight of it, and saying to himself, 'The boyos back home were right after all, this place is nothing but money, easy as you please,' and he bends to pick up the tenner when the thought comes to him. He straightens up, kicks it aside, and says to himself, 'Ah hell, it's Sunday. I'll start tomorrow.'"

Still Nora Lynch would have known I was one of her people. She would have sorted out that her grandfather was my grandfather's grandfather. Old Pat Lynch, whose heart failed at eighty on the twelfth of June in 1907, would be our common man. His body buried with his wife's, long dead, and Nora's twin who had died in infancy of encephalitis, and Nora's father who had died in 1924—all of them returning to dust in the gabled tomb by the road in Moyarta. We'd be cousins, so, twice removed. She could twist the relations back the eighty years, back to the decade before she was born when her father's brother Tom left for America. Old Pat had gone to America himself years before, stayed for several months, and returned to Honora and the children. Maybe he was the one who discovered Jackson, Michigan, and the huge prison, opened in 1838, the largest in the world back then, and all the work it provided for guards and cooks and the building trades. And Nora's brother Michael had gone to Jackson as a young man, following others from the west of Clare to "Mitch-e-gan." The records at Ellis Island show him landing there in 1920, off the *Adriatic* from Southampton. He'd married there and when his wife died, he returned to Moveen, where he died of a broken heart one warm August day in 1951 while saving hay. Nora would have had word from him about the Jackson crowd—about their uncle, Thomas Curry Lynch, and his wife, "a

Ryan woman, wasn't she?" and about his boys, Eddie and Tommy, and their sister Gertrude, raised at 600 Cooper Street. Hadn't he brought a picture of his first cousin the priest, Fr. Thomas Patrick Lynch, for whom I'd be named a dozen years after the young priest had died—my father's uncle—there in the wide-angled photo of them all gathered out front of St. John's Church on Cooper Street in Jackson, Michigan, in June of 1934 shortly after his ordination. My father, ten years old, wearing knickers and knee socks, is seated between his father and mother. And Nora's brother Mikey, somewhere in that crowd, posed for the camera with his young wife who would be dead before long, the way they are all dead now. Nora and Tommy four thousand miles away, in the prime of their lives, will get word from one of them, about the new priest in the family.

And years later she will sort it all out: her Uncle Thomas married Ellen Ryan, "a great stiff of a woman," she had heard, and their son, Edward, married Geraldine, "some shape of a Protestant, but she converted," and their son Edward married Rosemary, and then this Yank, twentyish, out of his element, in the black suit standing in the rain at the gate, the dog barking, the cab disappearing down the road, all family, "all the Lynch's," all long since gone, and now returned.

"So, Tom that went," she said, connecting eight decades of dates and details, "and Tom that would come back. You are welcome to this part of the country."

After the dog, Sambo, was subdued, we went indoors. There was a fire on the floor at the end of the room, a wide streak of soot working up the wall where the chimney opened out to the sky. And the rich signature aroma of turf smoke I'd smelled since landing in

Shannon. I was given a cigarette, whiskey, a chair by the fire, the household luxuries.

"Sit in there now, Tom. You'll be perished with the journey," Tommy said, adding black lumps to the fire. "Sure faith, it's a long old road from America." There were odd indecipherable syllables between and among the words I could make out.

Nora was busy frying an egg and sausage and what she called "black pudding" on the fire. She boiled water in a kettle, cut bread in wedges from a great round loaf, pulled the table away from the wall into the middle of the room, settled a teapot on some coals in front of the fire. She set out cups and plates and tableware. Tommy kept the fire and interrogated me. How long was the trip, how large the plane, were there many on it, did they feed us well? And my people would be "lonesome after" me. I nodded and smiled and tried to understand him. And there was this talk between them, constant, undulant, perfectly pitched, rising and falling as the current of words worked its way through the room, punctuated by bits of old tunes, old axioms, bromides, prayers, poems, incantations. "Please Gods" and "The Lord've mercies" and "The devil ye know's better than the one ye don't"—all given out in a brogue much thicker and idiomatically richer than I'd ever heard. They spoke in tongues entirely enamored of voice and acoustic and turn of phrase, enriched by metaphor and rhetoricals and cadence, as if every utterance might be memorable. "The same for some, said Jimmy Walsh long 'go, and the more with others." "Have nothing to do with a well of water in the night." "A great life if you do not weaken." There was no effort to edit, or clip, or hasten or cut short the pleasure of the sound words made in their mouths and ears. There were "Sure faith's" and "Dead losses" and "More's the pities."

And a trope that made perfect sense to Nora, to wit: "The same but different"—which could be applied to a variety of contingencies.

"The same but different," she said when she showed me the wallpaper she'd lately pasted to the freshly plastered walls of the room she had prepared for me. "The same as America, but different." There was a narrow bed, a chair on which to put my suitcase, a crucifix, and the picture of the dead priest I'd been named for. The deep window ledge gave me room for my briefcase. There was a chamber pot on the floor and a lightbulb hung from the ceiling. The room was five feet wide and ten feet long, like a sleeper on a night train or a berth in steerage class, snug and monkish, the same but different.

After tea she took me down in the land. Out past the cow cabins and the tall hay barn, we stepped carefully along a path of stones through the muddy fields. Nora wore tall rubber boots she called Wellingtons and moved with a deliberate pace along the tall ditch banks that separated their land from the neighbors'. She carried a plastic bucket. She seemed immediately and especially curious about my interest in farming. I told her I didn't know a thing about it. "There's nothing to it," she told me. "You'll have it learned like a shot. A great block of a boy like you, it'll be no bother for ye. You'd get a tractor, and a wife, and there'd be a good living in it."

"What do you grow?" I asked her.

"Mostly cows."

We made our slow way down the soggy land, dodging pools of standing water and thickening mud.

"Mind the fort, Tom," Nora said, pointing to a tall, circular mound that occupied the corner of the next field over. "Never tamper with a fort."

Then she knelt to an open well in the middle of the land, skimmed the surface with the bucket, then sank it deep and brought it up again with clear water spilling over the edges.

"Have a sup, Tom, it's lovely water and cold and clean."

We walked the half a mile uphill back to the house. I carried the bucket and was highly praised for doing so.

Back at the fire, Nora told me how she and Tommy had been the youngest of their family. How her father died young and all their siblings had left for America except for Nora's twin brother who died in infancy. Two sisters had gone to Buffalo, New York, married well, and never returned. Mikey had gone to Jackson, "Mitch-e-gan," and worked there in the factory and married but his wife died young and he came home to Moveen and died saving hay in the big meadow in 1951. He was fifty-three. So it fell to Tommy and Nora to keep the place going and care for their widowed mother who was always sickly and feeble. Neither married, though they had many chances, "you can be sure of that, Tom." Both had stayed. Now, nearing seventy, they had their health, their home, and their routine. "Thanks be to God," they wanted for nothing. God had been good to them. "All passing through life." Sambo dozed in the corner. A cat curled on the window ledge. Another nursed her litter in the clothes press near the fire. There was a goose in the storage room waiting on an egg. There was rain at the windows, wind under the doors. The clock on the mantel was tick-ing. The day's brief light was fading rapidly. The coals reddened in the fire on the floor.

Now I was nodding, with the long journey and the good feed and the warmth of the fire at my shins, and the chanting of cattle in the adjacent cabin and the story Nora was telling me of lives lived out on both sides of the ocean—an ocean I'd seen for the first time that day. I might've drifted off to sleep entirely, awash in bucolia, talk, and well-being, if all of a sudden Tommy didn't rise, tilt his head to some distant noise, haul on his tall boots, and disappear out the door. Nora quickly filled a large pot with water and hung it from the crane over the fire. She brought lumps of coal from a bag in the storage room and added them to the turf. She rolled a piece of newspaper and fanned the coals to flames in the turf. She brought a bucket of meal from a tall bag in the same room. I wondered what all of the bustle was about.

Within moments, Tommy was back in the door holding in a slippery embrace a calf still drenched with its own birthing. It was the size of a large dog, and shaking and squirming in Tommy's arms. Nora mixed meal in a large plastic bowl and filled it with boiling water—a loose oatmeal that she took out to the cow cabin. Tommy dried the new calf with straw and kept it close to the warm fire and tried to get it to suckle from a bucket of milk and meal. "Fine calf, a fine bullock God bless 'oo," he kept repeating, "that's it now, drink away for yourself." Nora reappeared and disappeared again with another bucket of hot meal. All of this went on for most of an hour. The calf was standing now on its own spindly legs. Tommy took it out to suck from its mother. It was dark outside; the night was clear and cold. The cow cabin, though it stank of dung, was warm with the breath of large bodies. Tommy squirted the new calf from its mother's teat and said, "Go on now, go on now, sup away for yourself, best to get the beastings right away, there's great medicine in the first milk." He got hay from the hay barn and spread it about and traded one of his Woodbines for my Old Gold. We stood and smoked and watched the new bullock suckle, its mother licking it with great swipes of her tongue.

"Haven't they great intelligence after all?" said Tommy. "That's it then, Tom, we'll go inside."

I was chilled and tired, tired to the bone. But Nora made fresh tea and put out soda bread and cookies and praised the good fortune of a healthy calf, God bless him, and Tommy who was a "pure St. Francis" with the animals. "None better. Ah, no boy. Of that you can be sure." Then she filled an empty brown bottle with boiling water and put it in my bed to warm the sheets. She brought out blankets and aired them by the fire then returned them to the room I was given to sleep in. I crawled in and despite the cold and damp could feel my body's heat beneath the heavy bed linens and was soon asleep.

Sometime in the middle of that first night I woke, went out the back door to piss the tea and water and whiskey in the dark, and looking up I saw a firmament more abundant than anything I'd ever seen in Michigan. It was, of course, the same sky the whole world sees—the same but different—as indeed I felt myself to be, after that first night on the edge of Ireland, in the townland of Moveen with the North Atlantic roaring behind the fields above, and the house full of its nativities, and the old bachelor and his spinster sister sleeping foot-to-foot in their twin beds and common room and myself out pissing under the stars asking the heavens how did I ever come to be here, in this place, at all?

IN THE LATE 1960s, my life was, like the lives of most American men my age, up for grabs. The war in Vietnam and the Selective Service draft made us eligible to be called up when between the ages of nineteen and twenty-six. For able-bodied suburban men, that meant going to college for the deferment. As the war grew increasingly unpopular, the draft was rightly seen as a class war being waged against the disadvantaged—mostly black or Hispanic or poor who were disproportionately sent into battle. In December 1969, Richard Nixon held the first draft lottery since World War II. The pressing need for more young men as fodder, the gathering storms of protest and public outrage, the inequities of the draft all coalesced into this theatre of the absurd. Three hundred sixty-six blue capsules with the dates of the year were drawn out of a fishbowl in Washington, D.C., on Monday evening, December 1. I was playing gin rummy in the student union of Oakland University. The first date drawn was September 14. Men born on that day were going to war. October 16, my birthday, wasn't pulled until 254. The first hundred drawn were reckoned to be goners. They'd be suited up and enroute for Southeast Asia before spring of the coming year. The next hundred or so were figured to be relatively safe. The last third drawn were the jackpot winners. They would not be called up for Vietnam. They would not be given guns and sent off to an unwinnable war and told to shoot at strangers who were shooting at them. It was like a sentence commuted. I was free to go.

Up until then, I'd been going nowhere. I was twenty-one, a lackluster student in a state university studying nothing so much as the theory and practice of pursuing women, a variety of card games, the pleasures of poetry and fiction and drink. I had been biding time, doing little of substance, waiting to see what would become of my life. I was living in a sprawling rental house in the country not far from the university with seven other men and the women they could occasionally coax to stay with them. We each paid fifty dollars a month rent and a few bucks for light and heat. The place had five fireplaces, a stream out front, half a mile of woodlands to the main road, acres of scrub grass and ponds out back. We had our privacy. We'd play cards around the clock, listen to the music of the day, drink and drug and arrange great feasts. I was working part-time at my father's funeral home to pay for the rent and the car and my habits but had steadfastly avoided making career choices yet. It was a life of quiet dissipation from which the number 10-16, the date of my birth, in concert with the number 254, delivered me. It seemed arbitrary, random, surreal. I could do the math— that 1016 was divisible by 254— but couldn't make out the deeper meaning. As with many of life's blessings, it was mixed. The certainty that I would not be going to war was attended by the certainty that I would have to do something else. As long as the draft loomed, I could do nothing. But I had escaped it. This was the good news and the bad news.

I considered the options. I had met a woman but was uncommitted. I had a job but no career. I was taking classes but had no focused course of study. I had a future but hadn't a clue as to what to do with the moment before me.

My closest friend, then as now, was the poet Michael Heffernan, with whom I drank, read poems, and discussed the fierce beauties of women and the manifest genius of the Irish. He had regaled me with talk of his own travels in Ireland and read me what he'd written about the people and the places. At his instruction, I read Joyce and Yeats and Kavanaugh. I switched from vodka to whiskey— it seemed more Irish. I asked my widowed grandmother for an address. She still dutifully sent Christmas and Easter greetings to her dead husband's distant old-country cousins.

Moveen West Kilkee County Clare Ireland

The syllables—eleven, prime, irregular—then as now belong to this place only: townland, town, county, country, place—a dot on an island in an ocean in a world afloat in the universe of creation to which I was writing a letter. No numbers, no street names, no postal box or code. Just names—people, places, postage—sent. Postmarked all those years ago now: December 10, 1969.

> *Tommy and Nora Lynch*
> *Moveen West*
> *Kilkee*
> *Co. Clare*
> *Ireland*

Like a telescope opening or a lens focusing, each line of this addressing reduces the vastness of space by turns until we get to this place, this house, these people, who are by degrees subtracted from the vastness of humanity by the place they live in and the times they occupy and the names they have.

Since 1970, everything here has changed. Ireland has gone from being the priest-ridden poor cousin of Western Europe to the roaring, secularized Celtic Tiger of the European Union. For the first time in modern history, people are trying to get *into* rather than *out of* Ireland, and a country of emigrants has become a nation of commuters. Once isolated as an island nation at the edge of the Old World, the Irish are wired and connected and engaged with the world in ways they never would have imagined even a decade ago. There are more cars, more drugs, more TVs and mug-gings, more computers and murders, more of everything and less time in the day. Ireland has come, all swagger and braggadocio, into its own as a modern nation. Its poets and rock stars and fid-dlers and dancers travel the wide world as citizens of the globe and unmistakably Irish.

Still, looking out the window my ancestors looked out of, west by southwest, over the ditch bank, past Sean Maloney's derelict farm, upland to Newtown and Knocknagaroon, tracing the slope of the hill to the sea at Goleen and out to the river mouth beyond Rehy Hill, I think nothing in the world has changed at all. The same fields, the same families, the same weather and worries, the same cliffs and ditches define Moveen as defined Moveen a hun-dred years ago, and a hundred years before a hundred years ago. Haymaking has given way to silage, ass and cart to tractor and backhoe, bush telegraph to telecom and cell phones. But the dark-ness is as dense at night, the wind as fierce, the firmament as bright, the bright day every bit as welcome.

Everything is the same, but different.

Everything including me. In my fifties, I imagine the man in his twenties who never could have imagined me. I consider the changes in this house and its inhabitants—my people, me.

IS IT POSSIBLE to map one's life and times like a country or topography or geography? To chart one's age or place or moment? To say: I was young then, or happy, or certain, or alone? In love, afraid, or gone astray? To measure the distances between tributar-ies, wellsprings, roads and borders? Or draw the lines between connected lives? Can the bigger picture be seen in the small? Can we see the Western World in a western parish? Can we know the species by the specimen? Can we know the many by the few? Can we understand the way we are by looking closely at the way we've been? And will the language, if we set ourselves adrift in it, keep us afloat, support the search, the pilgrimage among facts and reveries and remembrances?

Is it possible to understand race and tribe, sect and religion, faith and family, sex and death, love and hate, nation and state, time and space and humankind by examining a townland of the species, a parish of people, a handful of humanity?

It was in Moveen I first got glimpses of recognition, moments of clarity when it all made sense—my mother's certain faith, my father's dark humor, the look he'd sometimes get that was so distant, preoccupied, unknowable. And my grandmothers' love of contentious talk, the two grandfathers' trouble with drink, the family inheritance of all of that. And the hunger and begrudgments and fierce family love that generation after generation of my people makes manifest. And I got the flickering of insights into our sense of "the other" and ourselves that has informed human relations down through time. Can it be figured out, found out, like pointing to a spot on a peninsula between now-familiar points and saying: It came from there, all of it—who we are, how we came to be this way, why we are the way we are—the same but different as the ones that came before us, and will come after us, and who came from other townlands, peninsulas, islands, nations, times—all of us, the same but different.

Those moments of clarity, flickering wisdoms, were gifts I got from folks who took me in because I had their name and address and could twist relations back to names they knew. When I stood at their gate that gray February morning, going thirty-five years ago, they could have had me in to tea, then sent me on my way. They could have kept me for the night, or weekend, or the week and then kindly suggested I tour the rest of the country. Instead they opened their home and lives to me, for keeps. It changed my life in ways I'm still trying to understand.

Tommy Lynch died in 1971. He was laid out in the room I sleep in now. After his funeral I rented a TV for Nora from Donnelan's in Kilrush, thinking it would shorten the nights. Because she was an elderly woman living on her own, Nora got the first phone in Moveen in 1982. She added a roomlet out front to house the new fridge and the cooker. She closed in the open hearth for a small and more efficient firebox. In 1982, my friend Dualco De Dona and I ran a water line in from the road, through the thick wall, into a sink that sat on an old clothes press and gave her cold water on demand. "A miracle," is what she called it, and praised our "composition" of it all. In 1986, she built a room on the back in which went a toilet and a shower and a sink.

Nora died here in 1992 in the bed I sleep in now. She left her home to me.

P. J. Roche pulled up the old flagstones and damp-coursed underneath them, then knocked out an inside wall to enlarge the kitchen, put in storage heaters, a back-boiler, radiators, and new windows. The place is dry and snug and full of appliances. The civilizers of the twentieth century—toilets and tap water, TV and a kind of central heat, the telephone and tractor and motor car—all came to this place in the past thirty years. Still, little in the landscape out of doors has changed. The fields green, the cattle graze on the topography that rises to the sea out one window and leans into the river out another. The peninsula narrows to its western end at Loop Head, where gulls rise in the wind drafts and scream into the sea that every night the sun falls into and on either side of which I keep a home. Folks love and grieve and breed and disappear. Life goes on. We are all blow-ins. We all have our roots. Tides come and go in the estuary where the river's mouth yawns wide into the ocean—indifferent to the past and to whatever futures this old house might hold.

The plans for the new room include a sliding glass door out to the rear yard where the whitethorn trees my great-great-grandmother Honora planted a century and a half ago still stand. According to their various seasons, they still berry and flower and rattle their prickly branches in the wind. It was her new husband Patrick who brought them home—mere saplings then—from a cattle mart in Kilrush where the old woman who sold them told him it was whitethorn that Christ's crown was fashioned from.

There's shelter in them and some privacy for those nights when, here in my fifties after too much tea, rather than the comforts of modern plumbing, I choose the liberties of the yard, the vast and impenetrable blackness of the sky, the pounding of the ocean that surround the dark and put me in mind of my first time here.

Those rare and excellent moments in my half-life since, when the clear eyes of ancients or lovers or babies have made me momentarily certain that this life is a gift, whether randomly given or by design; those times when I was filled with thanksgiving for the day that was in it, the minute only, for every tiny incarnate thing in creation—I've measured such moments against that first night in Moveen where staring into the firmament, pissing among the whitethorn trees, I had the first inkling that I was at once one and only and one of a kind, apart from my people yet among them still, the same as every other human being, but different; my own history afloat on all history, my name and the names of my kinsmen repeating themselves down generations, time bearing us all effortlessly, like the sea with its moon-driven, undulant possibilities: we Irish, we Americans, the faithfully departed, the stargazers at the sea's edge of every island of every hemisphere of every planet, all of us the same but different.

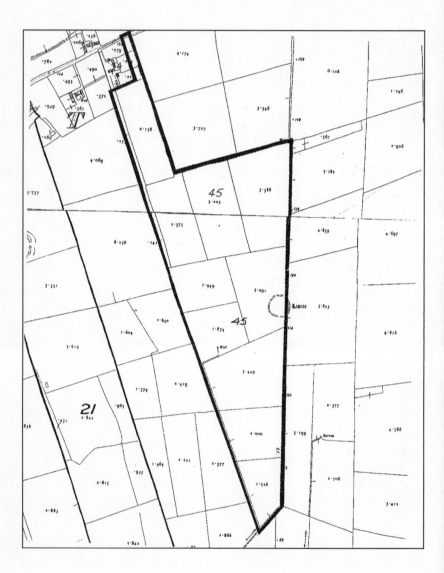

Inheritance

A Correspondence with Sile de Valera

Ms. Sile de Valera, T.D.
Minister for Arts, Heritage, Gaeltacht and the Islands
Department of Arts, Heritage, Gaeltacht and the Islands
Dun Aimhirgin
43 Mespil Road
Dublin 4
Ireland

6 September 2001

Dear Minister de Valera:
Am writing at the suggestion of Mr. Geroid Williams of the firm of McMahon and Williams, Solicitors, Kilrush, on behalf of certain constituents of yours, living and dead.

It had been my hope to see you in person, to which end I called at your office in Ennis twice in August and in both instances found it closed for staff holidays. I had been in Dublin in June, a guest of the Dublin Writers' Festival, and lodged at the Mespil Hotel, near the Ministry offices, but at that time was unaware that I would need your help. Last week I spoke to your office in Dublin and they were kind enough to put me in touch with Owen Lenehan who told me you will be in Ennis, in Chapel Street, on the 8th for a clinic. Alas, I had to return to Michigan at the end of August but will, if you can give me a date certain for an appointment, be on the next plane to Shannon or Dublin.

You and I met once before, at a wake. It was late March of 1992 in Moveen West, near Kilkee. It was my cousin Nora Lynch who had died and in her house that we met and I remember how touched I was that you had taken the time to call. Perhaps public servants in Clare, like politicos here in Michigan, find funerals fertile ground for politicking. But Nora Lynch was an elderly woman who had never married and had lived on her own for over twenty years and had neither children nor money nor influence left after her. So I knew you were there for genuine reasons, to pay respects to a woman of your grandfather's generation, a woman who was truly one of your people. I know that she often spoke of you, as "a mighty lady entirely, young and able, nobody's fool, well able for those prime boys above in Dublin, &c." Your being there to pay your respects to a woman who was, while precious to me, of no particular political estate, was a great consolation.

Indeed Nora Lynch's only estate was the small cottage we met in, there in Moveen, the haggards and out offices and cow cabins around it, enough money to wake and bury her well, and her belief that the 28 acres behind the house, the first freehold in that townland, worked by her grandfather and her father and her brother and that she had worked her entire life were hers to leave to whomever she pleased.

It is those few acres, Minister de Valera, about which I write in hopes you can help me to finally execute Nora Lynch's Last Will.

In May of 1968, Nora Lynch and her brother Tommy, 65 and 67 years old respectively, having spent years together working the farm, contacted Thomas Stapleton, an estate agent in Kilkee, with the intention of selling their land at public auction and going into retirement.

Tommy and Nora were the youngest son and daughter of Sinon Lynch and Mary Cunningham. While two older sisters and an older brother immigrated to America, Nora and Tommy stayed home, as was the custom, to tend to their ageing parents and the land. Neither ever married. Neither ever moved. Sinon died in 1926 and his widow, Mary, in 1950. In 1968 Tommy and Nora had thirty acres of grazing and hay and haggards. Nora sowed half an acre of potatoes, half an acre of oats, an eighth of an acre of turnips and a bit of cabbage. They kept, according to the inventory that appears on an Attendance Docket, "six good milch cows, 5 calves, 1 mare pony in foal and 1 ass." They also had "1 mowing machine, 1 rake, 1 slide and 1 haycar." The thatched house was three rooms and a kitchen, no plumbing, four lightbulbs and a socket for the radio and one for the kettle and a votive lamp to the Sacred Heart. No doubt you've been in hundreds like it.

Tommy rose early every morning to milk cows by hand

and ride by ass and cart the eight miles round trip to
Doonaha Creamery. Nora kept chickens and a couple geese
and tended the haggard. She did the marketing and prepared
the meals. They both worked the land long into their age. It
was, as you know, subsistence farming, bearing more resem-
blance in work and routine to three centuries earlier than to
three decades since.

It was the 25th of May 1968 that Thomas Stapleton, an
auctioneer in Kilkee, wrote to Michael McMahon, a solicitor
in Kilrush, to seek clear title to the land (which at the time
was still listed to Sinon Lynch) alerting him to Tommy and
Nora's intentions and his plan to "offer the holding by Public
Auction at my salesrooms on June 22nd."

(Mr. Williams has allowed me to copy the entire file on
this matter from his office records. Also I have, such as they
are, all of Nora Lynch's papers. So any quotations come from
actual documents, copies of which I will, on request, supply.)

Mr. McMahon then wrote to Tommy Lynch on the 31st of
May 1968 suggesting they meet in Kilkee "on some evening
that is convenient for you" to discuss "some particulars of
title." This they did on the 3rd of June. Everything appeared
to be proceeding apace for Tommy and Nora to sell their
land, keep their home, and settle into a deserved retirement
in the familiar landscape and friendly society of Moveen, living, they most likely hoped, into ripe old ages on their little
pensions and equities.

But this never happened.

On the 17th of June 1968, a fortnight after Tommy and
Nora Lynch met with Solicitor McMahon in Kilkee to discuss
the upcoming auction and the necessary updates to the Folio

in the Land Registry, a handwritten entry is made in that Folio, #22447, in Dublin, to wit:

"*The property is subject to the provisions prohibiting sale, transfers, lettings, sub-lettings or subdivisions without the consent in writing of the Land Commission contained in section 13 of the Land Act.*"

With this entry the rights of two honorable, elderly citizens to retain or dispose of the land that had occupied their lives and times and those of their parents and their parents' parents were lost.

The entry was made by a nameless Dublin clerk at the instruction, no doubt, of somebody who knew somebody who knew somebody who knew somebody else who, for reasons we might never know, had an agenda at odds with Tommy and Nora Lynch's.

They had committed no crime, done no dishonest thing, left no rate or rent unpaid. They had simply endeavored to sell their property by public auction or private treaty to whomever was willing to pay a fair price. And yet their right to do so was summarily removed by an entry in a ledger book by a Dublin bureaucrat.

You were, of course, a schoolgirl then, and I was not yet twenty. It was a tree, to paraphrase that Dublin churchman, that fell in the forest quietly. But fall it did.

On the 23rd of August 1968, Tommy and Nora were notified that the Land Commission had inspected their lands and had "decided to proceed with the acquisition of these lands in accordance with the Land Purchase Acts and the prescribed notices [would] be published and served on you in due course."

How the Land Commission came to be involved is anyone's guess. How does an agency in Upper Merrion Street in
Dublin 2 get wind of private dealings in West Clare? I know
that neither Tommy nor Nora contacted them. And I suspect
that the estate agent, Mr. Stapleton, didn't either, for surely
he looked forward to the commission he expected on the
auction of these lands, which he had by then advertised in
the *Clare Champion*. Would Mr. McMahon have any reason
to notify them? Was he required by any law or protocol to do
so? Had he other clients in Moveen? Did he stand to gain
anything by preventing a private sale or by protracting these
dealings? Who is to know? I never met the man. Mr. Williams
assures me his late partner was "punctilious" in every matter.
Years since his death his reputation for ethical and honest
dealings remains intact. So was it a neighbor who read Mr.
Stapleton's notice in the *Champion* and knew someone who
knew someone &c.? Indeed, who is to know? But there it is.

Nora always said it was a consortium of neighbors who
had "put in for it." She called them "grabbers" and said "they
wanted to get it for nothing." And I know who she said those
neighbors were. And I know why.

In any case, Nora and Tommy filed an Objection to the
Land Commission's action and in June 1969 a hearing was
held at the courthouse in Ennis at which they represented
that there was no reason for the Land Commission to be
involved in their property. They were working the farm to its
full capacity, the land itself was in good order, rents and rates
had always been paid, they'd never let any portion of the
lands and they expected that a young relation from America
would be coming to take it over for them. This last particu-

lar Nora made up. I think she was playing for time, hoping that the Land Commission's interest would disappear as quickly as it had appeared. Indeed, "after hearing the evidence of the Objectors, the Commissioners adjourned their further consideration of the objection for a period of two years."

No doubt Nora counted it a little victory. They wouldn't be able to retire but they wouldn't give into the "grabbers" or sell it for "worthless bonds." They filled their hay barn that summer, had their cows inseminated and hunkered down for the winter surrounded by neighbors with whom their relationship was now suspect.

This is where I came in.

In December of 1969 I was 21. I was a lackluster university student, doing English Literature and Psychology here in Michigan, trying mostly to avoid the draft and any life-changing decisions. My only attachments were to the work of Yeats and Kavanaugh and the new Irish poet Seamus Heaney and to the fiction of Joyce and John B. Keane and Flann O'Brien. My favorite American poets, John Berryman and Theodore Roethke, had both been to Ireland.

And I knew we had some family connections there. I suppose, like Nora, I was playing for time. I was in no hurry to begin a career or family or life's work. I believe she believed it was an Act of God by which the necessary fiction she'd told the Land Commission the summer before about "a young relation from America" became fact in the hapless person of myself, landed in the road at their gate in February 1970. In due course I was given the tour of the "first field" and the "far field" and the "fort field" and the "big meadow" and the spring well of "sweet water" that rose in the land; and told what a good living a man like me might get from land like this and how any woman would be happy to marry into such a place and after all it was my great-grandfather, Tom Lynch, who had left and only right that I returned.

It was clear Nora had a plan for my life. I told her I wasn't a farmer but that I thought it very generous of her to offer all the same. I knew nothing, of course, about her predicament with the Land Commission.

In the weeks that followed, I was taught to milk cows and to help with their calving, to clean the cow cabins and keep the fire, to cut hay from the hay barn and bring it to cows, and to make my way through the muddy fields for buckets of drinking water for the house. At Brew's in Kilrush, Nora bought me a pair of Wellingtons. I'd ride the bike alongside Tommy, on his donkey cart, to the creamery and out with Nora to visit neighbors.

Tommy taught me the management of dung and manure, the habits of cattle, fishing the cliffs for mackerel and twisting relations by the fire with Nora. I returned to America in early May, worked for three months, and was back in Moveen in August to draw turf with Tommy from the bog in Lisheen and enjoy the high season in Kilkee—open-air *ceili* dancing in the square, pony races on the strand, sing songs in the pubs.

And when neighbors would ask, "How long are you home for?" I'd tell them matter-of-factly, "not long enough." Nora would always insist that I "not present our business to any one of them. Tell them you might stay on altogether." I knew then there was subtext to her concerns. One night she told me about the Land Commission.

On the 9th of March 1971, Tommy Lynch died in his bed without medical attention of what was, I daresay, a treatable pneumonia. He was 70 years old and had been trying to work the farm like a younger man, to keep the Land Commission from taking it from him. His heart gave out. "A glass of water and a heave and he was gone, the poor cratur," is how Nora told it to those who asked. Nora biked into town to the Post Office and phoned me in Michigan. I flew over that night and was there for the wake and removal to Carrigaholt and the Mass and burial the following day.

It took a month to sell the stock and the hay barn and to get the roof slated and to go to Dublin for her passport. It was the first time she'd been in her nation's capital. And the first time she'd ever been on a plane. I brought her to America where she stayed with my family for a few weeks and then she rode out with my grandmother to Buffalo, New York, to see the two sisters she hadn't seen in over fifty years.

I don't know what happened there. My guess is it didn't go very well. It is the scourge of emigration—the guilt and shame on either side. Maybe their welcome was not warm enough. Maybe she was hoping they'd ask her to stay. Maybe there was old business never finished. Whatever it was, she called the visit "a dead loss" and flew home to West Clare the following day, determined to fight the Land Commission's efforts to take her land. She was frightened and alone, grieving and powerless and surrounded by neighbors she felt betrayed by. She was 68 years old and on her own.

That summer of 1971 whilst the appeal was pending, the Land Commission excluded the "dwelling-house and an accommodation plot" from "their proceedings," thereby giving Nora Lynch title to the roof over her head and the rooms she had lived in all of her life and the haggard and yards. They were apparently prepared to evict her from her own lands but not from her own bed.

At a hearing in Ennis that October her former objections were denied. Her brother was dead, the cattle were sold, the land was not being worked to its potential, the Land Commission's right to take up her land and re-distribute it among her neighbors was affirmed. So Nora began to quibble about the price and the method of payment. Again, it would seem, she was playing for time.

They'd offer one sum, she'd counter another. They'd offer land bonds, she'd insist on cash.

"I could be in America since my brother died," she wrote, "if they let me sell my land. I had plenty of buyers. We offered the land for full market value in cash as I am living alone and my friends are all in America and I have no one to fight for me. I have got my land valued and you know the value of land now. I'll have to get paid in cash and that's definite."

Nora was able to get the County Council to appeal the Land Commission's action on her behalf "upon the grounds that the price so fixed by the Irish Land Commission is inadequate and does not represent the true value of said lands."

In August of 1972 I returned to Ireland to see if Nora was making any progress. She was frightened and beside herself, bitter that a conspiracy of neighbors, through the Land Commission, was preventing her from a private sale of her land. She wondered if she should give up and join a convent but she felt it was her duty to fight for her rights in the matter.

In the space of four months, qualified buyers made no

fewer than four offers to Nora Lynch for the private sale of her land. In each case the Land Commission refused to allow the sale, though any one of them would have accomplished the stated goals of the Land Commission to consolidate smaller farms with larger adjacent ones so that they could be worked more efficiently. One can only assume that the Land Commission had another quite separate agenda with regards to this land.

Of course, all that follows from the Land Commission is enquiries as to "when possession can be obtained." For them, it is a closed matter. The price has been set at 4250 Punts.

On June 22, 1973, Iris Oifigiuil listed the 28 acres in question in its Final List.

The Land Commission sent notice in June that they would acquire the lands on the 17th of August 1973. But when they appeared at the gate Nora Lynch refused them entry. They could not gain possession of the land.

There's no telling why everyone seemed to back away from further confrontation at this point. Perhaps it was the look in Nora's eye when the Land Commission's agent appeared at her gate. Perhaps there was a change of policy in Dublin. Perhaps the people pressing for the acquisition decided that it would be easier to wait it out. Nora's brother had died in the midst of this imbroglio. She was getting older and had been under a lot of stress. And while I had been in Moveen frequently in 1970 and 1971 and 1972, marriage and career and family obligations meant I couldn't travel there in 1973. I did send for Nora and she made a brief visit to America in 1973. Still, maybe my absence was taken as a signal to them. Perhaps the consensus was that soon enough

Nora would die and I would disappear and then they could acquire the lands without having to further pester an old woman. I do not know. But I know that Nora believed that the Land Commission had withdrawn from the matter because they wouldn't pay her cash.

And I know that six years later, when I made my first trip back to Moveen in September of 1979, for whatever reason the case was suddenly reopened again. Two weeks after I left, a letter to Mr. McMahon from the Land Commission made known their intention to seek an Order of Possession. "Please let me hear from you without delay," it concluded.

At the suggestion of a friend, the late Paddy Murphy of Ballina, Co. Mayo, I contacted the Solicitor Adrian Burke. Paddy told me Mr. Burke was a friend and a fine attorney and that his sister, Mary Robinson, was a Senator and they were well connected.

Mr. Burke was representing a family in a legal case against the Land Commission for unfair acquisition of their lands. It was very similar to Nora Lynch's case. He told me that the case would work its way through the lower courts and eventually to the Supreme Court and that most likely, regardless of the outcome, there would be Appeals and that the whole process would take several years. For a small fee he agreed to attach our case to this other case. I sent him a check. He advised that Nora Lynch keep possession of her lands and under no circumstances give it up or take payment for it. I asked him about the wisdom of allowing a neighbor's cattle in the land and he said to go ahead, that it would prove the land was being used.

I confess at this point I was playing for time. I wanted

Nora Lynch to live out her life in possession of her lands. She was 77 years old, still living without transport or plumbing or central heat, in a damp climate in a damp cottage near the sea. She had refused our invitations to live in America. She had abandoned her plan to move into a convent. She wanted to live in her own house on her own lands and to exercise her rights as a hardworking, honest woman.

It was also plain why neighbors would want to get the land. All through the 1970s, emigration was the scourge it had always been, tearing families apart, banishing the young to England and America. As a parent, I could certainly appreciate a farmer's desire to expand the family holdings to keep as many of the children in the land as possible.

So I believed that if Adrian Burke's case could outlive Nora Lynch, everything might work out in the end. In fact, Mr. Burke was as good as his word. We never heard another word from the Land Commission. Nor did they ever attempt again to gain possession of Nora's land.

Nora came to Michigan for a visit in the summer of 1980. She seemed more relaxed. But still, after a month she began to worry that the Land Commission would take her lands in her absence. Every day her fear of this worsened. She cut short her visit and hurried back to Moveen.

Through the early 1980s Nora Lynch rented her land to various farmers for silage and pasturage. Relations with the neighbors, though occasionally tense, seemed to normalize. Whether it was local politics, Adrian Burke, or the Will of God, the Land Commission did not seem a present threat.

In 1985 she let the land to P. J. Roche, a young man from a townland between Cross and Kilbaha, who had recently married a woman from Ennistymon. He wanted to farm. He had a few acres just south of her land where he lived in a mobile home with his wife. Nora's letters were full of praise for this man. I believe P. J. reminded Nora of her brother Tommy. He rose early, worked late, tended his cows and improved the land. What is more, he would call into Nora mornings and evenings when he came by to check the cattle. And his wife Breda called in whenever she was going to town to see if Nora needed anything. At the birth of their daughter, Louise, they moved into their home in Newtown, at the edge of the ocean, from whence they could see Nora's lights and she could see theirs. When a cow was calving, she'd summon him at all hours, throw on the yard lights and make the tea. They'd talk farming and the price of things and the vagaries of the weather.

In 1988, after the publication of my first book of poems, I was given a fellowship to the Tyrone Guthrie Centre at Annaghmakerrig in Newbliss, Co. Monaghan. I cut short my residency there to go down to Moveen and visit Nora. She was nearly 86 years old but she was happier than she'd been in the long years since her brother had died. With P. J. and Breda Roche around, she didn't feel alone. There were still some tensions with some of the neighbors, but with the Roches' cattle in her fields, wintering out in her cow cabins, the fields being properly maintained and P. J. and Breda coming around with their infant daughter Louise, Nora Lynch felt once again engaged in the familiar life of her townland.

For me it was a great relief, having spent the most of twenty years concerned that Nora might fall ill or fall down or die alone and unhappy and under siege from forces over which she had no control; it was a great comfort to see that P. J. and Breda Roche treated Nora Lynch like family. She could not have lived on her own into her age without the daily kindnesses this young couple extended to her. Once, over pints in Carrigaholt, P. J. Roche made known to me his hope that if "God forbid anything should happen to Nora," he'd like me to know he'd like to buy the land from me. I told him I couldn't predict the future but "take care of Nora and I'll take care of you." In fact, Nora had made inquiries herself, with Geroid Williams, who had by now succeeded the late Michael McMahon as solicitor, to see if she could sell the land to Mr. Roche. He counseled against it. His advice was to leave well enough alone. The Land Commission had backed off their efforts to gain possession of Nora's land though they had in fact, for fifteen years, been recorded as the owners of it—a fact Nora Lynch never recognized. In her mind they hadn't any right to it, hadn't paid her a thing and she never allowed them inside the gate.

In 1988, Nora Lynch dictated to me her first Last Will.

It appointed me as the executor and charged me with the "distribution of her estate." It read in part:

Firstly it is my wish that the land that I and my late brother, Tommy Lynch, owned and worked all our lives be purchased at fair price and worked by Mr. Patrick J. Roche of Newtown. I have wanted to consummate the sale of said lands with Mr. Roche but am prevented by the Land Commission. I understand that as of August 1973, the land has been vested in the Irish Land Commission. However, I have never accepted payment of any kind from the Land Commission nor have I allowed them to take possession of the land since I believe they have no right to do so. Accordingly, I have rented the land to Mr. Patrick J. Roche since 1985 and he has taken good care of it. In the event of my death, should our dealings with the Land Commission not be finished, I instruct them to vest the land in Mr. Patrick J. Roche of Newtown. He has proved himself to be an honest, hard-working family man and has been kind to me in my latter years.

She left her home and haggards to me. As this was the home our common man, Pat Lynch—her grandfather and my great-great-grandfather—had been given as a wedding gift, and the home my great-grandfather left in 1890 to come to America, it was and remains a precious inheritance to me. Thanks to P. J. and Breda Roche, Nora lived out her last years a happy woman, vexed by the unfinished business of her land, but secure in the knowledge she had fought the good fight and stood her ground against the "grabbers" and "blackguards," whoever they were. She had taken no money, lived on her pension and foregone the comforts of retirement for the sake of principles.

In November of 1991 Nora was hospitalized briefly with what the doctors in Ennis called "gall stones." It was, we would figure out later, a cancer. I was in England on literary duties when Breda called my wife, Mary, in Michigan.

In February of 1992, Breda called with the news that Nora had fallen in her kitchen and was taken to the county hospital in Ennis and that the prognosis was very poor. I flew over to sort out what I could. With P. J. and Breda's help, we got her home where she was happiest.

Still Nora was worried about what would happen after her death. She asked me to go to Dublin and settle the business with the Land Commission. Through my friends, the poets Eilean Ni Chuilleanain and Macdara Woods, I'd met Paddy McEntee, the Senior Counsel, some years before. It was through his office I was directed to see Mr. Cathal Young in Lower Leeson Street to discuss what might be done with the Land Commission. I met with him on the 9th of March in 1992. Mr. Young thought Mr. Roche's chances to purchase the land from the estate—especially one executed by an American—were very poor. The Land Commission, though they had long since stopped acquiring properties and had begun in 1989 to sell off their land bank, still had vested themselves as owners of the lands in the Folio, leaving Nora Lynch a squatter on her own land.

I returned to Moveen with the matter still unresolved and gave the news to the dying woman. I suggested that she rewrite the Will and leave the land in question directly to the Roches, not for sale, but as inheritance. It seemed to me the correct thing to do. Their kindness and companionship had made it possible for her to live her life out in her own home, in charge of her own affairs, dependent on no one. If, indeed, the fight for that land must carry on, it seemed to me the case would be strengthened if a young Irish farmer were fighting for an inheritance of land he had worked in and had left to him by a woman who had worked it, rather than by a middle-ageing American poet. This made sense to Nora too.

On the 10th of March 1992, Geroid Williams came to

Nora in Moveen and prepared her new Last Will and
Testament. It appointed me sole executor, directed me to pay
the customary debts and expenses and reads, in part:

> *I do not accept that the Land Commission has any right to
> my lands at Moveen East and West. I have been in posses-
> sion of these lands all my life. Patrick J. Roche is at present
> tenant of these lands and has been very good to me. I give
> devise and bequeath all my lands at Moveen East and West
> to the said Patrick J. Roche and Breda Roche both of
> Newtown, Carrigaholt.*
>
> *I give devise and bequeath my dwelling house, haggards,
> out-offices and cabins registered in my name at Moveen
> West to my cousin the said Thomas Lynch absolutely.*

Nora died on the 27th of March in her own bed, in the
room she was born in nearly ninety years before, and was
waked there for three nights, it being wintry, and buried in
the vault in Moyarta among the bones of her people and
mine. Her obsequies, indeed the last weeks of her life, were
well attended by her neighbors, all old grievances having
been put aside in the name of still older friendships and
common struggles.

I've kept the house and, with P. J.'s help, made it more
habitable and able to withstand long absences. It has become
a kind of retreat for writers. Irish and English and Scots and
Dutch, Australian and American and one New Zealander—
poets and novelists and journalists—dozens of them have
benefited from the quiet and dark there and the friendly
ghosts. A. L. Kennedy wrote *On Bullfighting* there. Mike

McCormack did parts of *Crowe's Requiem*. Philip Casey wrote some of *The Water Star*. Mary O'Malley and Jessie Lendennie, Macdara Woods and Eilean Ni Chuilleanain, Robin Robertson, and Matthew Sweeney have all written poems there. Even the Heaneys had lobster there one summer evening a couple years ago. I think that Nora would approve. She regarded writing as an honorable trade, not unlike farming—"the poetry business," she always called it. I am there two or three times each year, whenever I've a good excuse. And my large extended family has restored its roots in West Clare for another generation. All to the good.

Still one bit of Nora's business remains unfinished.

It is going ten years since Nora Lynch died in Moveen. She never lived to hear the Celtic Tiger roar or see real signs of hope in The North, or watch the young come and go as they please around the country and among the countries of the world. Cell phones and central heat and holiday homes proliferate. It is another Ireland entirely from the one she knew. Nor did she ever have the certain knowledge that her lands would go to the ones she willed them to.

In West Clare now the question is not whether there'll be sufficient land for farmers but whether there'll be sufficient farmers for the land. The young will not be "grounded" in the way their parents were. They travel light now, like other Europeans through open borders, common markets, and virtual realities. No longer emigrants, they are ambassadors of Irish culture and competence.

P. J. Roche still works the land as he has for over sixteen years now. Like many Irish farmers he also works construction to make ends meet. He keeps his cattle and his horses.

He does masonry and plastering. His daughter Louise is in her teens. Breda works weekdays in the local shops. It is a good life and he is grateful for its blessings.

But he cannot stand in the land and call it his. Nor can he make the necessary improvements without clear title. The grants from the Rural Environmental Protection Scheme for the construction of a slatted house for his cattle are not available to him because he cannot produce proof of ownership. Nor will any lender loan him money against land that he works and occupies but does not own. Without clear title P. J. Roche is, as Nora was, a squatter on land he has long labored in. His work has not purchased any equity for himself, his wife or his daughter.

This is wrong.

It is a profound and longstanding injustice that quickened Tommy Lynch's death, cast a pall over Nora Lynch's life and severely limits P. J. Roche's future. Since 1968 the actions of the Land Commission have dishonored the honest labor of honorable people, made meddlers and quarrelers of good neighbors and served no defensible purpose for the State. It is long overdue to right this wrong.

For years, Mr. Williams has advised us to wait out the statute of limitations—thirty years. He has advised for years that the thirty years was up this year: thirty years since the land first appeared on the provisional list. But now he says, maybe thirty years since it appeared on the final list—2003! I ask why not thirty years since the Land Commission first made known their intentions, thus 1998? Or what if it is thirty years since they last sought an Order of Possession, which would bring it to 2010? Who's to know? Haven't we waited long enough to answer the simple questions?

Has not an Irish citizen and freeholder of land the right to dispose of that land in any reasonable way she sees fit? Or has the State the right to make her, for no apparent reason or compelling need, forfeit her title and rights in the matter?

Does an elderly, unmarried woman have fewer rights and protections than the young, the married or the male?

What other farms were seized in Moveen by government fiat? Was this case the exception or the rule?

Is it justice or politics that ought to determine these cases? Does cronyism trump honest labor and property rights?

Is there any legal, political, social or moral purpose to be served by letting the Land Commission's misadventures stand rather than giving title to Mr. Roche in accordance with Nora Lynch's wishes?

Which is why I write now, to beg for your intervention and good counsel, as my penultimate resort. My obligations to the estate of Nora Lynch and to her memory will not be met until this matter is settled.

Changing the world seems an impossible task. But changing twenty-eight acres is a start. The damage was done by the stroke of a pen, in a Folio in Dublin thirty-three years ago. Oughtn't it be undone just as easily? It is my hope you will help us do it. If so I will keep a record of it. If not, I'll keep the record of that too. I am a writer. It is what writers do.

Every goodwill,
Thomas Lynch
Moveen West, Kilkee
Milford, MI USA

In January a letter arrived, on government stationery with the
colored logos of the Ministry and the Dail:

> Dear Mr. Lynch
> Following my ongoing representations to my colleague, Mr.
> Joe Walsh, T.D., Minister for Agriculture, Food & Rural
> Development, concerning the procurement of title to the
> lands at Moveen West, Kilkee, Co. Clare, I am pleased to
> enclose the Minister's latest correspondence in this regard.
>
> I understand that on being asked to clarify the attached
> letter, the Department of Agriculture stated that title will
> revert to Nora Lynch and that a solicitor acting for P. J. and
> Breda Roche will then need to rectify title.
>
> Unfortunately, the Department of Agriculture could not
> give a timeframe as they have just begun the first case of this
> nature. They did, however, state that the "Lynch case" will be
> dealt with next and that they will then be in contact.
>
> I hope you are pleased with the above news and if I can be
> of any further assistance in the future, please do not hesitate
> to contact me.
>
> Kind regards,
> Yours sincerely,
> 'Sile'
> Sile de Valera, T.D.
> Minister for Arts, Heritage, Gaeltacht and the Islands

Settlement of "the Lynch case" came in February 2002 from the
Department of Agriculture:

Dear Mr. Lynch:

The Land Commission have submitted an application to us here stating while they became registered owners in 1973 of part of Folio CE22447, now CE999F (copy enclosed) they never took possession of the property. The lands remain in the possession of the previous registered owners. Sinon Lynch is full owner of property nos 1 and 2. Thomas Lynch and Nora Lynch are the owners of property 3.

We propose to reinstate Sinon Lynch as full owner of Property Nos 1 and 2 and Thomas Lynch and Nora Lynch as full owners of Property No 3.

We note on foot of your application in 1992, you became sole owner of the residue of Folio CE22447.

You may wish to lodge an application to become the registered owner of Folio CE999F if you are entitled.

We will proceed to register as stated above within 21 days.

Yours faithfully,
Daire Guidera

May 21, 2003

Dear Minister de Valera:

The last letter I wrote you was longish indeed, detailing the history of Nora Lynch's land and my interests in it. This will be briefer. Is it not always so—that please is always windier than thanks? Still these are thanks, underwritten and overdue, for your intercession on our behalf.

The slatted house that P. J. Roche has finished this year stands on his own ground. The greening of it, the grazing of it, the pride in it and profit of it all are his. His wife and his daughter are the more secure. The future is theirs to make of it what they can.

What is more, your representations on behalf of the estate of Nora Lynch, long deceased, restore a proper title to the past. The land was hers to give. And though it took ten years to make the gift complete, it is done now and there is justice in it.

Here in Michigan, the world and its wars and my own duties have kept me from travel to Ireland this spring. But my middle son, Michael, was over in February, taking advantage of the off-season, post 9-11 fares. He reported that February this year was much the same as I remember February there decades ago. The thought of him sitting in Nora Lynch's house, four generations removed from the young man who left there in 1890 and who started our family in America, fills me with a sense of the grandeur of Time.

You've used your time well, Ms. de Valera. Your grandfather would be proud of you. And my people are grateful to you always.

I'll be in West Clare, please God, the months of August and September and will call to your office in Ennis in due course to tender thanks in person. Or if you're out Moveen way, please pay a visit. You'll see what goodness your work has wrought.

All the best,
Thomas Lynch
Milford, Michigan & Moveen

Death Comes for the
Young Curate

A Pilgrim's Story

T HE PHOTO OF the new priest among his people is an
old one. Maybe it was Mikey Lynch who sent it home, to
let the brother and sister in the old country know that one
of their American cousins had been ordained. "First Solemn High
Mass," it reads in white handwriting in the top right corner, "of
Rev. Thomas P. Lynch," and on the next line, "St. John's Church,
Jackson, Mich., June 10, 1934." It is panoramic, seventeen inches
by seven inches, black and white, glossy.

Up on the steps in the middle background at the arching doorway of the church stands the celebrant, flanked by deacon and sub-
deacon, vested in albs and chasubles, with two cassocked and
surpliced men off to the right who must have been the altar servers
on the day. They are surrounded by a crescent of family and well-
wishers, five dozen or more, the front row seated on folding chairs
in the foreground, all posed, looking at the photographer with that

same grin folks get on their faces when they are saying, "Cheese!"
FedorFoto, printed at the bottom of the picture, suggests that Mr.
Fedor is, though nowhere to be seen, nearby squinting through his
lenses shouting, "That's it, hold it now, say, '*Cheese!*'"

The photo has hung here in Moveen for years, underneath the
picture of the Sacred Heart promising "Peace in the Family" and "A
blessing on the house where the image is exposed and honored"
and the little flickering red vigil light that is a fixture still in all the
country homes—remnants of a devotional past that may never
come 'round again.

It is the second Sunday in June in the middle of the Great
Depression between world wars, in the palm of the right hand that
is Lower Michigan. The print dresses, white shoes, and elegant
swooping hats make the women look fashionable and carefree. My
grandmother is wearing what looks like pearls. The men in three-
piece suits and ties sport straw hats. The morning light shines on
them all.

The Rev. Thomas P. Lynch is two months shy of his thirtieth
birthday. Though he survived the Spanish flu in 1918, he's been
sickly and susceptible ever since. His studies slowed by health set-
backs, he has been to seminary in Detroit and then, because he is
croupy and tubercular, his archbishop sends him to Denver and
then Santa Fe to finish his training in those high, dry, western cli-
mates. He has come home at long last, fully fledged, anointed, and
ordained to say a Solemn High Mass for his people—the family
and neighbors of his childhood. Within the week he will be returning to New Mexico and will die in two years of influenza and pneumonia, ten days short of his thirty-second birthday.

In front of him, smack in the middle of this assemblage, seated at the right hand of my grandfather, is my father, the priest's only nephew. He is ten years old, the only young boy in the frame, dressed in saddle shoes, knee britches, white shirt and tie, looking for all the world like his grandson and namesake, Edward J. Lynch, IV, a few years ago when he was ten.

These are Catholics, Irish Catholics—Higginses, Ryans, Murphys, and Flynns. They are immigrants or the children of immigrants who have brought with them the rubrics of the One True Faith of Holy Mother the Church practiced in the Druid-esque, idolatrous style of the Irish. This is the faith that saved them from England and Know-Nothings and Freemasonry, the church that buried their famine dead, stood firm against soupers and the Crown, educated their children, kept their women pure, their men sober and saved their immortal souls. And one of their own has just been made a lieutenant in the standing army that wages war on sin and evil and the flesh. It is an event worth hiring a photographer for.

FR. LYNCH WILL be stationed in Taos, New Mexico, at Nuestra Señora de Guadalupe. He'll be the assistant to the Rev. C. Balland and work with the five Sisters of Loretto at the Foot of the Cross who oversee the school with one hundred eighty-four pupils. He will marry and bury and baptize and teach young Apache and Hispanic children how to play baseball and avoid the deadly sins. He will do the rounds of the local missions—Arroyo Hondo, San Francisco de Asis, San Geronimo, and Immaculate Conception— before the paintings of Georgia O'Keeffe will make them all famous. He will bring forgiveness and communion and extreme unction to the sick and dying. After two years, his health will turn and he'll be taken to Santa Fe where, after three days in St. Vincent's Sanatorium, he will die on July 31, 1936. His body will be returned to Taos to be waked and prayed for and then a slow procession will take him down the mountains, along the river, to the cathedral in Santa Fe where the bishop will have another requiem. Then his body will be sent home in a box by train to Jackson, Michigan, where the people in this photo will follow him back into this church for the funeral Mass and out to St. John's Cemetery, where he'll be buried next to his father and mother.

When his brother, my grandfather, E. J. Lynch, goes to the funeral home to organize the local obsequies, he takes my father, twelve years old by now, along for the ride. While the men talk, the boy wanders through the old house until he makes it to the basement where he sees his uncle, the dead priest, being dressed in his liturgical vestments by two men in shirtsleeves, black slacks, and gray striped ties. Dead a week in the heat of summer, no doubt the corpse needed tending-to after all its travels. After alb and stole and mandible, they ease the chasuble over the cleric's head. They lift the priest's body into a casket, place his biretta in the corner of the casket lid, and turn to find the young boy standing in the doorway, watching.

It is to this moment in the first week of August 1936, standing in the basement of Desnoyer Funeral Home in Jackson, Michigan, that my father will always trace his decision to become a funeral director.

"I knew right away," he would always recount it, "that's the thing I was going to do."

For years I wondered why my father chose, given the scene as he described it, the undertaker's rather than the churchman's work. He was a devout boy, an altar boy, a fifth-grader being schooled by nuns. Surely he'd have been told to listen for his "calling." Why did he not choose to be a priest? It was years before it dawned on me—the priest was dead.

In the next ten years, my father will play right tackle for the St. Francis de Sales High School football team, learn to drive a car, fall in love with the redheaded Rosemary O'Hara, a girl he's known since the fifth grade, enlist in the Marine Corps, and spend four years in the South Pacific shooting a light machine gun at Japanese foot soldiers. He will return, a skinny and malarial hero, to Detroit, wed Rosemary, enroll in Mortuary School at Wayne State University, and go to work for William Vasu, a Romanian American who gives him, as part of his compensation, the rent-free use of a small apartment over the funeral parlor on Woodward Avenue in Highland Park. He promises his new bride that someday, just wait and see, they'll have a funeral home of their own, a house in the suburbs, "and maybe a couple of junior partners!" Within two months of their nuptials, she is pregnant with the first of their nine children.

Two generations later, grandsons and granddaughters of Rosemary and Edward Lynch are graduating from Mortuary School and joining the family firm of funeral directors that operates six mortuaries in the suburbs of Detroit, serving now more than a thousand families a year. They trace their calling to their parents who do this work. Their parents trace their calling to their father who traced his calling to the priest in this photo who died young and was sent home to Michigan and prepared for burial. Such are the oddities of chance and happenstance. Or such are the workings of the Hand of God.

"All things work together for good," is what Saint Paul has to say about such things. "God works in strange ways," my mother said.

WHEN I WAS seven, my mother sent me to see the priest.

I'd been fighting with my older brother, Dan, in the backyard. He was on top of me, holding my hands down, knees on my shoulders, bouncing on my belly, saying, "D'ya give?" I gave. He let me up. "God damn you, Danny," is what I said as soon as I had the breath back in me. Danny knew I had sinned grievously. "Damn *it*," was a venial sin. "Damn *you*," was worse but still not a deal breaker. But to implicate God in it was more evil by leagues. To ask God to send your brother into eternal damnation and the fires of hell forever and ever was, well, incomprehensibly depraved—a mortal sin.

We knew these things because we'd read *Fr. Murphy's Baltimore Catechism*, first published in 1885, its truths undimmed in the 1950s. Danny ran inside and told my mother, who came out roaring that I must go at once to see Fr. Kenny and make a good confession. I should be especially careful not to get hit by a car or killed in any way en route as it was certain that I'd be lost for good if I didn't get this good confession made before I died. Only an act of "perfect contrition" assembled from my dying breaths might save me in such a case and get me maybe a few thousand years in purgatory instead of the eternal damnation that mortal sins had coming to them. Perfect contrition was a true remorse, not motivated by a fear of punishment, plenty of which I had rightly coming to me, but by a genuine sorrow for giving offense to God. It was, I believe, beyond my ethical range at the time, to be so "perfect" in my regrets. I was afraid. I prayed for safe passage to the rectory.

The particulars of my confession and Fr. Kenny's absolution were not memorable. I only remember coming home with a clean slate, free of the worry over hellfire, saintly for the time being, looking for a way to get even with Dan.

Fr. Thomas Kenny came from Ireland. Born in Galway in the early 1900s, he came to Michigan to study for the priesthood at Sacred Heart Seminary, where he was a classmate of the dead priest I was named for. He looked like Barry Fitzgerald and Bing Crosby and Pat O'Brien and always wore a cassock and collar and biretta around St. Columban Church, newly built in a northern suburb of Detroit. The summer of 1956, when I was seven, he was probably just gone fifty. He had white hair, a red face, and a rich brogue. He spoke in beautifully constructed utterances with the precision I associate with nunnish training in Church Latin and diagramming sentences.

Perhaps because he knew the priest I'd been named for, and figured it was the Will of God that I finish that sickly classmate's foreshortened ministry, he made it his aim, in cahoots with my mother, to guide me toward a priestly vocation. Every parish priest knew that a constant flow of new recruits was required to keep the standing army of God at the ready and every Catholic mother knew that one of her sons should be a priest. Thus I'd been named and preordained, my foul temper and wicked tongue and often brutish ways notwithstanding. These were blamed with other tolerable imperfections on "being Irish."

And so I was sent in the summer of my seventh year on Tuesday afternoons at four o'clock to Fr. Kenny, who taught me how to say the Latin things that altar boys must say in response to the things the priest says at Mass. Fr. Kenny's housekeeper, a plump woman with chin whiskers, showed me into the priest's office off the entrance hall. A plate of cookies and a glass of milk were waiting on the table. The priest, in cassock and collar, sat behind his desk and began my tutorial immediately. I was to wear black shoes and dark pants and a white or light blue shirt, and a tie. "This is the house of God you're working in." I was to show up in the sacristy twenty minutes before Mass began. I was given a short course in pronunciation and a folded card with the priest's part in red and mine in black and told to come back next week with half of it memorized. I did. The foreign syllables in my mouth were deli- cious—*Et coom speery to too awh, Keer ee Ay Ay Lay E Sone.* My romance with words was just beginning. *Mea culpa, mea culpa, mea maxima culpa.* The cadence and rhyme and alliterative beauty of that phrase made its deeper meaning meaningless. Its rich acoustics were enough for me. I would confess to anything that sounded so good. *Confiteor Deo, omnipotenti.*

I was a very holy boy and served daily Mass for Fr. Kenny or his assistant priests two weeks out of most months for the next several years, walking in all weathers with my brother Dan, who worked the holy business with me because we were the holy elder sons of a devout Catholic woman and the local funeral director. It was good for our souls and good for business. My father was in the Knights of Columbus. My mother was in the Women's Sodality. We said the family rosary more nights than not. "The family that prays together stays together." We were all going to heaven with the help of God.

For six-twenty Mass we had to leave the house by 5:40 A.M. to appear at the church by six o'clock, get our cassocks and surplices on, light the Mass candles and put the patens, cruets, bowl, and towel out, and then assist Fr. Kenny with his vesture. We were not allowed to touch the chalice in those days because it had held the body and blood of Christ. We rang the bell as we processed into the sanctuary. Fr. Kenny would switch off the sacristy lights.

We'd genuflect in unison. The Mass would begin.

The attendees, pious women mostly, or pious men on the way to work, were there but did not participate. Fr. Kenny would say the red parts, Dan and I would give out the black parts, bowing low and striking our chests at the *Confiteor*, ringing the bells through the consecration and elevation, closing it out with a "Deo gratias," and everything went seamlessly from open to shut, without variation day after day. Fr. Kenny would pause at the same time during the Credo or Gloria, he'd fold the little hand towel at the Offertory, saying, "*Lavabo*," and give it back to me with the same indifference. He would turn the pages of the huge daily lectionary with the same affected contempt. At the appointed time, the shadows in the back of the church would shuffle forward for communion. I'd hold the paten under their chins, lest any of the sacred species fall to the floor, and look at their upturned faces, eyes closed, tongues out, waiting for the body and blood of Christ. Everyone was on their way by seven o'clock except for the widows huddled at the back in their private devotions, praying their dead husbands out of purgatory and into heaven. Fr. Kenny insisted we altar boys stay an extra fifteen minutes in the back of church, saying thanksgiving prayers for having received communion.

Sometimes I'd serve with one of the Duffy brothers, or Mulherns or Mullanys. There was no shortage, apparently, of devout boys with devout mothers. There were four Masses on Sundays, regular novenas, Lent with its Stations of the Cross, and Holy Days of Obligation. I was especially fond of Solemn High Masses, the Feast of St. Blaise with those crossed-candle yokes applied to the throats of the faithful against laryngeal scourges, and Good Friday, when we held the crucifix at the altar rail for parishioners to kiss the plaster feet of Jesus. It was our job to wipe the feet with a tiny white towel after every kiss, in a show of blessed hygiene. The blissful look on the faces of women as they bent to kiss the tiny tortured holy feet of Christ quickened in me a sense of the transcendent while the mugs of their husbands, unenthused but dutiful supplicants, restored to me a sense of the ordinary universe. Ash Wednesday, with its deep-purple penitential tones and the cruciform thumbprint of ashes on our foreheads, marked us as mortals and Catholics among the Methodist and Presbyterian neighbors who could only be pitied for not belonging to the One True Church. Best were the weddings and the requiems at which we servers were always tipped—no less than a dollar, sometimes five apiece—by the boozy groomsmen or the funeral director who, in the latter case, more often than not was our father. He'd sometimes wink at Dan and me at the back of the church where Fr. Kenny, draped in black chasuble and appropriately grim, would intone, "*In Paradisum*" over the black-palled casket and ritual tears of the immediate kin.

Fr. Kenny was in all ways precise, impeccably priestly, able to dispense guilt and shame, grace and goodness in regular doses as the situation demanded. He opened every homily with "My dear friends in Christ," and twice yearly gave his dear friends a good tongue-lashing from the pulpit for not supporting their priest or their church sufficiently. As my mother's confessor, he counseled her on her calling as a Catholic wife and mother. Long before the age of therapy, she would have taken to her parish priest her concerns—innocent and intimate—for moral and practical guidance.

Her children's discipline and education, her husband's drinking, the
pressures of a growing family and financial worries—whether or
not his advice was informed by the latest psychology made little difference. He had moral authority and he was unafraid to use it. The
Church was clear on right and wrong even when it was not user-
friendly. Probably he kept her in the marriage those times when she
wanted out. "Pray, Rosemary, for the strength to bear your crosses
gladly." Surely she had more children than she might have wanted
because the Church was unyielding on birth control: "The Good
Lord never gives us more than we can handle." Probably she gave
more money to the parish and the foreign missions and the archbishop than might have been sensible: "Be stingy with the Lord and
the Lord'll be stingy with you." I don't know. But I know that on her
deathbed she saw Fr. Kenny, dead himself for fifteen years, coming
to take her by the hand into heaven. She saw him plainly, called him
by his name, and smiled beatifically when she told us all about it,
the day before she died. My father harbored a wary ambivalence
toward the Church and its agents. He loved though mildly mis-
trusted the priest as a meddler and a friend. However jealous he
might have been of the cleric's long involvement in his wife's spiritual life, he knew Fr. Kenny was a good man and was grateful for the
comfort and the years of counsel, and grateful that the old dead
priest came out to meet his Rosie at the end.

As for me, I was advised to keep an ear tuned to "the call." Fr.
Kenny was certain I would have a "vocation." I'd know it when I
heard it—there in my heart of hearts—the voice of God saying,
"Come, follow me," or words to that effect. "Many are called but
few are chosen," is a thing he said not infrequently and often
pointed to a picture on the wall of Jesus knocking on a door to

which he would add a narrative caution, "and when our Blessed Savior knocks at the door of your heart, Tom, you'd better answer."

The knock or the voice, such as it was, would sound like the voice the nuns were always telling me that I should listen to—my conscience—that would tell me right from wrong. After our morning offices at St. Columban, Dan and I would walk to Holy Name School a mile and a half away. Fr. Kenny had not yet been able to raise what it would take to build a school for St. Columban, though he managed to do so before he left. At Holy Name, Sister Servants of the Immaculate Heart of Mary in their black and blue habits schooled us in the sacred and social wisdoms. They taught us to read and write and to avoid the near occasion of sin. We memorized the multiplication tables and the Ten Commandments, square roots and corporal works of mercy, cardinal sins, contrary virtues, the rules of punctuation and common spelling.

And everything was going well enough. I was learning how the pope was infallible and the Protestants were off the track and ours was the One True Faith and I was giving to the missions, making my First Fridays, serving early Mass, and every now and then I'd ransom a pagan baby or make a novena or a good confession and was listening for the "call," which I suspected would be coming any day. I was on the fast track to ordination until one weekday in 1959 or 1960 when I saw Sr. Jean Therese's breasts—well, not her breasts exactly, but that she had them, unambiguously. She was turning to the blackboard to underline some point she'd made there, perhaps about run-on sentences or past participles or dangling modifiers. She kind of swiveled, like, with one arm up to tap the chalk on the board beside the point she was trying to make and the other hand on her hip and there they were, denting the dull habit the good sisters wore—breasts. How had I not noticed them before? They were lovely, round, and soft, beckoning to me in wordless ways and now that I noticed, they were everywhere. Patsy Doherty had them unmistakably and Suzanne O'Connor to a lesser, less amplified degree but all the same, there they were, and the dark-haired girl in the front row with the great round brown eyes to go with them, oh! How had I never seen them before? Everything was, to borrow Yeats's phrase, changed, changed utterly. No longer did I see the world in black and white, right and wrong, good and bad, Catholic and everybody else. There were only those people with breasts and those who wanted to touch them in ways I could only imagine, of which latter denomination I was a willing and eager if ignorant catechist.

By the time of my matriculation from grammar school to secondary education, I was no longer listening for the call. I had quit confessing what the nuns called "self-abuse," as it was clear I had no intention of quitting what felt like a gift. I was biding time waiting for an opportunity to get my hands on someone's breasts. Perhaps sensing that I was in need of further disciplines, my parents sent me and the brothers off to the newly opened Brother Rice High School, operated by the Christian Brothers of Ireland. Sons of the immigrant Irish from the Bronx mostly, sons of cops and cabbies and civil servants, Brothers Murphy and Hallinan, Burke and O'Hare, McGowan, Kelly, and Kieley were given the job of turning us all into good Catholic men, fit for college and eventual careers.

These were tough years on Fr. Kenny, who had expected me to enter Sacred Heart Seminary after grade school and to be ordained ten or twelve years later. Equally off-putting was the opening, in

October 1962, of the Second Vatican Council in Rome. Called by Pope John XXIII, the council generated sixteen new documents on such subjects as divine revelation, the priestly life, the missions, the liturgy, and social issues. The altar was turned around, lay people were encouraged to participate, funerals became "celebrations" with white vestments and triumphant tunes, and everything was Englished.

Comfortable with the former things, meatless Fridays and ancient saints, and old enough to be set in his ways, Fr. Kenny had no interest at all in hootenanny Masses, parish councils, ecumenism, or vernacular. The world, he was certain, was coming to an end. In November 1963, Kennedy was shot. The war in Vietnam escalated. Civil rights and feminism were storming the old forts. The Beatles had landed. "Where was God?" the poor man wondered.

Whether it was my fall from grace or the Church's or the country's at large, by 1966 Fr. Kenny had had enough. He took his retirement from the archdiocese, packed his bags, and returned to Ireland with his Social Security and savings. He moved in with his sister in the family manse on Threadneedle Road in Salthill overlooking a golf course and Galway Bay and settled into his final years. He would never set foot in America again.

He found the Irish Church much as he'd left it years before— much as I found it in 1970—established, in charge, completely enmeshed with the life of the nation and its people. They'd retooled their liturgies and sanctuaries, changed some songs, even done away with Latin, all in compliance with Vatican II. But the social dynamic of the parish had not changed. The priest was and remained in charge. And his power extended well past the pulpit. He was connected to the culture by virtue of his collar and had easy access to any secular office. Chieftains of commerce, local or national politicians, all deferred to Holy Mother Church and to her favored sons.

WHEN I FIRST landed in Ireland, not only was the Church firmly rooted in the landscape but the landscape bore witness to its local holy men, celebrity hermits, and famous anchorites. In the firmament of saints in which the fifth-century Patrick (who banished the snakes) was the sun, and the sixth-century Brigid (who once turned her bathwater into beer to quench the thirst of a visiting bishop) was the moon, Senan (AD 488–544), who banished a sea monster and women from Scattery Island, was the saint of the West Clare Peninsula. Indeed, the River Shannon, in whose estuary the holy island sits a mile offshore of Kilrush, is believed to have been named after the ancient saint. The wells and churches named for him and ancient monastic sites and modern miracles assigned to him are numerous, the tales of his misogyny still well known.

Once, it is hereabouts storied, a certain young woman named Connara from the other side of Poulnasherry Bay, half a dozen miles downriver, came ashore and made "advances" on your (holy) man, known for his discipline and austerity; said advances were "repulsed." Her grave, at the low-tide mark on the west end of the island, remains as a testament to Senan's chastity and, one would guess, his sexual vexations.

AND THERE WAS Bishop's Island, which stood a hundred yards off the coast road in Moveen—a ten-acre rock on which the remnants of two stone huts held forth two hundred feet above the tide.

Nora told me that two holy men went out there "centuries ago," when it was still connected to the mainland, and prayed to have the ground removed that bound them to the land. Their prayers were answered. They remained out there, alone in their privations on their rock, drinking rainwater, feeding on seabirds they fished from the sky with hooks and lines on kites they made, praying for God knows what to God knows whom. When the first of them died, the other buried him, then died himself, of loneliness, some few years after that. His bones, of course, were blown into the sea.

"So mustn't there be something to it after all?" Nora posed the rhetorical.

"Why is it called Bishop's Island?" I wondered.

"That was later, Tom . . . ," she told me. "Some bishop came by and heard the story and made them saints and declared the holy island his. They're prime boys, the bishops, that's for sure."

In more recent times, and but a few miles westward in the River Shannon's mouth, the true history of "The Little Ark" at Kilbaha serves as witness to the fierce faith of the people. "Westerns," Nora called them—those who lived out on the narrowing strip of land between Moveen and Loop Head. It was in Famine times, decades after Catholic Emancipation (c. 1828), that the landlord, Westby, and his local agent, Marcus Keane, who had married the landlord's daughter, conspired to make Protestants out of the starving Catholics.

> The present parishes of Kilballyowen and Moyarta were one in 1849, and were called Carrigaholt after the central village. They embraced a stretch of the land which was almost twenty miles in length and three miles or less in breadth,

reaching from Loop Head to the boundaries of the parishes of Kilkee and Kilrush. To-day, as then, the district looks bare and, in the winter, poor; scarcely a tree breaks its monotony. On one side it is caressed or lashed by the Atlantic; on the other it is bounded by the Shannon, itself almost a sea as far inland as Carrigaholt.

The central church was at Carrigaholt; there was another at Doonaha; and a third (built in 1806) at Cross, which replaced a mud-walled building. These churches, as we could expect, were but poorly equipped. There was no church to the west of Cross, and Cross is eight miles from Loop Head.
—*The Little Ark*, V. Rev. G. Clune, C.C., D.Ph.

It seems the agent, Marcus Keane, established free schools run by Protestants for the Catholic children to attend. But the priest, Fr. Michael Meehan, was welcome to come and instruct the children in the tenets of their faith, though out of doors.

But almost immediately it became evident that there was something strange and sinister about the new education. The children began to bring home religious information that was new to the people of the Peninsula—that Confession was mere superstition, that the blessed Eucharist involved idolatry, that devotion to the Blessed Virgin was blasphemy.

It was now clear, to the consternation of the priests of the parish, that these schools were provided to proselytize the children, to wean them from their parents' faith.

Protestant clergy appeared, Bible-readers, a new Protestant church was built, and Marcus Keane, knowing the poverty of the

local people and controlling who might be evicted, gave free soup
and clothes to those who abandoned "their superstitions" and registered in the new Protestant "society."

Keane, remembered years later as "a local little despot who lived
near Ennis" and the "guiding spirit" behind the "souper" campaign—feeding soup to starving Catholics who would then
renounce their faith—had earned his reputation as "The
Exterminator General of Clare," so called by the *Limerick and Clare
Examiner,* for the thousands of people he put out of their homes
and off the land, many to an all-but-certain death, during the
Famine years. His summer residence at Doondahlin, overlooking
the estuarial harbor of Kilbaha, stands in ruin to this day. After he
died in 1883, the vault containing his corpse was robbed by night,
the remains removed, not to be found for eight more years.

Fr. Meehan in the meantime was prevented from saying Mass or
giving religion instructions anywhere in the western district. The
landlord would not give a site for the construction of a church. If
the priest used a home, the residents might be evicted. When Fr.
Meehan bought a deserted house, Marcus Keane burned it down.
Losing souls to the "soupers" and lost for a place to say Mass, Fr.
Meehan wondered what to do. One morning in 1852, traveling
from Kilrush to Kilkee in Moore's omnibus, it came to him that
something like the omnibus—"strong and covered in on all sides"
and set on wheels—might be rolled out on the beach at Kilbaha
between tides, in "no-man's land," and he could say Mass in it. He
hired the carpenter Owen Collins in Carrigaholt, ancestor to the
local undertaker there, who built it in the road in front of his shop.

> The removal of this omnibus [from Collins's shop in
> Carrigaholt to the strand in Kilbaha] was a triumphal pro-

cession. A large crowd from Carrigaholt accompanied it, and as it passed, the people came out to greet it and join the procession, for now they felt that at long last they could hear Mass without molestation from landlord or agent or superintendent. They would place it on the strand, between low and high water marks, a no-man's land, and from that position there could be no eviction according to law.

From 1852 to 1857, the priest said Mass in all weather on the strand. More remarkable than the structure was the fact that people came by the hundreds to watch and pray around the thing, with its tiny table and candles and makeshift tabernacle.

NORA TOOK ME to see The Little Ark in the old church at Moneen. She knelt at the place in the church where Fr. Meehan was buried, in front of the altar rail, in January 1878.

"The westerns," she told me, "were very holy. They'd rather've starved than take the sup of soup and change their religion."

So the west of Ireland that Fr. Kenny returned to and the one I first encountered in 1970 seemed to me a place still steeped in the comforting rubrics of my upbringing. None of the newly fashionable talk of ecumenism and "community." None of the post–Vatican II fashion blunders of the trendy, newly liberated clergy in America. West Clare still clung to the old ways of hermits and chastitutes and crazed spiritualists. It sounded like the language I'd been raised with—mysterious, miraculous, inexplicable, and old; and the tide of my apostasy, rising steadily since I'd discovered sex, subsided in Moveen, where Tommy would kneel on the stones and recite the rosary and Nora would shake holy water on me before I left for town and the Angelus sounded on the radio at noon and six o'clock and everyone blessed themselves a hundred times a day passing parish churches, graveyards, or local shrines; and the Infant of Prague, long framed in the low room where I slept, looked down upon my slumber.

WHAT LITTLE MONEY I'd brought to Moveen was going quickly. Nora had given me the use of a bicycle, an old Raleigh with a headlamp and chain guard, and three speeds, and I'd peddle off to Kilkee, three miles east. The Victorian resort town sat snug to the edges of the great horseshoe of Moore Bay, which can be spotted on the map on the northern edge of the southwestern peninsula. In the 1830s it was a fishing village growing slowly into a resort. The testimony of Mary John Knott, a Quaker woman from County Cork, first appeared in her little book, *Two Months at Kilkee,* in 1836:

> At present there are upwards of one hundred comfortable houses and lodges for the accommodation of visitors, independent of the cottages in which the natives reside; since that period the town has been gradually rising into importance, and it is probable will ere long, from the safety of its strand, and other peculiar circumstances, be one of the most desirable watering-places on the coast.
>
> The town, which commands a fine view of the bay, is built close to the sea, and assumes a semi-circular form from the shape of the strand, which presents a smooth, white sandy surface of above half a mile in length, where the invalid can, without fatigue or interruption, enjoy the exhilarating sea-breeze and surrounding scenery. The principal street runs nearly from one end of the village to the other, occasionally intersected by smaller ones; these extend to the strand, and at

every few steps afford a view of the Atlantic wave dashing into foam against the cliffs which circumscribe its power, and the rocks of Duggana, which run nearly across the bay. Some of the houses at the "west end" of the town, as well as a few in the village, are modern, with sufficient accommodation (including stabling and coach-houses) for the family of a nobleman or gentleman of fortune, and every gradation can be had down to a cottage with a parlour, two small bedrooms, and kitchen, the rent varying according to the accommodation and demand. A few of the largest, fully furnished, pay from £15 to £20 per month; but the average for comfortable, good lodges is from £6 to £8, and the smallest from £3 to £4, including a plentiful supply of milk, potatoes, and turf, according to the custom of the place.

To which might be added the report of Margaret Frances Dickson, in her "Letters from the Coast of Clare," which appeared in the *Dublin University Magazine* in 1841 and described Kilkee in a way that survives a century and two-thirds later:

> The air here is so light, so fresh, so briney, so inspiring, that it produces an indescribably charming effect on the feelings. One could almost imagine oneself to have emerged into some purer region leaving behind comparatively dull and heavy atmosphere, and shaking off the vexations, cares, pomps, vanities, etiquettes of life.

The place I most liked to shake off the vexations and etiquettes of life, such as they were that late winter of 1970, was in Egan's Marble Bar in O'Curry Street. I'd belly up to a Carlings Black

Label, which was an imported beer—these were the days before drink had been entirely globalized and an Irish pub was a pub in Ireland—and wait for the eventual conversation to strike up.

As it happened, David Lean was making his film *Ryan's Daughter* at the time, and the storm scenes, important to the story line and cinematography, were being filmed off the cliffs of Moveen. The film crew was hanging about Kilkee to take advantage of the agreeably violent weather. When a storm hit, they'd race out the Moveen road to the small bay at Goleen to film the scene where German guns come ashore during World War I. The scene is set in 1916 and England's enemies are Ireland's friends. On calm days, the film crew could be found in Egan's Marble Bar playing poker with the locals, one of whom, Danny Gorman, was a neighbor of Tommy and Nora's. His house sat high on Moveen Hill looking down on the townland. Danny's invite got me into the game and many was the afternoon I'd be late back to Moveen full of drink and out of money. No doubt Nora could see the life of dissipation and disaster before me and she'd warn me off the evils of drink and games of chance, warnings that I manfully ignored. So when my savings ran out and the cards and letters from family quit coming with ten- and twenty-dollar bills in them, the prospect of gainful employment reared its face before me.

The appointments page at the back of the paper promised work for skilled or experienced workers. I had neither skill nor experience. I'd worked in an asylum and a funeral home. I could write.

I wrote to the *Irish Times* thinking they might be in need of a reporter, and to several of the companies enjoying the Shannon tax-free zone around the airport—mostly German and Dutch firms. This was before the Common Market.

But Ireland couldn't employ enough of its own, who were leaving for America and England every day, much less offer work to a visiting Yank. Those who wrote back were courteous but uniform in their refusals. I took the fifty dollars that came in a card from my grandmother O'Hara and made for Dublin by thumb, thinking surely something would happen there, and besides I wanted to see the city that Joyce made famous. I checked into the Ormond Hotel in d'Olier Street near the *Irish Times*. I was lonely and tired and worried about my future. I applied at Eason Booksellers in O'Connell Street and Massey's Undertakers, who asked me if I could embalm. I couldn't yet. I rummaged the want ads without success. I didn't have enough money to stay and I didn't have enough money to leave. Lost for answers, I called Fr. Kenny in Galway.

After listening to the sad facts of the matter, Fr. Kenny told me to call him at the same time tomorrow, and when I did he gave me the address of an office in Dublin and the name of a man I should go and see there. I followed the priest's instructions, wore my suit, and came out of that meeting with a job as a night porter at the Great Southern Hotel in Killarney in County Kerry. I'd be working six days a week in ten-hour shifts, from 10 P.M. till 8 A.M., and be given my room and breakfast and thirty pounds a week, some tips, and free travel on the trains and buses I would take to get there.

We wore black pants, white shirts, and gold jackets provided by the Great Southern—an elegant nineteenth-century hotel attached to twenty acres of private gardens, framed by mountains, next to the train station in Killarney. Willie Clancy was my overseer, and it was our job to "Hoover" the downstairs lobby, dust the tabletops, empty ashtrays, keep the turf fire in the lobby going all night, and take drinks to guests who in Irish hotels could drink all night if they pleased. On the hour we were to turn keys throughout the building that said we were checking the place for fire safety, and we had to shine any shoes left outside guest-room doors. We would go to the larder early in the shift and make ourselves a meal from the evening's table fare. In the morning we would assist departing guests with their luggage to train or car. I have a memory of a fleet of purple Mercedes Benzes parked in front of the hotel, reputed to be part of Lean's entourage who were still shooting parts of *Ryan's Daughter* in Kerry. I never saw Sarah Miles and more's the pity. The film won an Oscar for cinematography but was generally a failure at the box office, though I saw it several times, for the scenes of Murray's Island and Dunlicky shot during fierce storms, which seemed plentiful in 1970. Once the day staff came in, we would eat breakfast and make for bed.

For most of a month I held this job, through the middle of February until the middle of March, and was thinking that working all night and sleeping all but a few hours of the day were not exactly what I'd had in mind and maybe I'd be better off working for American wages at my father's funeral home than Irish wages at the Great Southern, when I was called into the day manager's office for a chat.

Was I well, he wanted to know, and happy, and comfy in my quarters? I was, of course, and told him so. Had I been able, he further queried, to put aside some money from my month of labor? I had, of course, and thanked him sincerely. And had I noticed, he wondered, how most of the guests at the Great Southern Hotel were countrymen and -women of mine? I had, indeed, and more than once remarked on it. And might I imagine, his interrogation went on, how these neighbors of mine, from places like Miami Beach and Boston and San Francisco, might be in the leastways disappointed, having traveled so far across the Atlantic Ocean for a perfectly Irish, Blarney, and Belleek experience, how they might be ever so slightly let down to have their bags portered out to their hired cars by a fine young fellow from Detroit what with his midwestern patois and Michigan manners? I could, of course, though it pained me to say so. And mightn't I, therefore, comprehend, he carried on, the terrible dimensions of the dilemma this placed him in—to wit, here I was, a sound man entirely, wanting in no way in the requirements of a night porter, steady on the job, scrupulous in its performance, tidy in every habit and circumstance, and yet, through no fault of my own, nevertheless by virtue of the tongue in my mouth and the talk that came off of it, unsuitable for the very job for which he'd hired me, in every good faith, at the direction of his superiors above in Dublin, who themselves would never have contemplated such a contingency as the one he was after outlining for me? The man's genuine discomfort was manifest. He was folding and refolding a piece of paper on the desk, looking like a man trapped between the rock and the hard place. So I said, yes, yes, of course, whereas I never once considered it before now, it did make, after all, perfect sense, now that he explained it. So would I, he wondered, in observance of this unforeseen and regrettable circumstance, ever be able to find it in my heart to forgive his having to make me redundant? Well, yes, yes, I told him, I suppose, with profound regrets, I could. He produced at that moment an envelope that contained a brief letter of recommendation on the hotel stationery addressed, "To Whom It May Concern," and a severance package of one month's pay. This doubled my income for the past four weeks, and when I questioned the generosity, he simply said he had instructions from Dublin. I did not press the matter but packed my bag, said my goodbyes, boarded the train for Limerick, and returned by thumb and shank's mare to Moveen.

It was not until nearly twenty years later, at my mother's funeral, that one of Fr. Kenny's former curates, Fr. Joe Killeen, dear to my people in the way Fr. Kenny was, filled me in on the entire story. It turns out that when I called the old priest from Dublin, out of money and on the ropes, Fr. Kenny called my mother back in Michigan. A retired priest, in a country and time where priests still ruled, could have placed me in any number of jobs. It would take a phone call, little more. My mother told him she did not want me to have to come home a failure. This was several years before the "self-esteem" craze in schools and parenting, but she trusted her instincts on the matter. Neither did she want me to have suffi- cient success to "go native" in Ireland as she called it. So she and the priest had conspired to get me enough work to say I'd "gotten on," but insufficient work to allow me to stay. Not a word of this was ever whispered by either of them. I never saw their plotting, from Galway to Michigan, in these happenings in Dublin and Killarney and County Clare. They went to their graves content in their conspiracies, certain that not only had they meant well, with only my best interests in mind, but that good came from their machinations; certain, too, that their wills were, by dint of faith and prayer and the tenets of the One True Church, aligned near as could be with the will of God.

The plot they hatched had worked exactly as they'd planned. I stayed on in Ireland with Tommy and Nora in Moveen, day-trip- ping up the west coast, until the money ran out in the middle of

April. Then I flew back to Detroit on money my parents lent me for a ticket.

There was an American wake in Moveen for my leaving, the cottage filled with neighbors—Denny Tubrity playing the tin whistle, Johnny Hickey on the fiddle while sets were danced and songs sung and pints drunk and sherry sipped in the kitchen and teas and cakes and sweets served in the bedroom long into the wee hours of the morning. And when Flan Carey came to take me to Shannon, there was a crowd at the gate at 6 A.M. to keen a little and wave goodbye and shake holy water on the car and its occupants. Tommy and Nora saw me to the Departures Hall at Shannon and wept real tears at my going, as was the form and habit of their country and their time.

Within four months I'd paid my parents back, saved enough for another tour, and came by way of Italy and Greece, in a car with my Italian-American friend Dualco De Dona for another visit to Moveen. My mother's plans and Fr. Kenny's kept me from going native, but kept me, just as certainly, coming and going ever since.

I got the truth of it from Fr. Killeen when he came to do my mother's funeral, and not only did it explain the generous severance packet, it made me love and miss both of the blessed schemers all the more. Irish priests and Irish-American mothers were more willing collaborators years ago, and each more powerful in their separate realms.

In her excellent book *Goodbye to Catholic Ireland*, journalist Mary Kenny charts the currents of this change and notes the dynamics of the former culture that awarded moral authority in the home to the mother and in the larger society to the priest.

This culture of Holy Fathers and Blessed Mothers waging the

battle against temptation and the world was transported by immigrants largely undisturbed to the Irish Catholic communities across America. A photo of a new priest's first Solemn High Mass and the circle of family and friends in communion with him served as a template for those images of priests and the faithful in "Angels with Dirty Faces," "Boys Town," "Going My Way," and "The Bells of St. Mary's," where the comfortable Catholic ghettos of home and church and school maintained safety and order in an often-hostile world and trained generation after generation in the doctrines and rubrics of the Church.

THE PICTURE ON the front page of the *Clare Champion* for the Ides of March 2002 seems a throwback to the former age—a plump bishop in his crimson and black regalia and pectoral cross—a common image here a few years ago when the clergy appeared for every newsworthy event.

But the headline this week reads, "Clare Bishop in U.S. Sex Scandal."

> The Clare born bishop at the center of the latest sex scandal to rock the Catholic Church in the United States is this week in seclusion, having submitted his resignation to Pope John Paul II. It is understood that sixty-three year old Bishop Anthony O'Connell will travel to Rome in the near future to meet senior figures in the Vatican.
>
> A native of Lisheen, Ballynacally, the Bishop of Palm Beach, Florida, last week admitted to having "an inappropriate relationship" with a fifteen year old seminarian as well as his possible involvement, in similar circumstances, with another person around the same time, twenty-five years ago.

The admission by the bishop has devastated family members and friends in the closely knit community of Ballynacally to which he returned on a regular basis. According to a family spokesman: "Shock, hurt and disbelief has been the reaction."

Bishop O'Connell contacted his immediate family in advance of his press conference on Friday last, at which he admitted to allegations made by Christopher Dixon, his former student at St. Thomas Aquinas Seminary in Hannibal, Missouri, that the two had touched inappropriately in bed after the teenager sought out the then college rector for counseling.

"He expressed contrition, pain and anguish over what he has done and asked them for their prayers and support in this difficult time," said the spokesman. "They are inclined to believe Bishop O'Connell in his explanation of acting 'foolishly, stupidly and naively' at the time."

It is understood that Bishop O'Connell will not face criminal prosecution arising from the incident as the statute of limitations has run out.

In point of fact, His Eminence in Seclusion has confessed to nothing but a kind of ignorance and claims that his primary interest in Mr. Dixon was to provide good counsel. The *Champion* quotes him, thus:

"Foolishly and stupidly and naively, I attempted to work with him, to help him deal with his problem. . . . But I've always been a do-gooder. I've always been one who thought you could change things."

"There was nothing in the relationship that was anything

other than touches. There was nothing beyond that. So in the
ordinary understanding of sexual activity—no, there wasn't—
and I certainly want to make sure my people know that."

There is something vaguely Clintonesque about the bishop's
pronouncements. That these counseling sessions—what Bishop
O'Connell calls his "experimental approach to therapy"—
occurred while both were naked in the cleric's bed is apparently
the "naivete" for which the bishop agreed to pay his former coun-
selee $125,000 in 1996.

Lent in 2002 was all penitence and reparations, on both sides of
the Atlantic. In the United States, Fr. John J. Geoghan, Jr., of the
Boston Archdiocese, accused of molesting more than a hundred
children over thirty years, was sentenced in February to nine to ten
years in prison for fondling a ten-year-old boy. Cardinal Bernard
F. Law, archbishop of Boston, was under pressure to resign for having shifted Fr. Geoghan from one parish to another, fully aware of
the complaints against him, thereby placing the young in peril of a
predatory sex offender. He turned over to local prosecutors the
names of eighty priests in his archdiocese—one in seven of the
total—accused of sexual abuse over the years. The cost of settling
all the cases of priestly abuse in Boston could reach $100 million,
and across the country's one hundred ninety-four dioceses, possibly a billion dollars.

Bishops across the country have all been vetting their local ros-
ter of priests formerly treated or accused.

In New York, Cardinal Edward Michael Egan was defending his
record on handling abusive priests in a Palm Sunday letter to the
faithful:

Let me be clear. I regard any accusation of sexual abuse with the utmost seriousness. Should the Archdiocese be approached with an allegation, we will make the appropriate report to the proper authorities if there is cause to suspect abuse and the victim does not oppose the reporting. I would strongly encourage, however, anyone with an allegation of sexual abuse to bring it to the proper civil authorities directly and immediately. —*New York Times,* March 23, 2002

Cardinal Egan was responding to a St. Patrick's Day article in the *Hartford Courant* that accused His Grace of a failure to act when he was bishop of Bridgeport, Connecticut. His letter addressed the matter directly:

First, in every case discussed in the article, the alleged abuse occurred prior to my appointment as Bishop.

Second, the policy and practice that I established for the Diocese and followed in every instance required anyone accused of sexual misconduct with a minor was, after preliminary diocesan investigation, to be sent immediately to one of the most prominent psychiatric institutions in the nation for evaluation. If the conclusions were favorable, he would be returned to ministry, in some cases with restrictions, so as to be doubly careful. If they were not favorable, he was not allowed to function as a priest.

It seems what Cardinal Egan didn't "get" in Bridgeport is that in addition to what he calls "an abomination," the sexual abuse of children is a crime and whilst abominations are left to bishops, crimes are turned over to the civil, not the episcopal, authorities. What Cardinal Egan didn't "get" is that the days when criminal misconduct could be handled "in house" are long since over in America and long since over in Ireland, too.

THE PARALLEL SOCIETY of Catholicism that, of necessity, unified and identified the colonized faithful in Ireland and the ghettoized faithful in America through the eighteenth and nineteenth and early twentieth centuries could not survive the rapid secularization of the last half-century. The separate schools, separate banks, separate graveyards, separate media, separate moral laws and leaders that once protected them from the manifestly unfriendly larger culture—mostly Anglo, mostly Protestant—have become redundant. In a world that sees humanity as consumers of "common market" goods and services and globalized info-tainments, access is more important than ethnicity, bottom lines more compelling than belief systems. What was parental and protective and refining in earlier times is seen, in latter days, as patriarchal and authoritarian and intrusive. The Father Flanagans and O'Malleys, on both sides of the ocean, known for their rough-and-tumble manliness, have been replaced by a sensitized bunch of Fr. Pats and Fr. Mikes and Fr. Teds, and have been made clowns, fops, and sexual suspects by a culture, within and without the Church, that has traded moral authority for therapeutic models. Confessors become counselors, sin becomes sickness or dysfunction, repentance becomes recovery. A confessor has the sacramental magic to forgive and cleanse. A priest worked by the will of God. A counselor works by training and wit—some better than others, all human, all flawed, all with feet of clay.

In Ireland, the scandals that have only lately racked the Catholic

Church in the United States have been going on uninterrupted since the remarkable case of Bishop Casey broke in May 1992, beginning a process that has, in the space of a decade, disestablished a church that had rooted for centuries. While the Church had certainly been losing the skirmishes with modernity since the early 1960s, the all-but-fatal blows were largely self-inflicted. No social or political initiative could have done what the coincidence of clerical misconduct and the opening forums of television and radio did loosen the Church's hold on Holy Ireland.

In point of fact, the exile of Eamonn Casey was more about clerical embarrassment than public mistrust. Like so much in Ireland, it had a transatlantic connection. A young Irish-American woman had come to stay with him twenty years before. The predictable element of Mighty Nature took its course. His Grace was the father of her nineteen-year-old son. What is more, the bishop had been buying her silence and supporting his son on money that belonged to the archdiocese. All of this came out and Annie Murphy made a very public tour of Ireland, speaking to anyone and everyone about her fifteen moments of fame. Like St. Columcille centuries earlier, the hugely popular bishop of Galway vanished; he has not been seen in Ireland since the spring of 1992 except for a rumored visit to Limerick, in 2002, for a class reunion. He spent some years in Ecuador and now lives in England.

A bishop who behaves like a man in Ireland would be readily forgiven, especially by Irish men; no less a man who behaves like a cad. People understand a scoundrel anywhere and while folks thought the bishop behaved badly toward his son, and unleashed the dogs of public comment, they could certainly understand how a middle-aged cleric could be seduced by a young American beauty and were willing to blame it on the media or the Church's requirement of celibacy or the wiles of the temptress, or to forgive him outright. In Irish pubs and country kitchens, Bishop Casey's sin was "only natural."

The Casey affair, however, showed the Dublin media how deep the ambivalence really was toward the institution of the Church that claimed more than ninety percent of the citizenry. Beneath the religious conformity was a current of popular contempt, growing stronger for two decades, that had not been previously exposed. Apart from the soap opera of the Bishop and the American Divorcee, there was the clear lesson that such matters could be taken up in the press, on the radio and TV news, and not only would the sky not fall but papers would sell and ratings would soar. There were, apparently, deep reserves of anger and resentment toward a clergy that had "lorded it over" the people for far too long.

If the Irish could tolerate Bishop Casey's affair, what they would not tolerate was the litany of physical and sexual abuses that followed. Reports of Christian Brothers and Sisters of Mercy acting anything but Christian or merciful to the children in their care filled the broadcasts through the 1990s. The low-grade hum of clergy misconduct that has always attended the priesthood became in the 1990s an amplified plainchant out of every quarter.

Mary Kenny gives a condensed sampler in *Goodbye to Catholic Ireland*:

August 1993: 'Two Catholic priests have been jailed this year after being found guilty of child sexual abuse. A third priest, who has admitted charges involving thirty incidents of indecent assault on an eleven-year-old boy, is currently awaiting trial.' November 1994: 'A priest has been given a fifteen-month suspended sentence by Dublin Circuit Criminal Court for sexually assaulting a male hitchhiker.' The priest had claimed that the teenage boy had consented to what had taken place, but the claim was rejected by the court. November 1994: 'Dublin priest dies in gay sauna. Liam Cosgrave, a native of Co. Cork, who was in his sixties, collapsed and died in the Incognito Sauna Club in Bowe Lane, off Dublin's Aungier Street, shortly after 6 p.m. The club owner, Mr. Liam Ledwidge, said two other priests gave him the last rites. He said that priests made up a significant number of the club's membership, after barristers and solicitors.' Father Cosgrave had been a regular visitor to the gay club for several years.

November 1994: 'Fr. Daniel Curran jailed for seven years for abusing children. RUC says it wants to interview thirty Catholic priests and brothers in relation to child abuse. Nearly a dozen are in jail or under investigation.' November 1994: 'Church silent on alleged assault by priest. The Archdiocese of Dublin has refused to say whether it gave Gardai [Irish police] information on the past activities of a priest who has been the subject of a Garda investigation into an alleged sexual assault against a boy earlier this year. Gardai have prepared a file for the Director of Public Prosecutions on the assault against the thirteen-year-old boy, which is alleged to have occurred in a hotel following a funeral.'

7 December 1994: 'Sex abuse victims sue Archbishop Connell. The Archbishop of Dublin Desmond Connell, and a priest who was convicted of indecently assaulting young

children in the North Dublin parish of Ayrfield, are being sued by two of the priest's victims. Because the priest had a history of sexual abuse of children prior and subsequent to his tenure in Ayrfield, the victims claim that the Church has a responsibility to face.' April 1995: 'Church's new sex scandal. £27,000 paid to man abused by priest. Former Altar Boy tells of Ordeal.' June 1995: 'Fifteen sex charges against priest. A priest appeared in court yesterday on fifteen charges of indecently assaulting a youth.' The forty-year-old curate was making a remand appearance at Tuam Court. Initially he had been charged with one count of attempted buggery of a youth, more than six years ago.

November 1995: 'Alan O'Sullivan, now a thirty-three-year-old architectural draughtsman, told the newspaper that Father Patrick Hughes had raped, buggered and taken pornographic photographs of him between the ages of nine and eleven.' Patrick Hughes, aged sixty-eight, made an out-of-court settlement of fifty thousand pounds to his former pupil. The abuse had come to the attention of the Archdiocese and Hughes had been sent to a psychiatrist. He was allowed to continue in his ministry.

THAT FR. HUGHES was allowed to continue in his ministry is the part that makes the Church seem to more than a few parents nowadays like a security risk for their children. Sexual misconduct occurs across the culture, and people of faith have learned to separate the sin from the sinner. But they also want the sinner separated from those sinned against as a safeguard for the young and powerless and have had to look to the civil authorities to do what the Church authorities wouldn't do. What bishops in Ireland and in America have in common is their effort to stonewall, silence, buy off, or ignore reports of priestly misconduct in an effort to "not give scandal."

It is argued by the Church that "scandal" will shake the faith. But the secrecy that has surrounded these cases has allowed criminal behavior to proliferate and victims of crime to be bullied by bishops into silence and intimidated by Church attorneys into "settlements" that require them to say nothing. Such misconduct does not shake the faith, it kills it.

In Boston one in every seven priests has been investigated for the abuse of teenagers or children. One chance in seven is more of a risk than even the most devout of parents can be expected to manage.

In Ireland the case of Fr. Sean Fortune, a serial abuser, is associated with five suicides, four of his victims and his own. Bishop Brendan Comiskey, his superior, was criticized for attending Fr. Fortune's funeral in May of 1999 and for ignoring the credible evidence of the priest's crimes for years. The faithful have pressed for the bishop's resignation.

Holy Week in Ireland and America in 2002 was full of reports of settlements between do-nothing archdioceses and the victims of abusive priests. The *Irish Independent* headline read, "Abuse victim settles for 'six figure' payout from diocese," and, as evidence that the clergy still didn't grasp the magnitude of the problem, immediately below this article another headline read, "Materialism killing vocations to priesthood, says bishop," in which the bishop of Cork laments that if trends continue, his diocese, which now has one hundred thirty-three priests, will only have forty-three by 2015 and many parishes will be without a priest.

In Ireland—a country with fourteen hundred parishes—only

fourteen priests will be ordained this year. Many more will die or resign or retire. The country that once sent young priests out to England, Australia, Africa, and the Americas, now faces the prospect of importing priests from Nigeria and Uganda and South Korea just to manage the sacramental workload of the nation. As in America, nothing in the immediate future will reverse the trend toward fewer and fewer men "hearing the call," or leastways, fewer and fewer answering.

In his book *The Changing Face of the Priesthood*, Donald B. Cozzens estimates that between thirty and fifty percent of the priesthood, and those studying for it, are gay. There are, of course, many gay priests who are living sexless lives in service of the faithful. And one would assume that sexual abuse should, sadly, achieve gender neutrality—as to both victim and abuser. But since nearly ninety percent of the reports of priestly misconduct involve abuse of teenage boys, it would appear that fewer and fewer heterosexual men have been drawn to the priestly life. And as reports proliferate, it is feared, even fewer will.

The math of the decades since Vatican II is finite. The number of Catholics increases as the number of vocations falls. Of course for many Catholics a shortage of priests is no bad thing, increasing as it does the role of the laity in the Church's mission. Still, the questions are genuine.

Must one have a bishop to have a God? Can faith thrive without the clergy? Is hierarchy an impediment to holiness? Are priests— distanced by celibacy, social and sexual suspicions from the ordinary lives of parishioners—more trouble than they are worth? Might the Church achieve a postclerical stage in its development? Could Christians do church without churchmen?

For John O'Donohue, a neighbor in Connemara, the answers to these questions would be nuanced not only by organizational studies but also by theology. A poet and writer and holy man, he has, it would seem, evolved past his own parish priesthood into a Christian mystic with a good dose of the Druid, and Hegel, and environmentalism, at odds with the commercial and ecclesiastical milieu of his time, at one with the stone desert of his home place in Caherbeanna, near Black Head in the Burren, about which it has been written famously in *Lloyd's Tour of Clare*: "There is not Water enough to drown a Man, Wood enough to hang him, nor Earth enough to bury him." His books on Celtic spirituality are best sellers in Ireland and America and he has connected with Catholics and non-Catholics alike who are religiously distanced from their orthodoxies but spiritually alive and well.

Years ago, we read together on a Friday night in Ennis Bookshop. He was kind enough to share the venue and provide for the turnout of locals, among whom he is famous and loved. He invited me to return with him to Galway, stay the night at the rectory, and read poems from the pulpit of his church the following day. I was glad to return the favor. But I could see that his priesthood wouldn't last. He was alive in ways the Church would only encumber and the range of his curiosities went beyond the pale of approved concerns of the Irish parish priest. He wrote and published poems. He studied the mysticism of Meister Eckhart. His scholarship, contemplative habits, and compassion for the flawed fellow humans that brought their fears to him in the confessional augured against the pat answers and corporate policies of the Church. And women found him—though I doubt he knew it—relentlessly attractive. When *Anam Cara—Spiritual Wisdom from a Celtic World* was published in 1997, it made him famous and well heeled, neither of which much humored his bishop, who stopped paying him his monthly pittance. When we met for coffee in a Galway café in the spring of 1997, he seemed to me the happiest of pilgrims, grounded in his faith and constantly searching for the God in things. More books followed, tapes and videos, and when I saw him some years later at a conference in New York, he seemed like the circuit-riding homilists who brought the good word to the frontiers of America years ago or a latter-day incarnation of Columcille, that vexed and blessed monk, self-exiled and the better for it. On the "longing to belong," our search for meaning and intimacy, he has much to say:

> Here in the west of Ireland I was born in a valley, so there were always horizons around us. As a child I often dreamed of climbing to the line of the horizon, and I imagined that I would be able to see the whole world from there, when I was big enough. And finally the day came when my uncle was going with sheep over the mountain and he needed help, so he brought me with him. We climbed up alongside the valley, and I was in great anticipation about the line of the horizon. But of course when we got up to where the line of the horizon should be, the line had disappeared and there was a whole host of other horizons waiting for me. I came back home that night disappointed that I hadn't seen what I had anticipated, but kind of excited and fascinated that there was so much more to be traveled. It echoes this lovely remark by a German philosopher, who said, "There's a horizon towards which we travel, but it also travels along with us." I think that's the nature of human identity—that we are constantly

on this pilgrimage, from experience to experience, and from territory to territory within us.

Those times when I've met John O'Donohue since, for dinner and talk in Galway or Connemara, it is clear that his pilgrimage has brought him to a place where he seems most alive and well, a concelebrant of all those elemental gifts of creation that link us in one "great belonging" to memory and vision, the present moment and the earth.

For many of my neighbors in Moveen and in Milford, the "great belonging" is to the Church. For others it is to Family. For others it is to Nature. For others it is to the Nation. For others it is to the species.

An increasing number of Catholics in Ireland and America believe in the core teachings of a Church they can no longer belong to. Perhaps the pastoral model of John O'Donohue and men and women like him is a harbinger of an evolving Church and priesthood, a return to the traditions of exile and contemplative life within a community made global by technology—men and women for whom the quiet and the distant and the darkness allow for visions they might otherwise never have had, who are nonetheless "connected" to the wider world of faith by broadband and modem and common quest.

GOOD FRIDAY IS the anniversary of the agreement in The North that was brokered by George Mitchell on behalf of the Clinton White House in 1998 and established a framework for governing that province where more than thirty-six hundred people have died in the past thirty years. Their names are read in

Dublin at the Unitarian Church in Stephen's Green. The reading takes longer than the three hours Catholics believe Christ hung on the cross.

There is little doubt that the disestablishment of the Catholic Church in the Irish Republic has made the peace process easier in Northern Ireland, where among the things that had to be decommissioned were the border patrols of religious identity that have divided these people for hundreds of years.

As certainly as faith unites, religion just as certainly divides, and a united Ireland, if there is ever to be one, will only thrive in a post-denominational context.

IN ST. SENAN'S Church, uptown from the gorgeous bay in Kilkee, Holy Week starts with Palm Sunday Mass on Saturday night. About a third of the church, built in 1963, is filled. It has pews to seat more than eleven hundred. Men stand, as they have always stood, at the back, near the doors. In Penal Days, guards were always posted. The old custom gives the latter-day sentries an early dispensation, breaking for the public house at communion. Beads hang from the hands of the women. All of the statues and crosses are covered in deep purple satin. The Passion According to St. Matthew is read in a dramatic reading by the priest, who takes the part of Christ, and two lay lectors from the parish. It is a story of betrayal, suffering, and death. All kneel when Jesus "gives up the ghost." Coins ring in the collection baskets. Bells ring for the elevation of the host. Some go to communion. More remain in their pews. The evergreens that are distributed will go home to be hung around holy pictures and crucifixes, as a yearlong reminder of the Easter season. What is evident to the blow-in observer, standing in the back with the other men, is that an entire generation is miss-ing here. The old and the young are here in numbers, the over-fifties and under-fifteens, the stalwart mothers on their own. But the others—courting couples, newlyweds, young parents, middle-aging householders—are gone missing. For the Irish of the Common Market generation, the first to grow up with surfeit rather than shortfall, television rather than the bush telegraph, a country of commuters rather than migrants, to be Irish no longer means to be Catholic. To be Catholic no longer means to be here.

ON EASTER MONDAY, Fr. Culligan says the Mass I arrange for every year to commemorate Nora Lynch's death. It is the first of April in Carrigaholt, the fishing village on the Shannon that is our parish seat—jackdaws cawing in the breezy air. Only a few of the faithful are here: Rose Green, one of the eucharistic ministers, Mrs. Lyons from the local wholesale seafood shop, Mrs. Morrissey from the pub, Maureen and Eithne McGrath who own the lands on which the ancient castle sits at the end of the pier that angles into the little harbor here, and Mary Sullivan, Fr. Culligan's house-keeper, who kneels in the front pew and will kneel here again tomorrow, please God. It is women who keep the church doors open, at least this Monday in Carrigaholt.

The Gospel is the one about the empty tomb.

Like my mother and sisters, the women here in West Clare have been taught that their devotions will help save their husbands' and children's souls. Keeping the faith will keep their families together, maintain peace in the home, and provide their daily bread. But more and more women are feeling betrayed by a church that refuses them access to full liturgical participation, doctrinal decisions, and administrative roles. Holy Mother the Church, it turns out, is a men's and boys' club that mostly approves of women who are virgins, martyrs, or repentant sinners. And though up and down the episcopal ladder, from pope to bishop to parish priest and curate, few of these men or boys has supposedly had a mature, adult relationship with a woman, these very men presume to hold forth upon the intimate lives of women—their spiritual, sexual, and reproductive lives. More and more Irish women are asking, "What exactly is wrong with this picture?"

"What is wrong with this picture?" is the question that has vexed Patricia Burke Brogan all of her life. A devout child of devout parents, raised with a social conscience and Catholic ideals and a brother who would become a priest, she entered the novitiate of the Sisters of Mercy in Galway in the late 1950s. She was sent, at the instructions of her Mother Superior, to one of the order's local "branch houses" to assist the Mother Superior there. She remembers the long hallway and the rattle of keys that hung from the belt of the nun's habit and the huge door opening into a room, ill lit and shadowy, full of girls and women and machines.

"It was as if the ground opened under me," she says now. "And their eyes, their eyes—there was such hatred for me in them, because they saw me as their white-veiled jailor."

For the young novice, "high on idealism" and good purpose, it was a loss of innocence, to be let into this "secret place where women, girls like me, were imprisoned. I was only there a week and all I could do—I couldn't be 'over' them—was work along with them." She was never the same.

Three years later, she left the convent, torn from her calling by a tortured conscience. Thirty years later, Patricia Burke Brogan's play, *Eclipsed,* opened on Valentine's Day in 1992 at the Punchbag Theatre in Galway. It dealt with "what was wrong with that picture" that shattered countless innocent, idealized youths—her own included. Later that year—the year the Bishop Casey imbroglio hit the news—*Eclipsed* won first place in the Edinburgh Fringe Festival and has been staged now fifty-seven times around the world, including New York, San Francisco, and London.

In 1993, when the Sisters of Our Lady of Charity sold their property holdings in North Dublin to a developer, they had to apply to the Health Board for permission to disinter one hundred thirty-three bodies buried in unmarked graves on the convent grounds. When the firm of Dublin undertakers hired to do the job began, they found, alas, one hundred fifty-five sets of remains. Further research showed that fewer than half of these deaths had ever been recorded with a death certificate. No names, no dates, no records kept—only the bones of the anonymous dead buried on the North Dublin convent grounds. The good sisters amended their application to reflect the new count of corpses; permits were quietly granted and the bodies were just as quietly cremated and buried in a common grave at Glasnevin Cemetery at dawn one morning in boxes marked with names like, "Magdalene Number 354," or "Magdalene of St. Jude," or "Unknown Magdalene."

These were among the first layers unearthed in the sad story of the Magdalene laundries in Ireland—an institutional witness to the Church's culture of shame and control over the unpredictable powers of female sexuality and the systemic misogyny of Irish society.

From the mid-nineteenth century until the last one closed in 1996, various religious orders in Ireland—Sisters of the Good Shepherd, Sisters of Mercy, Sisters of Charity, and others—ran asylums in which young orphaned girls, unwed mothers, and girls too pretty or precocious could be sent to work as penitents, washing away their sins by doing the dirty laundry that was brought to them from hotels and prisons and churches and schools. These "Magdalenes" were named for Mary Magdalene in the scriptures who repents of her sins and washes Jesus's feet with her hair. She was a witness to Christ's Crucifixion and the first witness to his Resurrection. But before all that, she was purported to be a sexual sinner. The "Maggies" of Ireland, if not outright sinners—about forty percent were pregnant on admission—they were, because of their beauty perhaps, or their simplemindedness, likely to tempt some man into sin. In any case, it was generally figured better to put them away than let them go astray, or worse still lead some man astray with their charms and wiles.

In October 1994, Joni Mitchell released her *Turbulent Indigo* CD, which included her song "The Magdalene Laundries."

> *I was an unmarried girl*
> *I'd just turned twenty-seven*
> *When they sent me to the sisters*
> *For the way men looked at me.*
> *Branded as a jezebel,*
> *I knew I was not bound for Heaven*
> *I'd be cast in shame*
> *Into the Magdalene laundries.*

The story of Mary Norris, reported in the *Irish Times* (October 5, 2002) by Patsy McGarry, is not untypical:

Mary Norris was born Mary Cronin in Sneem, Co Kerry in 1933. The eldest of eight children, all was normal with her young life until her father died. He left behind a young wife with two boys and six girls, aged between six months and 12 years.

Life was difficult, but the family coped. A man began visiting their house, occasionally staying overnight. The children noticed their mother was "a little bit happy" again.

One morning, a car drove up to their farmhouse, with a garda and a "Mr Armstrong" from the Irish Society for the Prevention of Cruelty to Children inside. "The Cruelty Man" is how Mary refers to him without a trace of irony.

He announced they were taking the children, as they considered Mrs Cronin an unfit mother. Everyone was screaming. They were even going to take the baby, but realised she was being breastfed, so left her. (She too was taken, when she was weaned.) The other seven children were brought to Sneem courthouse and committed to "a place of safety" by a judge.

Mary was taken to the orphanage in Killarney where, as she cried hysterically, she was given the routine disinfectant bath on arrival and ushered to a dormitory under the supervision of Sister Laurence.

"I don't know what you are crying for. Your mother's a tramp, an evil woman, and I hope you don't turn out like her," said the nun. To her undying shame, Mary responded: "Yes, sister."

She began to wet the bed and was made to carry the mattress on her head to the drying room every day. At bathtime every Friday Sister Laurence would beat her around the lower back (where the weals would not be visible) with a belt, as the wettings continued. There was no education, except for Christian Doctrine, and they were kept apart from the town children at the school there.

At 16, Mary got a job as a servant to a retired school-teacher in Tralee, a sister of one of the Killarney nuns. There she did all the cleaning for her employer and her employer's two nephews, and blind sister, for 2s 6d a week. She was allowed out once a week.

The film *My Wild Irish Rose* arrived in town midweek and she wanted to see it. She was told No, but sneaked out to see it. The next day "the very same Cruelty Man" came to take her away. She was told she had been "a very bold girl" and was brought back to Killarney.

"I knew you were a tramp. I knew you'd turn out like this," said Sister Laurence, and dispatched Mary to see a local doctor. He examined her intimately, painfully, and told the woman sent along to supervise the visit: "I don't know what's wrong with the nuns. This young woman is intact." No one explained to Mary what he meant.

The nuns dispatched her to "the Good Shepherd" Magdalene laundry in Cork. In the orphanage in Killarney, "the Good Shepherd" had always been the ultimate threat. Mother of Our Lady O'Mahony greeted her there. "We can't call you that here", she responded when Mary gave her name. Instead she was called "Myra".

An older resident stripped Mary. Her bra was replaced with a piece of buttoned-down calico which flattened her breasts. Her long dark hair was cut short. She was given a grey dress, boots and a white cap, and brought to the sewing room where she sat "among these old women, crying and making scapulars".

At supper she saw "all these young pretty girls" coming from the laundry, and heard them refer to her as "the new sheep". No talking was allowed, and even during recreation time discussion to do with life outside was forbidden. Just the rosary over and over again; sometimes hymns, and prayers were read to them by a nun at mealtimes.

They got up at 6 a.m., went to Mass, had breakfast, began working in the laundry at 8 a.m., broke for lunch at 12.30 p.m., resumed at 1 p.m., and finished at 6 p.m. They had an hour's recreation until 7 p.m. when, in theory, they could talk, but there was not much to talk about. Not least as "particular friendships" were forbidden. Few of the approximately 130 women there were unmarried mothers. Most were from orphanages.

Mary was told she couldn't write to her mother. Only to Sister Laurence. She did so, begging to be taken out of the laundry. There was no reply. After one petty misdemeanor, Mary was punished after prayers in the dormitory one night, when she was made lie on the ground between the two lines of praying girls and made repeat "through my fault, through my fault, through my most grievous fault" again and again until the nun conducting the prayers finally announced, "You are forgiven" and she was allowed resume her place among her praying colleagues. She faked a toothache once in a half-baked plan to run away. The dentist removed the perfectly good tooth. She was so desperate she considered suicide.

She discovered later an aunt of hers in the US had been inquiring in letters—money enclosed—of Sister Laurence

why Mary was not getting in contact. She was told Mary had
a job in Tralee, had left it, and no one knew where she was.

Sister Laurence got Mary a job in a laundry in Newcastle,
Co Limerick around this time. Soon Mary was back in
Sneem, where she worked for two years before heading off to
England. She remained there until 1993 before returning to
Co Kerry with her husband, Victor.

Her mother had married the man who had been visiting,
but it was not a happy affair. She too had gone to London
and lived on the same street as Mary for eight years, dying in
1989 surrounded by many of her children.

Another layer was unearthed by the British documentary filmmaker Steve Humphries, whose program, *Sex in a Cold Climate,*
aired on British television in March 1998. (RTE in Ireland twice
refused to run it.) It told, in their own words, the stories of four
women who'd been inmates of these places. Phyllis Valentine spent
eight years in the Galway Magdalene asylum because she was
"pretty as a picture" and the nuns were afraid she might tempt
some man into sin. Her hair was shorn upon arrival. Christina
Mulcahy gave birth to a boy after a wartime romance. When he was
ten months old, her son was taken from her and she was placed in
the Cork asylum. It was fifty-five years before she saw him again.
Martha Cooney was raped by a cousin and considered "tainted" by
her family, who banished her to the good sisters. Brighid Young,
brought up in an orphanage attached to the Magdalene laundry in
Limerick, was beaten by the nun who caught her speaking to one of
the Magdalenes. Forced to look at her swollen face in the mirror,
she was told by the nun, "You're not so pretty now."

It was watching *Sex in a Cold Climate* in his Glasgow home that led Scots actor and filmmaker Peter Mullan to write and direct the feature film *The Magdalene Sisters,* which won the 2002 Venice Film Festival Golden Lion Award for Best Picture. The Vatican called it "an angry and rancorous provocation." Before its release in America in August 2003, the U.S. Conference of Catholic Bishops rated the movie "O" for "morally offensive" for its "exaggerated theme of abusive nuns, brutal beatings, sexual violence including rape and forced oral sex with a priest, an extended scene of dehumanizing full female nudity, an attempted suicide, sporadic rough language and brief profanity." Indeed, the film is an unflinching indictment of the patriarchies, domestic and ecclesiastical, that gave parish priests (in league with embarrassed fathers) control over the sexual conduct of girls and young women.

THE POWER OF femaleness—to attract, seduce, pleasure, and reproduce; to mother, mold, inspire, and educate—has always posed a threat to the Church. From the earliest centuries, Church fathers have sought to silence or sideline the voices of women. Indeed, the particulars of Mary Magdalene's discipleship—her relationship to Jesus, her supposed sexual sins, her teaching and writing and ministry—are still the subject of much debate. Evidence in the Gnostic Gospels suggests that Mary was more intimately attached to Jesus than any of the twelve apostles. That she ministered and preached and wrote and spread the "good news" in the early years of the emerging Christian Church seems incontrovertible. That one way of silencing her teachings and diminishing her standing among Christ's disciples was to taint her memory with sexual sin—a thing accomplished by a third-century churchman who first suggested she was the prostitute described in Luke 7: 36–50—seems likewise incontrovertible.

In Ireland, the Church has long sought to keep women "in place": tucked safely into marriages, tethered to large families, tied to land owned by their husbands and then inherited by sons. The willing emigration of single women for centuries from Ireland to England, the Americas, and elsewhere has been not only to escape famine or poverty but also to get free of a system that disallowed their full participation in the established Church and the established order while indenturing them to home and child care. If nuns were the wardens of the Magdalene asylums, it was priests and bishops and popes who made the rules by which women in the Church are divided into good ones and bad ones, virgins and whores. Women have had to fight in Ireland for education and careers, contraceptives, property rights, political parity, and divorce. Every year, more than two thousand young women travel to England for abortions, which are not allowed in the Irish Republic. The sense of betrayal by the Church is palpable. And yet it is women in Ireland who remain the most faithful, as they are this morning in Carrigaholt.

ST. MARY'S CHURCH is gray and vaguely Gothic, overlooking the Shannon, sheltered by a stand of ancient trees and surrounded by the graves of long-dead churchmen. The interior is freshly painted. The sanctuary is post–Vatican II, though the accessories—votive lamps and tabernacle, candles and communion rail—are nineteenth century. Sunbeams angle through the tall stained-glass windows on the eastern wall of the old church, which is built in the shape of a cross and has the high-vaulted acoustics of a mausoleum. Altar servers, a boy and a girl, put out the water and wine and lectionary.

Fr. Culligan processes out from the sacristy, quenching the light. The faithful stand. The Gospel is taken from the 27th and 28th chapters of Matthew, detailing the burial and Resurrection of Christ. Joseph of Arimathea, the patron saint of funeral directors and grave diggers, petitions Pilate for the body of Christ. Most often the executed were denied burial. But Pilate agrees. Mary Magdalene and "the other Mary" are there with Joseph when he "rolled a great stone to the door of the tomb and went away." Pilate orders the tomb "sealed" and guarded after the chief priests and Pharisees caution him about Jesus's disciples coming to steal the body and claim a miracle. Two mornings later, the Marys return. They have come to anoint the dead body of Christ in keeping with the customs of the Jews. There is an earthquake, a lightning bolt. An angel appears. The soldiers are dumbstruck with fear. He shows the women the empty tomb and tells them Christ has been raised from the dead. They hasten back to tell the rest. On the way, Jesus appears to them and they fall to worship at his feet.

The soldiers guarding the tomb tell the authorities about the missing corpse. They are told, according to St. Matthew's version, to say the body was stolen by the dead man's disciples while they slept. They are paid to tell this version of it. "And that is still the story that is told down to the present among the Jews," concludes Fr. Culligan.

"The Gospel of Our Lord," says Fr. Culligan.

"Thanks be to God," the handful of women reply.

"Thanks be to God," I say with them.

That seems the simple crux of the matter—the version of the

story that separates Catholics from Muslims, Hindus, and Jews and all the people of other faiths—grave robbers or the Son of God? Trickery or miracle? And of course there are other narratives that separate Catholics from all the other Christians—faith or works, king or pope, scripture or liturgy, how Easter is reckoned in the calendar; and others that separate Irish Catholics from all the other Catholics—Byzantine, Polish, Italian, African and Asian and South and North American.

Why has this never much mattered to me—this central tenet of the church where I am kneeling on Easter Monday in West Clare because here is where I've come to commemorate Nora Lynch? Am I missing something?

The great entanglements of the Church in Ireland, over the past thirty years, have not involved the private faith of the people but the public policy that involves their private lives—whom they might marry and sleep with, how they might manage their fertility, what's to be done when vows cannot be kept. Divorce and abortion and contraception would seem, I am not the first to say, odd topics for manly celibates to get so embroiled in.

IN NOVEMBER 1991, I went to the holy island of Iona in the Hebrides. I had four days off between readings I was doing in England and felt drawn to the place associated with the great sixth-century saint Columba, or Colum-cille. He was a native of Donegal, in Ulster, born of royalty and raised by a priest who taught him to read the psalms. There were the usual signs of sanctity. He cursed a man to death once and once turned spring water into wine. It was certain he would have an important future. Later he studied with St. Finnian at Moyville whose psalter he copied

and was going to keep until Finnian found out and objected.
Columba insisted that he had made the copy. The book was
Finnian's, the copy his. The two saints could not come to agreeable
terms. The case came before the Irish high king Diarmud, who
ruled famously: "To every cow her calf, to every book its copy."
Columba, a bard and prince and bookish man, and apparently not
much of a sport, returned the psalter but went to war with
Diarmud and defeated him in a battle in which hundreds died. In
penance for the bloodletting, Columba exiled himself from his
beloved Ireland and vowed to convert as many pagans as men who
died in the battle. The Picts of Scotland seemed handiest, so with
a boatload of twelve kinsmen and brother monks he sailed off the
north coast of Ireland in AD 563. He went from island to island
among the Inner Hebrides until he could no longer see his beloved
Ulster coast, so that his exile would be truly penitential. He came
ashore in a small bay on the west side of Iona and, looking back
into the fog, saw nothing and so decided to stay.

I'd always wanted to see this place.

The long train ride from London to Glasgow, thence northwest
on a far less elegant train to Oban, felt to me like a pilgrimage. I
went without a plan or reservation, drawn to it by an aching to be
there that I could articulate but not explain. I felt I had to go.
Arriving in Oban late at night, I took a room in a hotel overlooking the esplanade and in the morning made the first boat to the
Isle of Mull, thence by bus to Fionnphort on the far side of Mull,
and finally by smaller ferry across the mile-wide Iona Sound to the
tiny treeless island where the saint had founded his community
and from which he launched his evangelistic missions among the
Scots and northern Anglo-Saxons. It was noonish in a place where

the light would only last until four o'clock so late in the year. The hotels were closed for the season. I was directed to a woman who operated a guesthouse near the pier who was happy to take me in but, since the power was out, could offer a bed but neither heat nor light beyond candles and a bit of turf. I paid her and went out to make what I could of the remaining daylight.

I walked out the road a mile or two to the small bay where the saint had first landed. I met no one on the road and saw no one in the fields, only the cattle with their abundant horns. When I got to the sea's edge, I sat among the large rocks that littered the deserted strand, looking south and west the way the saint was said to have looked. I was alone in the off-season on an island in the sea, ready and willing and eager for God, such as I had come to understand Him or Her to be, to speak to my innermost self and soul. The tide surged, gulls circled overhead, the gray light of the sun behind the clouds was cold. I was ready.

Presently in my vigil I saw a small dot growing larger down the beach and as the figure of a man approached, I assumed he would, as must be the international custom among spiritual tourists, walk his own path, leaving me to mine and to my soul's own reveries. In this I was, alas, mistaken. On spying me, the man—for he had the surly, determined, duty-bound walk of a man—adjusted the angle of his ambulations so as to arrive in no time in the space I occupied, holding forth a hand and a hearty, "Hello there," in an accent I took to be East Anglian. The voice of God, I told myself, might not be heard today.

In short order and without solicitation, I was possessed of the man's particulars: He was thirty, he told me, the son of Irish parents who'd emigrated to England; he was a priest, on leave from parish work in a suburb of Glasgow where he'd been the curate for a year, sent here by his bishop for a little rest, "you know, to recharge the batteries, you know, emotional, spiritual, etcetera, you know!"

He proffered his right hand: "Peter, Fr. Peter."

"Tom Lynch," I told him and shook his hand.

"May I take from your name you are a Roman Catholic?"

Before I could answer, he carried on. He was so glad to find another Catholic here. He'd been staying at the abbey for a fortnight now among an array of Anglicans and Presbyterians and Protestants of an unspecified sort from "somewhere on the continent."

"All very nice, you know, but not the same."

The abbey, once a Benedictine monastery, had fallen over the centuries into ruin. In 1938 the Reverend George MacLeod, a minister from Glasgow, founded the Iona Community, rebuilt the medieval abbey, and began its mission "to rebuild the common life, through working for social and political change, striving for the renewal of the church with an ecumenical emphasis, and exploring new more inclusive approaches to worship, all based on an integrated understanding of spirituality." Its brief at the close of the twentieth century was determinedly liberal, open to any and all.

Fr. Peter thus found himself tucked away in remotest Iona, a month after even the abbey had ceased its program offerings for the season, among the other variously wounded souls who were sent here to winter out for their own reasons, sharing household chores and meals and dorm rooms; he was clearly in need of a co-religionist.

"I don't mind the cooking and washing up and keeping the fire going, Tom, not even the bunk beds and shared loo. But this push,

push, push to be 'community'—I came here to be alone, you know, with my thoughts and prayers. You know, St. John in the desert, or Our Lord."

Yes, I told him. I understood.

"And the worst of it is I'm stuck here till the bishop sends for me and I don't know which of them here is his inside man. Or woman for that matter, for we are, after their fashion, a mixed company. It'd be just like him."

I said I thought it would make the "community" better to have women in on it.

"And what brings you to Iona?" the priest asked.

"I don't know."

I told him that I'd just felt drawn to see the place, that my life, such as it was, had achieved of late a kind of calm I'd never been accustomed to, and that my faith, for reasons I was only beginning to isolate, was deepening—the sense that whoever was in charge of things in the larger sense was in charge, likewise, of things in the small and was, I could only hope and had some reason to believe, keeping an eye on me and mine and that this filled me with a sense of safety and connectedness I had never discerned in my life before, but for which I was, here, now, right in the moment, filled with thanks.

Fr. Peter looked curious.

I said I was grateful at the moment for the good death my mother had gotten two years before, for the tenuous hold on life my father then enjoyed, for the kinship I felt among my brothers and sisters, for the connection I had to the neighboring island and the life of my cousin Nora there, with whom I'd be visiting, please God, in a matter of days. What's more, I could count as an abundant blessing the writerly life I was allowed to lead, catch as catch can, among my other duties—to be reading things written in private in public forums felt like a kind of affirmation.

The priest looked perplexed.

Mostly, I told him, I was thankful for the lives of my three sons and my only daughter and the love of the woman I'd married just months before, after years of fear and procrastination. I was grateful for her beauty and good counsel and the peace she had brought to our household where, at the moment, she was tending to my children.

The cleric, I could see, was calculating.

Finally I counted, a proper confession required my telling, as a coincident and no doubt correlated blessing, the sobriety I had enjoyed for two and a half years, as an addendum to the litany of blessings I was after reciting, and the release, just recently noticed, from the cycle of guilt and shame, fear and anger, regret and distemper my drinking life had become for me. I knew, of course, and could bear witness to the fact that life, each life, had its share of suffering and the future was full of uncertainties. But what my sobriety had given me was the sense that God, whoever that was, would handle the lion's share of these, if I only handled what was given to me.

By now it was clear to me that this was what I'd come here for—to take an inventory of my life and times much as Columba had done in his early forties, fifteen hundred years before; to stare into a sea devoid of any familiar island or vision, and to say out loud into the void what Job of old had said in the midst of his worst days and his best, to wit: Blessed be the name of the Lord, whatever name it is he, or she, as the case may be, answers to.

Further it occurred to me that Fr. Peter, whom I'd but moments before regarded as a bore and an intruder, might actually be an agent of God sent to this holy place to facilitate this fresh epiphany, and I was in that moment nearly overwhelmed with appreciation for his priestly ministry, for the gift he'd given me outright when he'd asked what it was I was doing here.

"Did your first wife die? The mother of your children?"

His question caught me by surprise.

"No, no, of course. . . . No, thanks be to God . . . divorced. We were divorced. Years ago now."

"And was the marriage annulled, then?"

"No," I told him. I could never bring myself to turn over to a group of men who had never been married the job of deciding if we, my former spouse and I, had been. I remember the erstwhile parish priest, once he got word the ink was dry, coming by with the forms for the annulment. He was fulfilling, no doubt, his sense of pastoral duties in the matter. I told him I needed a housekeeper more than the approval of a bunch of chastitutes downtown. I wasn't very grateful for the trouble he'd gone to.

"Well, you know, don't you, that the Church still recognizes your first marriage as valid and binding."

By the time it was over, I assured Fr. Peter, it was completely invalid, and so were we both, hobbled with mistrust and mutual contempt.

"You know, of course, that as far as the Church is concerned, you're living in adultery with this other woman."

"This 'other woman' as you call her, Father, is my heart's true love and beloved wife."

"Not in the eyes of the Church, I'm afraid."

I said we hadn't done it in the Church. We'd gone to the court-house where a friend of mine, the local judge, sentenced a fellow before us to ten years in prison for dealing in cocaine; then went in and changed his robes from black to white, came out of his chambers smiling, and told us we "were sentenced to life!"

"Of course that was only a 'civil' marriage," Fr. Peter said.

"Well, that would be an improvement on the one before," I told him.

"It has no standing in the eyes of God."

The eyes of Fr. Peter seemed oddly glazed over, as if he'd gone into a kind of automatic pilot, giving out with the cant of a mind colonized by years of clericalism.

Just then I found my own eyes looking around the beach for a stone or a board or something with which to bang the man at the place on his face from which these godawful words were issuing forth. "Snap out of it," is what I wanted to tell him coincident with a mild pummeling. I told him the Church would be wrong about that—our "standing in the eyes of God," etc.—and that maybe he'd want to be moving along now, surely some of his inmates at the abbey would be keeping his dinner warm and worried about him.

"And all that AA business—nothing but cults," he carried on. "I see them in the back hall at St. David's, all smiling and pious, hugging each other and smoking like chimneys, and never once would you see them at Mass."

Something my father used to say about there being no shortage of assholes in the world came into my mind just then.

"Everybody's got at least one, Tom," he used to tell me. "It's just more obvious on some than others."

And almost miraculously I could see that Fr. Peter had an
asshole too, maybe two of them—more pronounced than any
other member or mannerism—one of which was opening and
closing and giving out with shit in the middle of his face where
his mouth should be and I was figuring the distance between it
and my fist and preliminary to the attack I was planning, I said
some especially righteous if patently un-Christian things, incor-
porating words and phrases I'd not used before or since and not
one of them surplus to requirements or worthy of repetition
here.

On hearing same, he backed away, shocked, blushing, muttering
something about not blaming the messenger, clearly unpracticed
at being told what he could do and where he ought do it. I could
feel the fist forming with which to smite him and the overwhelm-
ing urge to do the needful thing was forming too. To every cow its
calf, I told myself; to every asshole its thumping. I stood up
straight and took a step in his direction. He turned on his heel and
walked off briskly, shaking his head.

The light in the western sky was declining. I waited for another
half hour to lessen the chances of meeting him in the road on the
way back. By the time I'd returned to my quarters, it was dark and
cold and there was no power.

"Never meddle with a priest," is what Nora told me.

"Don't ever cross one, Tom, you'll come to grief."

In these parts a priest could curse as well as bless and those who
believed in the power of one believed in the power of the other.
She had stories of priests who had called down some mayhem
upon the lands or family of someone who didn't pay their share or
who failed to give them drink or refused to come to Mass.

"The devil you know's better than the one you don't."
Liam O'Flaherty writes in his *Tourist's Guide to Ireland:*

> He is the great and only power in the district. Confident in the
> blind worship of the peasants and the village loafers and the
> fishermen of the seaside, he forces the wealthier people to
> obey him in the most minute matters. He is practically mas-
> ter of the body and soul of every individual. When they are
> born they are brought before him and he baptizes them for a
> few shillings. When they begin to go to school they come
> under his supervision. He hires and sacks their teachers at his
> discretion, very often at his whim. He flogs them if they mitch
> from school or if they fail to learn their catechism. When they
> become striplings he watches them carefully lest they make
> love clandestinely. When they reach marriageable age he mar-
> ries them for a few pounds. If they don't get married he nags
> at them, eager for his fees. He abuses them from the altar
> unless they pay him what he considers sufficient money at
> Christmas and Easter. When they die he buries them, but
> before doing so, he levies a further toll in hard cash over their
> dead bodies. This toll is levied from all their relatives.
>
> From their first yell at birth until the sod falls on them in
> their grave their actions and thoughts are under his discre-
> tion. He is, almost invariably, himself of peasant extraction
> and almost invariably he is just about as well informed as a
> well informed peasant. So he is not burthened by a very
> refined religious conscience in the civilized sense of the
> word. Being mentally on a level with his peasant flock, he is
> up to all their tricks. He knows what is passing in their
> minds, of what they are afraid, how to tickle their greed, how

to overawe them with threats of hell, or to enthuse them with promises of indulgences and eternal happiness. So they are proud of him, as of something that has sprung from their loins, that satisfies their innate greed by giving a promise of Heaven and that is just a little cleverer than themselves. Not too clever, for too much cleverness inspires a peasant with distrust. —pages 19–22

It was just such a priesthood, satirized by O'Flaherty in 1930, that the young priest in the picture no doubt aspired to at his first Solemn High Mass in Jackson, Michigan, on that bright June morning in 1934—a ministry of gossip and goodwill, moral authority and fear of the Lord, shame and salvation, tribal bias and beatitudes, deep humanity and flawed humans. It was a priesthood of a people and a faith familiar to his father, who'd brought it from the small house in West Clare he'd left in the decade before the new priest was born. It was the faith known to those who stayed put in these western parishes at the edge of the world. It was Irish and Irish American. It was Hollywood and Holy Roman, icon and idolatry. It was the faith of my youth and instruction. All my life I have been dogged by priests whose voices I hear when my conscience speaks. I think of them as fellow pilgrims, placed at random or by the hand of God at intersections in my own journey. However imperfect these men have been, all they've ever done was good to me.

When I meet Fr. Culligan in Carrigaholt, I hear Fr. Kenny in his voice, and Fr. Killeen, and Fr. Murphy and Fr. Walsh and Fr. Lynch. It is the same language that Fr. Ron and Fr. Bill and Fr. Leo in Michigan speak. It is a dialect of faith I understand. It is the language I first learned as a child, safe in the arms of my Blessed

Mother, my Holy Father, the curious syllables of secret, sacred speech rolling off my tongue by rote. And there's a comfort in it, a return to the safety of my childhood, to the certainties I had then that someone was in charge and watching out for the likes of me.

But faith, it turns out, is not child's play, seasoned as it must be by the facts of life—love hurts; we die; hope falters; God, it seems, goes missing sometimes.

This is where the smarmy and narcissistic doxologies of the day fail us. Faith is not for dealing with God's grandeur—the sunset, the candle flame, the child's face. God is manifest in a lover's eyes. Faith is rather for the hours of God's absence, when we are most alone, betrayed, in pain, afraid. The life of faith is less a journey into ever-more-pleasant horizons or agreeable truths, and more a kind of rummage through the doubts raised by mere existence. This is when the discipline and traditions, the rubrics and language of religion provide a necessary infrastructure for our own voice, crying in the desert, at one with pilgrims everywhere. But more and more our churches have become a kind of spiritual country club or theme park or religious mall endeavoring, as everything in the marketplace does, to entertain, excite, comfort, or soothe us. What faith is after is not comfort but salvation.

For many of the faithful, the politics of the Church and the failings of churchmen and religious have made their religion at best a distraction, at worst an impediment to the life of faith. They cling to the disciplines and language, observe the rubrics and rituals, say their prayers, and go about their lives keeping an arm's length between their religiosity and spirituality. They are Catholic by birth and baptism, training and temperament. They simply have little to do with the Church.

On Ash Wednesday of 2004, when two reports commissioned by the U.S. Conference of Catholic Bishops revealed the scope of clergy sexual abuse since 1950 in the world's largest Christian denomination, Bishop Wilton D. Gregory, president of the conference said, "The terrible history recorded here is history."

Like those who proclaim "closure" at a memorial service, often just before the Merlot runs out, thus suggesting that grief is "finished," the prelate's declaration seeks to make finished history of all-too-current events. But history is a perspective that, like closure, is achieved, not proclaimed. Unless and until the Church deals not only with the scandal of problem priests but also with the vastly more egregious conduct of a hierarchy that has failed the faithful badly, lay and ordained alike, Catholics are right to be wary of this old boys' network of company men.

That Boston's Cardinal Law resigned in December of 2002 is little comfort to those who believe he should have been arrested. That he was restored by Pope John Paul II, early in 2004, to a cushy and largely ceremonial post at St. Mary Major Basilica in Rome is an insult and further proof that at its highest levels the Church still doesn't "get" it. That good men of God, servants to their parishes and communities, innocent and heroically kind practitioners of the corporal and spiritual works of mercy have been made sexual suspects and left hanging in the wind by the cover-ups and cronyism of their ecclesiastical uplines is wrong, wrong, wrong.

Hard times, these days, to be a parish priest in Ireland or America—indeed, around the world. Damned if they do and if they didn't, in ways the old movies never foretold, they are called to imitate Christ: to bear the beating due the sins of others, to take a scourging in the public square, to suffer all the large and little deaths and to live in the ever-present fear that God is watching or that God isn't.

WE CATHOLIC BOYS all listened for the call—the voice of God exquisite in our ears: *Come follow me,* or, as it was with Paul, thunder and lightning, or to Noah, *Build an ark.* Even when God speaks in riddles, as in "Be fruitful, but not the apples," there is comfort in the conversation. Belief is easy when God speaks to us. The ordinary silence—there's the thing—the soul-consuming quiet, the heavens' hush that sets even the pious wondering. Lord, spare us all, we doubting Thomases who, even with a trembling finger in the wound, still ask aloud, "My Lord? My God?"

Once in the basement of my grandparents' house, I found the dead priest's cassock and Roman collar hanging from a rafter, blessed and bodiless. I was the age my father was when his uncle was ordained. And under it, a trunk of priestly things, surplice and biretta, bright chalices, a sick-call kit and leather breviary. I tried them all. Though nothing seemed to fit, all the same, I kept on listening.

Fr. Thomas Kenny—never "Tom"—that Holy Roman Irish Catholic Man who never wavered, never doubted in the least but lost his bearings when they Englished everything, taught me to pray to know God's purpose in my life. "Discernment," he called it, and I keep praying for it.

It was a language I learned to speak, lovely and Latin, a sort of second tongue, given by my parents and people, nuns and priests, that lingers in the air like incense and song, ghostly and Gregorian—memories of which are always flooding then fading, coming then going, but never gone.

WHEN THE YOUNG priest in the picture died, that last day of July 1936, they took him, I'm told, back the high road to Taos from Santa Fe past the holy shrine at Chimayo and the mission churches in Cordova, Truchas, Las Trampas, and Penasco. And after a wake on Saturday night and Mass on Sunday in Our Lady of Guadalupe in Taos, they took him back the low road for Mass in Santa Fe at the Cathedral of St. Francis of Assisi. The route meets the Rio Grande southwest of Ranchos de Taos and works its way south through Velarde, Arcalde, and San Juan Pueblo, with the river to the right and mountains everywhere. A reporter for the Santa Fe paper, Katharine Darst, wrote it down and sent a copy of the article to my grandfather. Along with a handful of photos sent home with his things, it was the only document we ever had that brought to life the man who went out West and died and wore the cassock that hung in the basement of my grandfather's house on Montevista Street in Detroit.

PATHOS IN BURIAL OF YOUNG PRIEST
UNTIMELY DEAD AT TAOS

While eastern tourists flocked to the horse show, or drove gaily off to Jemez for the Indian dances, a somber little procession wound down the mountainside from Taos *Sunday*—a procession carrying the Rev. Thomas Patrick Lynch to burial.

These black draped Mexican women with withered faces, these young boys, and mothers with babes in their arms, were the people the young priest had come west to serve. At their head rode Father Balland, weeping.

Two years ago the young Irishman from Detroit had made

the journey up to Taos for the first time. Full of hope he was starting his life's work in the missionary parish. And that work was not entirely one of preaching. When Father Lynch had ministered to the spiritual needs of his little flock he had a way of taking off his Roman collar and his coat, and giving the boys a few pointers at baseball. And they respected his advice, for here was an athlete, a virile man. And he loved them. Why else had he come?

When the little procession started from Taos Sunday no relative accompanied the body of Father Lynch, but all that little band of mourners. Slowly, carefully, they bore their friend down through the chasm cut by the Rio Grande. Somber skies and the great black mountains cast a shadow of their own upon them.

In Santa Fe they bore the casket through deserted streets. Silently the Dominican monks, children from the orphanage, the nuns, His Excellency Archbishop Gerken, friends from Taos and Father Balland bore Thomas Lynch into the Cathedral for the last time. There his hands, as the hands of a saint, were touched to their rosaries.

A few people returning early from the horse show looked with curiosity on the quaint procession. Stray motorists who were stopped by traffic police, paused before they turned their cars down the detour. But nowhere was there a Willa Cather to make immortal the passing of this boy. She who had felt so poignantly the death of an old archbishop with his life work accomplished, was not here to witness the infinitely more pathetic exit of this boy whose life had been shut off "'ere half his days were done." Here was a sorrow which needed her pen, and alas, only I was there.

Let this be my excuse for touching something so far
beyond the ability of a simple newspaper reporter.

When they were through in Santa Fe, they put the dead priest
on the train back East to his people. Bishop Gerken fronted the
hundred dollars, which was later reimbursed by the dead priest's
estate, which also paid the undertakers in Santa Fe three hundred
dollars for the embalming and coffin. It was late on Tuesday when
the train arrived in Jackson. It was Wednesday, August 5, 1936, that
my father's father—the dead priest's brother—took his twelve-
year-old son along to Desnoyer Funeral Home in Jackson to
organize the requiems and burial. And it was that morning, while
his father talked details with Mr. Desnoyer, that the boy who
would become my father wandered into the basement where he
saw two men dressing the dead priest in a fresh white alb and green
chasuble in preparation for the wake that night and ten o'clock
Mass at St. John's in the morning. That vision—a young boy's witness of a dead priest and living men lifting him into his casket—
shaped his life and my life and my family's life for going seven
decades now. Who we are, what we do, our lives and times have
been shaped by it. Were it not for that moment in our father's life,
when his journey intersected with his dead uncle's journey home,
God only knows what we'd all be doing these two-thirds of a century since.

What if, there in the doorway of the embalming room, my
father had been "called" to become a priest instead? Or what if,
after all of Fr. Kenny's plotting and prayers, I'd gotten the vocation
he'd in mind for me?

"'What if's a mug's game," Nora would say. "Things happen the way they're supposed to happen. Of that you can be sure, my boy."

But in truth my people's pilgrimage, across oceans and countries, from Ireland to America, Michigan to New Mexico, up and down mountains, through the desert and distant places and home again, wherever those homes were, began here in this small house in Moveen, where Fr. Thomas Lynch's father, Thomas Lynch, first had a vision of a future in America. He only had the testimony of his father who'd been there, briefly we figure, in 1875; and others from the townland who'd gone out before. But it was 1890 now. His mother was dead. His roots to the home place loosened. His prospects in the familiar parish dimmed. The future, like Michigan, was a far country—a leap into the distant and unknown, oceans and rivers full of loops and turns, tides and repetitions, ways that widened and narrowed and crossed themselves. He took it all on faith, as pilgrims do.

Bits & Pieces

Messages

Nora rode a Raleigh bike. It was black and basic—three gears, hand brakes, a pump for the inevitable punctures. A gray leatherette bag hung from the handlebars. Every day or every other she'd ride into town for "messages."

She would return with some muttonchops and rashers, the day's provisions, staples and necessities, ten Woodbines for Tommy, Maguire & Patterson matches, and a newspaper. The spuds and onions and cabbage all came from the haggard out the back door beyond the whitethorn trees. The eggs came fresh from her own hens. Bread she made—plump loaves of soda bread, crossed like a good Catholic, baked in her covered cast-iron pot with turf coals on bottom and on top. Milk was their business. Now and then she'd kill a goose.

But it was that trope, "going for messages"—not marketing, not shopping—that best described the difference between the "custom" in West Clare and "consumers" in Michigan.

"Pa Hawk's" was her first stop—Pat Haugh's Central Stores. Neighbor ladies from town and country would be there, Mrs. Haugh, and her daughters. She'd buy Lyons Green Label tea, some biscuits and a pound cake for the inevitable guests, a tin of peas and corn, Chimo for the soot—bits and pieces. There'd be talk of the weather—"We're perished with it"—and news of the world, "Godhelpus." Were there visitors in town, someone gone off, anything happening to anybody? "Now Missus," she'd say, holding forth the payment. "Now Nora," with the change. "And many thanks."

To the Irish House then for an *Independent* or *Ireland's Own* or the *Champion,* maybe a Confirmation or First Communion card, some sweets—Scots Clan—and talk. Someone in hospital? Someone to Dublin? Someone home?

"The weather's very broken."

"By cripes, 'tis true for you."

Then up O'Curry Street to Peggy Starrs Off License for a half bottle of Paddy to keep in the house and word of anyone that Peggy knew that Nora knew. Across to the Bank of Ireland to leave the pension in and chat with the others waiting in line. Who was pregnant? "Is she?" Who was courting? "Go 'way out of that." Who was getting married soon? "Musha lovely Nora!" Who died? "Did you hear what I'm after hearing below?"

To Maloney's the Draper for a look at the latest, a new tablecloth, stockings, or shirt. "Any word from the crowd in America?" Then to Nolan's Victuallers for the meat—some banter and barter—"Fresh eggs, Mr. Nolan, for a bit of beef. What say ye?"

Nora's was an information economy—her news in trade for the other's news—the pleasure of each other's words, the pleasure of their own.

By then in America we went to "super" markets for the stuff and filled the back of cars with a month's provisions and spent the time at the checkout watching the charges as the clerk rang them up, or rummaging for the coupons, or sighing in commiseration with our fellow shoppers and sellers for whom the transactions had become just work, just getting it—the money and the stuff. In trade for "messages" we got discounts, "paper or plastic?" and "have a nice day," all in the one monotony of corporate good manners.

The market is common, global, and dull. We buy in bulk, bank by machine, and couldn't care less about the name on the sign. More and more, we point and click our way past any human interaction. Everything is logo and commercial-faux. Even the pubs are pretend. A good Italian restaurateur in Milford just opened his very own Irish pub. "Stouts," he calls it, because "Angelosanti's" mightn't bring in the pretend-Paddys. He heard about it all at a convention, took a crash course at Guinness's in Dublin for a week, and went for the real look—the dark woody snug, the dartboard, and folksy posters. He does Irish music and it's going great guns.

Oh for the days when Mrs. Egan pulled warm pints at Egan's Marble Bar or when Tom Ketts held forth at Ketts' Lounge, and Pearce Fennell, "that old communist" shared the barman's spot with his German shepherd at the Anchor, then the Dolphin, and now no more. And thanks for the days that are still there—with Michael and Mary O'Mara behind the bar at O'Mara's, and Mary Hickie at the Bayview, and the Lynches at Lynch's in Kilkee; and below in Carrigaholt, Mrs. Morrissey reading palms at Morrissey's, and Dodo Carmody at Carmody's with generations now, and Jack Lynch, home from the Bronx, at the Anchor, and Keanes at Keane's and lobster at the Long Dock and chowder at Fennell's and the stop at Foley's or Boland's in Cross, a bowl of mussels at the Lighthouse in Kilbaha or songs at Keating's, the last pub out the west. Thanks for the known place, the known face, the talk and table fare, powerful houses and publicans, the uncommon decency of the common place.

Nora came home the long road from Kilkee with a small bag of things, a day's worth of perishables, a night's worth of news—her messages. We return bulging with our bags and boxes of stuff—our newer faster brighter bigger better-than-ever right-priced stuff—laden and empty, grim and wordless.

Kilrush, County Clare

THE KILRUSH RACES
[Author unknown]
Come all you decent people and listen to my lay
We'll have the Kilrush races on the 24th of May
And if you gather round me I'll tell you who'll be there
There never was such fun before, in the good old County Clare

Chorus
So come to the Kilrush races
On the 24th of May
And if you do, upon my word
You'll spend a pleasant day.

There'll be horses there from Galway, and also from Tralee
Boys from every barony, from Feakle to Kilkee
There'll be ladies there from Dublin, dressed up in style so grand
With their racing glass and powder puffs and fine young men at
   hand.

There'll be suppers in the kitchens, the finest ever seen
Cold boiled beef and cabbage and a thrupenny crubeen.
There'll be fiddles making music, to fill our hearts with joy
And old maids will get husbands and the bachelors get wives.

Every year in August, this old market town on the Shannon, just upriver from the sea, has set aside a weekend to honor the memory and music of Lizzie Crotty, who owned, with her husband Miko, a pub on the square at the corner of Henry Street.

She played the concertina—the diminutive cross between a button accordion and a harmonica—which is essential to traditional music. She was better by all accounts than anyone of the day. But her concertina was not made with concert halls or recording studios in mind. It was the woman's instrument, handy and demure, intimate and intuitively played, made for the kitchen and cottage nook, and the back rooms of public houses. Same for the fiddle and tin whistle, pipes and spoons, like bluegrass or zydeco: lovely but local, old, in many ways, before its time.

By the time she died, in 1960, Mrs. Crotty had been made famous by Ciaran Mac Mathuna, who traveled the country in the 1950s, recording local heroes for Irish Radio with RTE's new "mobile" unit. "The Wind That Shakes the Barley" and "The Reel with the Beryl" are among Mrs. Crotty's original jigs and reels, frequently covered by new-millennium musicians.

Kilrush, with its powerful shops, good hardware, dry goods and fishing gear, pubs and music, is a regional hub. It is well known for cattle marts and horse fairs.

When Nora Lynch was alive, we'd make a day of it. Many's the time we'd call into Crotty's for tea or a drink and there'd be music on, in the back kitchen, quite by happenstance. Traditional musicians would often call in to pay their homages and to say they'd played at Mrs. Crotty's. A few years ago the pub was bought by Rebecca Brew, daughter of the hardware Brews in Henry Street. After working the family shop and going to school and stints with the United Nations and the EEC, she returned to Kilrush, married James Clancy, and bought the famous bar from Mrs. Crotty's people. Rebecca Brew's travels in the larger world brought her by turns back to the home place to labor over the modern Irish dilemma of how to manage too many choices rather than too few, plenty rather than shortfall, and lines of people wanting to get into rather than out of Ireland.

The food is better. The décor is the same. The price of a pint is mostly taxes. Some things change. Some things never do.

The notion of an annual festival—the *Eigse Mrs. Crotty,* as it is called—seemed to grow out of the ancient Irish interest in music and the recent Irish money to pour into the arts and community festivals. Ms. Brew was one of the early organizers of this festival. They got local sponsors and help from their T.D. (senator), Sile de Valera, then minister for Arts and granddaughter of the Irish Republic's first president.

There are workshops for budding concertina players, and serendipitous consortiums—sessions—of tin whistlers and fiddlers and bodhran players, and a visit to Mrs. Crotty's grave in the old Famine cemetery at Shanakyle overlooking Scattery Island from which the local saint, Senan, banned women ages ago. He ruined a sea-monster there as well. And there are open-air *ceili* dances in the town square and plenty of "open mike" events in the local pubs, which all enjoy extensions for the festival. There'll be a fiddler in the snug, a tenor in the lounge, and from the bar a flutist holds forth for anyone listening. Everyone has a song or story, a poem or party piece. It is late summer in West Clare and the place is full of Limerick suburbanites, Euro-tourists, returning Yanks, and locals.

Saturday night is the Mrs. Crotty Memorial Concert. We all squeeze into the gymnasium of the primary school to sit and listen whilst pairs of apprentices come out to play in a concertina extravaganza. They play but do not perform, in the way that traditional dancers remain expressionless except for their feet. Once the music is delivered, they stand, smile, bow, and leave. The regimen of a recital fits the space we're in.

Then Slide—three Dubliners and a Corkman—come on to wow the audience with their highly energized, neotraditional set of reels and jigs and originals. They have just launched their CD—*The Flying Pig*—that promises to put them on the elaborate map of Irish music. Aogan Lynch, Daire Bracken, Mick Broderick, Eamonn de Barra—Slide (say *schlide*)—are taking no prisoners. They have brought an arsenal of old and new tools. This is no recital. Theirs is the poetry slam of the trad music scene—a full-body, large-muscle, amplified articulation of "traditional" forms. One imagines statues moving in the school.

After an encore and much applause, Slide give over the stage to the night's headliners, Martin Hayes and Dennis Cahill, on fiddle and guitar respectively, who are joined by Mary McNamara on the requisite concertina and Pat Marsh on the bouzouki. They begin with three reels, elegantly played, but measurably down-volume from Slide's performance.

"Think of us," says Martin Hayes in the hushed-parlor talk of his East Clare roots, "as a cup of cocoa after the night's reveries." The crowd laughs. Then he praises the young men of Slide, "any one of whom has more energy than the four of us." We laugh again. Hayes's generosity is genuine. He sounds the thinking man whose CD jacket notes are manifestos of artistic intent. In the County Clare of former generations, Martin Hayes would have, like his father, played maybe a hundred nights a year—weddings and dances, American Wakes—most within bike range or bus range, always back for the cows and creamery to the home place in Feakle where Brian Merriman of *The Midnight Court* is said to have come from. And Rebecca Brew would have pulled pints, raised children, and learned the till and the routine of the tourist season. But they belong to a new generation of Irish men and women who export the nation's culture but bring its far-flung people home. Now there is a pair of reels that highlights Mary McNamara and her concertina as if Mrs. Crotty were incarnate in the pretty woman's round knees, closed eyes, slight smile, and meditative airs; and everything is working toward the quiet evening by the fire in a kitchen full of familiar tunes that none of us has time for anymore.

Then Mary rests the squeeze box on her lap and folds her arms, and Pat sets his bouzouki aside, and Martin and Dennis begin a slow air in the lyrical Clare style that Hayes has claimed as birthright. The air bridges by a single chord to "Kilnamona Barndance," which in turn becomes "Ship in Full Sail" and then

picks up pace with "Jer the Rigger" and the jaunty "The Old
Blackthorn," then "Exile of Erin"—the transitions are seamless,
thanks in no small measure to Cahill's perfect accompaniment of
Hayes's virtuosity. Each piece quickens the pace and raises by
degrees the emotional ante. Everyone in earshot is aware that
something very magical is happening. Hayes and Cahill are telling
a story that is generations old and has no end in sight. Hayes is lost
now inside the music, which seems like nothing so much as the
soundtrack for much of Irish and Irish-American life in the last
two centuries—the pain of departure, the adventures of going, the
joys of the open larger world, the hunger and hope of return to the
home place. As they work their various ways through "Humors of
Tulla" and "Fitzgerald's Hornpipe," Hayes has achieved a kind of
ecstasy, his face cast upward, his mouth partly agape, as if communing with all the friendly ghosts of this music—Martin
Rochford, Junior Crehan, Tommy Potts, Micho Russell, Francie
Donnellon, John Naughton, and dozens, hundreds more who
brought this music through good times and bad to its present
postmodern incarnation. Hayes has become one with his instrument and the strings bounce and soar toward flights of sound we
have never imagined within the range of fiddling. He is scrutinized
and anchored by Cahill's guitar percussions. Knees and feet are
keeping a kind of blissful overtime. It is clear that nothing "traditional" is being done here with the fiddle or guitar. Hayes eases
through "Rakish Paddy" into the mad-paced "Finbarr Dwyer's
Reel No. 1" and finally into "P Joe's Pecurious Pachelbel Special"—
written by his father P. J. Hayes, the famed leader of the Tulla Ceili
Band who died in May 2001. By the time this set finishes, it is
nearly half an hour and the cup of cocoa seems the bottle of the

finest sipping whiskey. The audience roars with gratitude and approval. They clap and stomp, whistle and hoot and stand. Hayes, still hovering between the music and the place, dripping with sweat, nods and smiles, restored apparently to ground level. He wipes his face, counts to Dennis, and they take up the next tune.

The Weather in West Clare

"Grand day thank God," is what the Moveen crowd says whenever they wake to anything within the range of tolerable miseries.

"Not as bad as the night of the Debbie," is what they'll say when slates fly off the house, or the power goes down, or the rain makes a puddle out of everything. It was August 1969 when Hurricane Debbie rose up out of the Caribbean and made its way across the North Atlantic to sweep hay barns and knock some ancient walls in West Clare.

"Grand day thank God," is what they mostly say, grateful to be up and out in it. Or "soft day," or "it's very broken." One rarely hears the out-and-out complaint that the weather in West Clare is severely damaged compared to, say, Cuba or Connecticut or Melbourne or East Clare, where trees can stand and gardens thrive and people can go about their business.

More menacing than the forty days of rain in every month of every season, and the gale-force winds that pound the place, are those odd stretches, known to go weeks on end, of unseasonably kindly weather—the sweet breath of the Antilles in the air, so gentle on the skin that the skin rejoices, the light so magic that the eye can hardly bear such beauty, the heart aching with thanksgiving for the day that's in it. I've seen it hit in March or April or November and once near the feast of St. Serenus, in late February. The day-trippers come in their cars to Kilkee. The seafront lodges fill with weekenders. The merchants open for unexpected trade. The pubs grant themselves a dispensation. Everyone thinks of it as a bonus.

For the first few days there is the usual greeting, punctuated with authentic glee. "Grand day thank God, entirely!" But after several days in the one week of such relief, the locals take a different view, knowing as sure as heaven there's hell to pay and that too much good requires much more bad to balance it.

"Grand day," they say with the wary look of the long-suffering, waiting out old peril and new doom, "Grand day, indeed, the Lord've mercy on us all."

Fair Play to Charming Billy

From Moveen, I sometimes look across the Shannon Estuary to the Kerry hills. From the end of the peninsula, I can make out Ballybunion where Bill Clinton golfed in September of 1998 in the midst of the Lewinsky imbroglio. Back in Washington, Senator Joe Lieberman was calling Clinton's behavior "immoral." But in Ireland a beauty parlor named Monica's, on the road to the famous golf course, removed its sign lest it embarrass the motorcadians. The Irish know what's in a name. They know that words can hurt or heal old wounds.

Whatever history says of William Jefferson Clinton, let it say he did the right and difficult thing by Ireland.

The Protestant and Catholic questions are giving way to "Visa or MasterCard?" "Cash or charge?" Expanding markets and lines of credit breed goodwill toward men in ways that God on Our Side or the Other's never did. And the Celtic Tiger purring in the Republic trumps the old begrudgers and hateful rhetorics.

In Belfast this month, the shoppers come and go between storefronts without opening their bags or standing for the old inspections. The worry over bombs and armaments has given way to the welcome extended to coin of the realm. Dublin is bulging at its seams: cars, computer wares, trendy bars, and multinationals. It is one of the dividends of even a fragile peace—the marketplaces thrive. And though there are growing pains, more, it turns out, *is* merrier than less. If Clinton did not invent this truth, he had the courage nonetheless to come and preach it in these contentious parishes.

THE GOSPEL ACCORDING to your man—equal access to a promising future, investments in jobs and education, forsaking of the old tribal alliances and wars in pursuit of peace and creature comforts—these things took root in this ancient, rocky place. In the three decades of the current "Troubles," Bill Clinton was the first, the only, U.S. president to take the Irish predicament to heart. Campaigning in New York in April 1992, he promised to do something about it, and then he did. From the granting of a visa to Gerry Adams in 1994 to the appointment of George Mitchell, a peace envoy disguised as an economic advisor—all things done against the odds—Mr. Clinton deftly handled the dicey relations among London and Belfast and Dublin and Washington, D.C. By bringing the weight of his office and intellect and charm to bear on both sides of the divide, he opened the dialogue of cooperation if not conciliation. What peace there is in this green place, and much of the prosperity that has followed, owes as much to Bill Clinton as to any other American or Irish American.

And in Ireland they know it. They have forgiven him everything: every moral failing, every political duplicity, every personal foible in trade, in *thanks* for the moral high ground he helped to clear where no side wins but none is vanquished. The peace, however shaky, holds. The talk goes on. The future seems full of hope and possibilities. For the first time in two hundred years, the young of this country may go or stay as they please. People are trying to get *into* Ireland for its opportunities. For the first time ever, the Irish have to contend with the perils of too much rather than too little.

Fair play to charming Billy, he had a hand in all of this.

Little wonder, then, your man would find, in the ever-shortening days of his watch, the comfort and commisery of home fires among people who, like himself, are known for their enigmas, their excesses and abuses, long suffering and kindnesses, their gifts of gab and blatherments, their poets and politicos, their shame and guilt, their hunger for forgiveness, and the deeper gifts of history—peace on earth, goodwill toward men—even if they are their own worst enemies.

Party Piece

THE CLIFFS OF MOVEEN
[Author unknown. To be sung to the tune of "The Cliffs of Duneen."]
I have traveled far far from my own native home.
Far away o'er the mountains far away o'er the foam

Many places I've traveled and great sights I have seen
But none can compare to the cliffs round Moveen.

'Tis a grand place to be on a fine summer's day
Where the apples and cherries they never decay.
The towns of Kilrush and Kilkee can be seen
From the high rocky slopes round the cliffs of Moveen.

Take a view o'er the Shannon, great sights you'll see there
And the high rocky mountains on the west coast of Clare
The hare and the rabbit are plain to be seen
Digging holes for their homes round the cliffs of Moveen.

Fair thee well old Moveen, fair thee well for a while.
And to all the grand neighbors I am leaving behind.
May my soul never rest 'till it's laid on the green
Near the high rocky coast round the cliffs of Moveen.

Water

We plumbed the place in 1982, Dualco De Dona and I. Nora told us they'd brought the water up the road the year before and sure enough we found it there under a plate outside the gate. We cobbled together the parts we'd need from Williams in Kilkee and Brews in Kilrush—a length of PVC, some copper fittings that came from Poland, a shiny tap and a used stainless-steel sink we'd bought from a barman in Kilkee. There were no shops with vanities and housewares that sold anything that suited Nora's tastes. Everything was far and away "too dear." So we emptied a small clothes press, cut off the top, and set the sink there in its place. We drilled a space through the east wall off the house—and worked the piping through and hooked it up. When Nora turned it on, we took a picture. It replaced the long walk down the land to the open spring well, the bucket-at-a-time return uphill, or, in a pinch, the rainfall in the barrel by the downspouts off the roof. Nora said it was a miracle and praised the "composition" of it.

The only bill left after Nora when she died a decade later was the one she owed to the Clare County Council for the water. Noel Grogan was local rates collector. The bill was huge. I thought there must be some mistake. Nora was scrupulous about her debts and was proud of the way she'd sold eggs and new potatoes to pay off her father's little debts when he had died. And she'd left plenty of money after her, for the wake and funeral and the rest.

When I went to his office in Kilkee, he said, "I knew I'd meet you sooner or later." He said that Nora Lynch would never pay for water. He'd gone out to Moveen to work out payments years before and Breda Roche had tried to convince Nora that she should pay the bill. But Nora was steadfast in her refusal.

"Why would I pay anyone for water in West Clare?" she protested. "There's never been a shortage of it. There's buckets of it raining down on Moveen every day. Will you stop? It has the land destroyed. And why would I ever pay the County Council anyway? It was Tom Lynch put water in this house."

Thus tongue-lashed and a kindly man, Grogan decided he would bide his time. "There's no fear, I knew you'd sort it."

We laughed. I paid. Some months after that, the County Council did away with household water rates.

BUSH OUT

Front page center, below the fold, in living color, thanks be to God, the April 11, 2003, issue of the *Clare Champion* is a picture worth its thousand words. It is an aerial photo of forty-seven naked women lying belly-up on the greensward of Clare, in the shadow of the Burren's great mountain, Mullaghmore. They have assembled themselves in such a way as to scrawl BUSH OUT across the treeless, bushless landscape in the memorable script of their lovely bodies—aged twelve to sixty, says the report. "Grin and Bear It, George," reads the photo's caption.

The group, calling themselves Bare Necessities, according to the *Champion*'s ace reporter, Joe O Muircheartaigh, is hoping that the U.S. president, en route to his Belfast summit with Mr. Blair, will "get the picture" while flying over Clare.

"We were sending a message to George Bush that we were appalled that he was coming to Ireland talking about peace while he was waging an illegal war in Iraq," Bare Necessities pioneer Ruby Wallace is quoted as saying.

Shannon Airport continues to be the scene of protests over the use of that airport for the refueling of American troop transports.

Great Hatred, Little Room

Out of Ireland have we come.
Great hatred, little room,
Maimed us at the start.
I carry from my mother's womb
A fanatic heart.
—from "Remorse for Intemperate Speech," W. B. Yeats

THE PLANE I am trying to get on is United. Flight 373 from O'Hare to Detroit. I never intended to be here at all, nor did any of my fellow pilgrims, all dumped here in Chicago by an act of God. Last night it was raining ice in Lower Michigan. The airport in Detroit was closed. So here we are, the morning after, the cranky and unshaven stranded from the canceled flights. There are travelers from Baltimore and Newark, Boston and New York who overflew the storm in Michigan. There are folks trying to return from Orlando and the Carolinas and the cities of the West, trying to get home, just like me.

I was en route from Reno where I'd given a speech to OGR—The International Order of the Golden Rule—an association of funeral directors whose slogan is "Service measured not by gold but by the Golden Rule."

Do unto others, etcetera, etcetera.

I've lost track of the time zones and geographies.

Surely we are nearing the end. The news is booming from the TV screen: War in the cradle of civilization, the great cities under siege. The miserable weather is relentless. We're bombing the enemy. There's friendly fire. The dead are everywhere.

EVER SINCE THAT godawful Tuesday morning, that September in 2001 when United and American Airlines planes were flown into the World Trade Center and the Pentagon and a field in Pennsylvania, the nation has been bombing what it can, the Afghans and Iraqis, who knows who is next? *Those to whom evil is done do evil in return.* Who said that?

Not only did they die, they disappeared—our dead that day— 9–11. There's the terrible fact of the matter. We never got them back to let them go again, to wake and weep over them, to look upon their ordinary loveliness once more, to focus all uncertainties on the awful certainty of a body in a box in a familiar room, borne on shoulders, processed through towns, as if the borderless countries of grief and rage could be handled and contained, as if it had a manageable size and shape and weight and matter, as if it could be mapped or measured. But we never got them back.

There are thousands dead and gone, Godhelpus.

We know this the way we know the weather and the date and dull facts of happenstance we are helpless to undo. There are many thousand bits and pieces, salvaged from the Fresh Kills landfill site. Families keep vigil at the city morgue. Good news is when they get their portion of the precious body back.

IN THE PAPERS this April is the image of a man kissing the skull that was found in the dirt of a shallow grave outside a prison in the city of Baghdad. The number on the grave corresponds to the number in the gravedigger's log and the names of the people that are tallied there. The name and the number and the grave and the skull belong to the man's son. He was taken away years ago. There is a hole in the back of the skull the size of a bullet. There is a litter of other bones, femurs, and ribs, and the man in the photo is strangely pleased. This is the seeing—hard as it is—that is believing. It is the certainty against which the senses rail and to which the senses cling. This is the singular, particular sadness that must be subtracted from the tally of sadness. The globe is littered with such graves as these, people killed by others of their kind, by hate or rage or indifference. Most of the graves will never be found and the dead wander in and out of life, never here and never really gone. Whether they are victims of famine, atrocity, terrorism, casualties of a widespread war, part of a national or global tragedy, they are no less spouses and parents, daughters and sons, dear to friends, neighbors, and fellow workers; they are not only missed in the general sense but missed in their particular flesh—in beds, at desks and dinner tables, over drinks and talk and intimacies—the one and only face and voice and touch and being that has ceased to be. And their deaths, like their lives, belong to the precious few before they belong to the history of the world.

THE PRESIDENT AND the prime minister are meeting in Belfast to discuss the future of Iraq—how warring factions of that invaded nation might be brought together when the "hostilities" have stopped. The clerics are rallying the faithful to the streets. The politicos are holding forth. The corporations are moving in. The press is embedded.

"Hate," the president says, "and vengeance and history can be put aside in trade for a peaceful and prosperous future." He says the Irish have shown us that. He's never been to Belfast before. He's never been to Iraq.

It sounds lovely, of course. Who's not in favor of that? Forget the past. Let's just all try to get along.

But really I just want to get home. I've been too long in this airport, too long in transit, too long up in the air. I want to go home now. I am standing by.

Sitting next to me, also standing by, also listening to the ugly, ubiquitous news blinking from the monitors, is a handsome woman from Los Angeles. Well, actually from Michigan. Well, actually from Belfast. She's a traveler, too.

"I was born in Belfast," she says when the news mentions Belfast.

She moved to Canada when she was a girl. Then to Michigan. Then to Los Angeles, from whence she was flying to Detroit yesterday when the ice storm forced her to land at O'Hare. She is going for her son's twenty-first birthday. He was born in Michigan and still lives there.

We are all just waiting for our names to be called. The 7 and 9:30 A.M. flights were packed out. We're hoping to get on the 10:55.

"I was born in Belfast," the woman says.

"I have a house in Clare," I say. She reminds me of my youngest sister, strawberry blonde, freckled, blue eyes, and a squarish, pretty face.

"Really!" she says. "What part of Clare?"

"Near Kilkee, in the West, a wee cottage only." The *wee* is an adjective I've stolen from friends in Ulster and in Scotland, from whence many of the Northern Irish families came. The *only* at the end, trailing the adjective—instead of "only a wee cottage"—is another affectation. If not a brogue, I have achieved a mid-Atlantic syntactical style. Talk of Ireland makes me talk like that.

"I've heard the seaside in West Clare is lovely."

"Lovely," I tell her, "entirely."

She left Belfast as a girl. She was ten. It was 1964. Her father and mother could see what she called "the handwriting on the wall."

She says she has promised never to teach her children to hate. She'd been taught to hate as a girl.

"I can't believe my parents did that to me," she says. "It was crazy. It hurt."

It is the thing she remembers about her childhood.

"'I'd know them by their eyes,'" my mother would say, "'those squinty eyes.'"

"Which had the squinty eyes," I ask, "Catholics or Protestants?"

"Oh, Catholics," she says.

"I see, I see."

"I'm Lorraine," she says.

"Tom," I say. "Nice to meet you."

Lorraine had a friend who was Catholic, a girl named Eileen who lived down the street. That was fine with her parents until Lorraine went with Eileen to "chapel." When her father got word of her going into a Catholic church, he beat Lorraine in the way that other parents might spank their child for running into a busy street, only harder.

"As if I might 'catch' something there," Lorraine says now, still embittered by the injustice and betrayal of it. "God, where does such hatred come from?"

She looks out over the thickening traffic of stranded travelers.

"I might as well turn back and head for home. I have to be back to work day after tomorrow."

"Have faith," I tell her, as if I had it, "you'll still make it for dinner."

"It snowed like crazy the day my son was born. They closed the schools. Amazing, April of '82—twenty-one years—seems like yesterday." Lorraine has lost any semblance of a brogue. She has the accent of the network news. "I never taught him to hate."

SIX MONTHS AFTER the towers fell, I am in New York City at the invitation of David Posner, senior rabbi at Temple Emanu-El, the largest Jewish house of worship in the world. He has asked me to speak on the Book of Job. I rise early from a night's sleep in a room on Bleecker Street and go out for a morning walk, drawn to what has come to be called Ground Zero. I walk down Broadway to Fulton Street, where a "viewing platform" has been constructed so people can look over Church Street at the gaping wound. Some days, twenty-five thousand people come, lining up like mourners at a wake, for a look. They have to see. The recently constructed ramp is for people to queue up alongside St. Paul's Chapel, with its churchyard of eighteenth- and nineteenth-century stones. George Washington prayed here after his inauguration. It is Manhattan's oldest public building in continuous use. There is a broad deck facing east from which groups of maybe twenty can take a look at what isn't there. It has become, in most ways, negative space. Cameras click into the open air. Men in hard hats work below, in the pit, in the massive open mass grave. Everything stops when "something" is found. Something flag-draped and horizontal is carried slowly up out of the hole to an ambulance. Work resumes. On the boardwalk that leads back to Broadway, there is a wall on which the names of the dead are listed alphabetically. It begins with Gordon M. Aamoth, Jr., and ends with Igor Zukelman. There are Murrays and McMahons, Collinses and Keanes, Curtins, Maloneys, and Mahoneys, all names of my neighbors in Moveen and names from the far-flung and neighboring townlands: Doherty, Dolan, Doyle, Crotty, and Curry. Like the dead, the Irish are everywhere. And when I come to the Lynches in this grim litany, I am shocked to see the names of my own boys—Sean and Michael—I count them all: *Farrell Peter Lynch, James Francis Lynch, Louise A. Lynch, Michael Lynch, Michael F. Lynch, another Michael F. Lynch, Richard Dennis Lynch, Robert H. Lynch, Sean Lynch, and Sean P. Lynch.* Ten of them—a bond trader, a property manager, stockbrokers, firemen, and cops; and two brothers of immigrants who worked together at Cantor Fitzgerald. One over fifty, two over forty, the rest in their thirties—primes of their lives—all murdered in the one madness, in the same sixteen-acre killing field at the south end of an island city of the world between 8:46 and 10:28 on a Tuesday morning. The only name with more murdered there was *Smith*. There are a dozen Smiths. There are ten Kellys, too—James and Joseph and Richard and three Toms—and ten Murphys—Raymond and John Joe, Edward, and Kevin and strangely, as I read it, no Michaels or Seans. In all, sixty-four names that begin with "Mc"—McAleese and McCourt, and McSweeneys. Four O'Briens, four O'Connors, one O'Callaghan, two O'Keefes, an O'Grady, O'Hagan, O'Sheas, and O'Neils. Oh God, it seems so Irish and American. So very sad and beautiless. It seems like a chapter from the Book of Job.

I walk down Church Street from the plywood wall of names crossing Liberty into Trinity Place and slip into the old Trinity Church there, High Church Episcopal, where Dr. Deirdre Good, officiating at Morning Services, was giving a homily on Christians and Jews—how they must achieve reconciliation. At the time I remember thinking that Jews are having more trouble with Muslims of late. For Jews the Book of Job is real.

"WHY DIDN'T YOU take the Jews to America?—There's plenty of room."

So asked the man who drove the cab that brought me to the airport this morning from the Best Western Hotel in Des Plaines, where I was able to get a room last night after they diverted our plane to O'Hare. He is Palestinian, angry, and named Mohamed.

"It's all about oil and the Jews. Bush and Blair are criminals. Why do you think people blow themselves up? Because they won't live like this!" He's lecturing the rear-view mirror, shaking a finger. "They'd rather die."

He thinks of Jews as colonizers, foreign occupiers, settlers sent by a larger power to dominate an indigenous population, the way Sinn Fein thinks of the Presbyterians who were planted in Ireland generations ago. Or the way Native Americans or South Africans think of white Europeans or the way white European pilgrims thought of the ghetto Irish in New York and the way the ghetto Irish thought of freed slaves, or the way white Detroiters thought of blacks from the South who came north for work in the last century, or the way the blacks think about the Jews, or the Jews the Arabs, or the Arabs the infidels, or the Koreans the Japanese, or the Tibetans the Chinese, or the guy without the boarding pass, the guy who does—

everyone fighting for his piece of the rock, his bit of the planet, his vision of the truth, a seat on the bus or boat or plane.

I'm feeling a little cramped in the cab, hostage to Mohamed's increasing rage. Great hatred—Yeats was right—and little room.

My mother's dearest friend was a Jew. Renee Friedman and Rosemary O'Hara grew up in brick bungalows next door to each other on Eileen Street in Northwest Detroit. Renee's mother, a Russian, and her father from Hungary met and married in New York then moved to the Midwest at the end of World War I. My mother's parents, children of Irish immigrants who worked in the copper mines in Michigan's Upper Peninsula, met as students in the class of 1918 at the University of Michigan, where he played in the marching band and she studied music. Renee's mother kept a kosher kitchen. Rosemary's served no meat on Fridays. Both of the mothers upheld the other's rules for each other's daughters. They kept different Sabbaths, different customs, and different holidays but shared a respect for faith and rubric and devotion. Renee and Rosemary grew up constant friends. They prayed together when their boyfriends went off to the war, rejoiced together when they returned. And married within a few months of each other, both wearing the one dress, each barred by the other's religion from "standing up" for the other. Renee raised seven children; Rosemary nine. The families shared bar mitzvahs, bat mitzvahs, First Communions and Confirmations, Passovers and Easters, wakes and shivahs, Christmases and Chanukahs. They tried to teach their children not to hate.

"Jews and oil," Mohamed says, grabbing my bag from the trunk of the cab. "That's why they are killing Iraq. For the Jews and oil." The fanatic heart beats in every breast. He hates them all—Jews and the president and the life he has. And though I do not share his particular hatreds, I know what an adrenaline high it is—to hate and rage against the facts of one's life. I try to commiserate but I'm spending my hate this morning on having had to bunk in Des Plaines last night, on the time lost to an ice storm, on the lines already forming at the curbside check-in booths, and on the fact that I'm a middle-aged white man, with more money than time, and I'm willing to pay whatever it takes and still I'm stuck here, standing in this endless line, trying to get a boarding pass, here only two hundred fifty miles from home. I don't need an upgrade or exit row or aisle seat. I'm not looking for anything special at this point. Can't they understand? I just want to get home.

And the more time I spend in the airport, standing by, the more I'm beginning to dislike everyone with a ticket and a boarding pass and the sureties that belong to such as them. And I'm beginning to hate the airlines and the professional sangfroid of the agents at the counter with their "have a nice day" corporate-speak and the industrial-strength smiles behind which they are paid to keep the reasonable contempt they have for me for showing up here looking for some kind of guarantee when the whole room full of us are standing by and there's not a thing anyone can do about it.

I hate the woman calmly reading in the seat across from me and the young man next to her who will likely outlive me and the inconsolable child on the other side of the room yelping at the top of her lungs with an earache or sore gums or God-knows-what discomfort. I hate them all and am more or less certain that they hate me, until I meet Lorraine, who is stuck in the same predicament as I am and is, like me, made crazy by all of this. I can see it in the way she is just barely hanging on to the slimmest thread of civility.

Maybe we were maimed from the start. Maybe it is the little rooms.

I think of the cramped quarters in Moveen; my great-great-grandparents huddled around a fire on the floor with their expanding family, all of them afloat between intimacy and aggravation, familiarity and contempt—the weeping baby, hungry toddlers, the adolescents fighting for their place by the fire, in the family, in the room. They sleep on straw, in earshot and arm's length of each other's dreams and flatulence, masturbations and copulations. Their defecations and urinations are done outside. They eat potatoes mostly, sea grass, periwinkles, a bit of herring or mackerel, meat at Easter and Christmas. There's a bucket of water in the corner, a few sods of turf stacked in another. There is one table, one fire, one candle, a pig. There is never enough of anything—food, warmth, privacy, space. They have rent and penances to pay. Sometimes they count their blessings. Sometimes they fight over the shortfall. Some days the struggle fills them with fellow feelings. Some days it fills them with a quiet rage. Is this where the hair trigger of my temper comes from? The low-grade, ever-present fever in the blood—was it carried from my mother's womb, my own fanatic heart?

More battles are waged over the morsel than the meal. Is it the little rooms or the privations? Poverty or lack of open access? Jews in the Warsaw ghetto, the Famine Irish, West Africans in slaving ships, oppressed Shiites, slaughtered Kurds, the homeless Palestinians—all want, all hunger, all hate.

There's new looting in Baghdad, old contentions in Belfast, suicide bombers in Jerusalem. CNN is everywhere.

Detroit is full of Iraqis and Irish, Jews and African Americans;

there are Asian and Hispanic and Native Americans too. It was the factory work and the easy borders with Canada that brought us all here. There are mosques, synagogues, and churches of every kind—Sunnis and Shiites, Chaldeans and Kurds, Catholics and Protestants, Black Muslims, Black Christians, Black Buddhists, and Jews. There's more than enough religion to go around. There's sufficient history. There's no shortage of anger, no shortage of fear.

YEARS AGO I joined a men's Bible study group.

"We're looking for a good Catholic," Larry said when he called. He's Lutheran, an attorney, a neighbor and friend, and good on all counts.

"Let me know if you find one," I half-joked, then asked the who and when and wherefores.

Larry told me we'd meet Tuesday mornings at half past six, a dozen of us, like apostles, at the Big Boy restaurant.

I figured on two weeks maybe, two months at the outside, before we'd come to our senses. But twelve years since and it's still going strong. A couple have died, a couple moved away, a couple quit. They've been replaced. There are three attorneys, some retirees, sales reps, engineers, local businessmen. We've done the letters of Paul, the Acts of the Apostles, Genesis and Exodus, Kings, Chronicles, and Revelation. When it was all the rage, we did the *Prayer of Jabez*. We open with prayer and close with oatmeal. By half past seven, we're on our way.

Lately we've been studying the Book of James. It has things to say about the rich and the poor, faith and works, and intemperate speech:

How great a forest is set ablaze by a small fire! And the tongue is a fire. The tongue is placed among our members as a world of iniquity; it stains the whole body, sets on fire the cycle of nature and is itself set on fire by hell. For every species of beast and bird, of reptile and sea creature, can be tamed and has been tamed by the human species, but no one can tame the tongue—a restless evil, full of deadly poison. With it we bless the Lord and Father and with it we curse those who are made in the likeness of God. From the same mouth come blessing and cursing. My brothers and sisters, this ought not be so. —Chapter 3: 5–10

But so it is.

Between Tuesdays we forward things—jokes and stories, preachments and prayer requests—by e-mail and the Internet. Recently the following made the rounds, forwarded from one of our twelve, who got it from his pastor who got it from some other "reliable" source.

Allah or Jesus?
by Rick Mathes

Last month I attended my annual training session that's required for maintaining my state prison security clearance. During the training session there was a presentation by three speakers representing the Roman Catholic, Protestant, and Muslim faiths, who explained each of their belief systems.

I was particularly interested in what the Islamic Imam had to say. The Imam gave a great presentation of the basics of

Islam, complete with a video. After the presentations, time was provided for questions and answers.

When it was my turn, I directed my question to the Imam and asked: "Please, correct me if I'm wrong, but I understand that most Imams and clerics of Islam have declared a holy jihad [holy war] against the infidels of the world. And, that by killing an infidel, which is a command to all Muslims, they are assured of a place in heaven. If that's the case, can you give me the definition of an infidel?"

There was no disagreement with my statements and, without hesitation, he replied, "Non-believers!"

I responded, "So, let me make sure I have this straight. All followers of Allah have been commanded to kill everyone who is not of your faith so they can go to Heaven. Is that correct?"

The expression on his face changed from one of authority and command to that of a little boy who had just gotten caught with his hand in the cookie jar. He sheepishly replied, "Yes."

I then stated, "Well, sir, I have a real problem trying to imagine Pope John Paul commanding all Catholics to kill those of your faith or Dr. Stanley ordering Protestants to do the same in order to go to Heaven!"

The Imam was speechless.

I continued, "I also have a problem with being your friend when you and your brother clerics are telling your followers to kill me. Let me ask you one more question. Would you rather have your Allah who tells you to kill me in order to go to Heaven, or my Jesus who tells me to love you because I am going to Heaven and He wants you to be there, too?"

You could have heard a pin drop as the Imam hung his head in shame.

Needless to say, the organizers and/or promoters of the 'Diversification' training seminar were not happy with Rick's way of dealing with the Islamic Imam and exposing the truth about the Muslims' beliefs.

I think everyone in the U.S. should be required to read this, but with the liberal justice system, liberal media, and the ACLU, there is no way this will be widely publicized. Please pass this on to all your e-mail contacts.

This is a true story and the author, Rick Mathes, is a well-known leader in prison ministry.

Whether it was the "gotcha" religiosity, the thumping triumphalism in this codswallop, or the haplessly appended anonymous commentary in the last three paragraphs that put me in mind of the letter of James and what he had to say about the fire of tongues—it made me think of my youth among the nuns. Our Protestant neighbors—the parents of my pals Mark Henderson, Jimmy Shryock, and Mike McGaw and their sisters who taught me precious truths—had heard it rumored that we Catholics kept a stash of guns in the basement with which we would someday during the Kennedy presidency rise up and take over the nation in the name of the pope. In the meantime, I was taught that Mike and Marcia, Jimmy and Cathy, Mark and his older sister Jane, were no doubt bound for a certain hell for their failure to believe in the One True Faith. The world, this scurrilous e-mail showed, was a larger, World Wide Web–connected version of the old neighborhood with its grudges, mistrusts, and xenophobes, blessed and cursed in exactly the way James wrote it was. The Catholic crusaders who rode off to save the Holy Land from "Mohammedans" centuries ago, like the Episcopalians gleefully hanging Quakers in the New World, bore in their hearts and minds the religious passions and the species blindness of the *jihadist* and holy warrior who fails to see the creator in all of his creations.

WHEN LORRAINE'S PEOPLE left Belfast, the Protestant majority made no effort to hide the fact that "Roman Catholics need not apply." It was there in bold print in the shop windows and newspapers. It was the subtext in every conversation. It was the quite boldly spoken ugly truth that there was a cultural and religious divide between those with access to education, employment, finance, and power and those without.

In Detroit it is done on black and white, or variations on those themes of race and ethnicity. In London it is done on "class." In Calcutta, "caste." In Baghdad as in Belfast, it is sect and tribe and party politics.

The president and the prime minister are telling the world that Iraqi oil will benefit Iraqis. The president is anxious to prove his critics wrong. It is not about oil and Israel but liberation and democracy. There's looting in Baghdad, the statues are falling. No one seems to know exactly who is in charge.

My last time in Belfast, two years ago on literary duties, I was struck again by the Irish gift for understatement. To call the decades of damage in Ulster "Troubles" is like calling cancer "difficulties." What has happened in "The North of Ireland" or in "Northern Ireland," depending on your politics, is trouble indeed, and difficult, and cancer. It is hate.

In Belfast a standing joke goes:

"Are ye a Catholic or Protestant?"
"God knows I'm an atheist."
"Sure, but are you a Catholic or a Protestant atheist?"

In Belfast as in Baghdad, there is no choice to opt out of the conflict. Everyone is *something*. Everyone believes or disbelieves in something. Whether lapsed or devoted, militant or indifferent, orthodox or not; whether disbeliever or misbehaver, nonconformist or reformer, everyone is bound by ancient codes of tribe and blood, belief and conflict. And hate, like love, forms its habits and attachments.

Among the young writers, teachers, and professionals I know in Belfast, there is always talk of the comfort of going south, into the Republic, or farther still, to the Continent or Canada or the United States, and the chance it gives them to "turn the radar off"—to disengage that terrible wariness of what they might say and whom it might offend or infuriate. These are well-meaning people who are sensitive to their neighbors' sensibilities, who hunger for peace, who abhor the posturing of extremists but who are, nonetheless, to various degrees, Loyalists, Nationalists, Protestants, Catholics, damned if they do and if they don't say anything. Damned for their beliefs or lack of them, targeted for the faiths they profess or renounce. Among these border towns where flags and banners and the writing on the walls proclaim the differences, the "other" is said to "dig with the wrong foot." The road signs are variously defaced. One side crosses LONDON off of LONDONDERRY while the other crosses the DERRY out. "What's in a name?" we ask. The answer in most places is, "What is not?

MY FATHER'S MOTHER became a Catholic mostly to marry my grandfather. The priest shook water on her, she always told us, and said, "Geraldine, you were born a Methodist, raised a Methodist, thanks be to God, you are now a Catholic." One unseasonably warm Friday evening the following spring, she was grilling burgers in the backyard when the neighbor, Mr. Collins, one of my grandfather's brother knights from the K. of C., leaned over the back fence to upbraid her on the subject of what other people would think about a Catholic woman preparing meat for the dinner on a Friday in Lent. With water from the garden hose, she "converted" the beef, saying, "You were born a cow, raised a cow, thanks be to God, you are now a fish."

"All God's children," she would often say.

IS IT DERRY, then? Or Londonderry? Is it *The North* of Ireland or *Northern Ireland?* Is it Sean or Sidney? Mabel or Maeve? Lorraine or Kathleen? Do you dig with the right foot or the wrong one? Are you wide-eyed or squinty? Are the violently conflicting views of Ulster rooted in race or sect, language or doctrine, poverty or pride or power-lust? "Whatever you say," wrote Seamus Heaney famously of this painful case, "say nothing."

WE HUMANS HAVE these troubles everywhere. Religion, race, and nationality; gender, age, affiliations—these define and divide us. We are ennobled and estranged by them. These "conditions" are, unfashionably, not matters of choice. I am Catholic in the way I am white and American and male and middle-aged—irreversibly, inexorably, inexcusably. However lapsed or lazy or lacking in faith I am on any given day, I am, at the same time, a lapsed, lazy, and faithless Catholic. I sin and am forgiven according to the language I learned as a child—a dialect of shalts and shalt-nots, blessings and beatitudes, curses and prejudices. Surely it is no different for the children of observant Jews, Muslims, Methodists, and secular humanists. Religion is the double-edged sword that unites, protects, and secures while it divides and conquers and endangers, always and ever in the name of God. The subtextual message of all religions is that, while we are all God's children, God likes some of his children better than others, and that heaven, wherever it turns out to be, will be populated by those of one kind and not another.

Of course in Belfast, as in Baghdad or Jerusalem, the issue isn't doctrine or observance. There are fewer true believers than we like to think, and true believers honor true belief in others even when it is not a belief they share. The issue is "otherness." How we separate ourselves from other human kinds. Religion is just one of the several easy ways for the blessed and elect to remain just that. The haves and the have-nots around the world maintain their status—as victimizer and aggrieved—on the narrowest grounds of difference. Race, religion, tribe, caste, class, club, color, gender, sexual preference, denomination, sect, geography, and politics—everything we are separates us from everyone else. In the border counties of Ulster, where it is hard to tell Kenneth from Sean, or Alison from Mary, where everyone is fair and freckled, "he digs with the wrong foot" and "she has squinty eyes" are both the sublime and the ridiculous truth. It is the same in Baghdad, where it is impossible to say who is Sunni and who is Shiite, who is Baathist and who is not. Everyone on the news looks the same to me. Does it have something to do with the headgear, the eyes? What's in a name? Everyone here is Muhammad or Ali.

LAST YEAR I read in the *Irish Times* about Muhammad Ali's Irish roots. Ms. Antoinette O'Brien of the Clare Heritage Centre in Corofin had traced the connections.

Was there ever any doubt?

"The Greatest," it will come as no surprise to Claremen and Clarewomen 'round the planet, has roots in the Banner County. Like my great-grandfather, Ali's great-grandfather came from that poor county bordered by the River Shannon and the North Atlantic, famous for poets and dancers and knock-down handsome men who float like butterflies and sting like bees.

"Up Clare!" is the only thing to be said about it.

Born in the gray city of Ennis in the 1840s, as grim a decade as ever was, Abe Grady left for the New World in his twenties. He got the boat at Cappa Pier by Kilrush—not ten miles upriver from my ancestral hovel in Moveen—and made west for The Better Life.

Mr. Grady found his way to Kentucky, where he was smitten, in circumstances undocumented by Ms. O'Brien, like men of the species since time began, by the dark beauties of an African woman. Like my great-grandfather, in his youth Abe had never seen a visage that wasn't freckled, blue-eyed, pale-faced, and blushed-red. Little wonder that he found her lovely and exotic, enchanting altogether. She was, to quote my late and sainted cousin Nora on this theme, "pure black."

A son of their union, an African Irish American, it is reported, also married a black woman, and one of their daughters, Odessa Lee Grady, married Cassius Marcellus Clay the elder in the 1930s and settled in Louisville, where The Greatest, formerly known as Cassius Marcellus Clay, Jr., was born to them on January 17, 1942.

The world, of course, has been the better for it.

The *Irish Times* reports that Michael Corley, chair of the Ennis Town Council, would be extending an invitation for The Champ to visit.

"We would like to honor him because the town is proud and

delighted to have played a part in producing one of the heroes of the twentieth century," the councilman is quoted as saying. No doubt they plan a suite at the Old Ground, a feast at Bunratty, and a tour of the Turnpike area where Abe is reported to have hailed from, though all of the thatch-roofed lodges have been leveled.

The Champ, who like me lives in Michigan, has not said when he intends to return to the country of his ancestors.

What part did Ennis play, we might sensibly ask ourselves, in the production of Muhammad Ali? Is there something in his dance, his duck and weave, his combinations and his "rope-a-dope" that might be traced to his roots in Ireland? What got Abe Grady to Cappa Pier with his ticket and tin box marked, as my great-grandfather's was marked, "Tom Lynch—Wanted," meaning, I have often supposed, that the contents were precious to him?

History is a sad and instructive study. The County Clare that Abe Grady left was, per capita, the most decimated by emigration of any county in Ireland. They did not leave as tourists. They left like the Jews of Europe left a century later for Israel—withered, starving, having just survived. They left like Somalis and Iraqis and Cherokees and Bosnians—because they had no choice. For most emigrant Irish of the nineteenth century, the choice was fairly simple: stay and starve, surely, or leave and live, maybe. Abe, we might imagine, was in the same circumstances.

MY GRANDFATHER SAID "nigger" the way Mark Twain wrote it, or LBJ or Harry Truman said it, the way I used to say "tinker" before I was told that I oughtn't talk like that. He said it the way you might say "February" or "pomegranate" or "twelve." It was a word, like any other word, that he had learned to say from hearing it said, or reading it. He was unaware of the hurt and harm it could do.

He worked with black men and women, who all looked the same to him, in the way he looked, to them, the same as his Polish and German and English fellows—white. They said "cracker" and "mick" the way he said "nigger," not so much in hate as ignorance and indifference. Micks and mackerel snappers, kikes and hebes, spics and Polacks and wops and chinks and jigaboos and hunkies and honkies and spades and guinnies and all the other derisive derivatives of our melting pot—such was the vocabulary of kind and color and identity.

Ali's great-grandmother's people came as slaves, in boats built in Belfast, like the one that Abe took down the Shannon and across the sea. Colonization, abject poverty, forced emigration by starvation, eviction, and political domination—all close and distant cousins, of a kind—bondage done up in the Sunday dress of steerage, slavers turned into coffin ships, the human cargo stacked like chattel in the hold, a third of them dead en route or on landing, all of them well below tourist class, all of them looking for a class of people worse off than themselves.

FOR THE IRISH—starved, evicted, long oppressed, spewed out on the docks of America—the only ones they could find worse off than themselves were the blacks they had never seen before. If the Irish owned nothing, they owned themselves. "Darkies" were chattel.

Needing more fodder for the Civil War, the Republican president Abraham Lincoln ordered a military draft. The Enrollment Act of Conscription, issued in March 1863, like drafts that followed, weighed most heavily on the poor. Married men were exempted, as were those who could provide a substitute or those who paid a three-hundred-dollar fee. The Irish of the northern city slums were too poor to marry and too poor to pay the "commutation fee" and were losing their lowest-rung-of-the-ladder jobs to the influx of former slaves moving north. Prejudiced and living in poverty and urban squalor, and shocked by reports of the horrors of Gettysburg, the immigrant Irish found the prospect of going to war to free slaves who would compete with them for down-market jobs was all tinder for the riots that broke out in New York City in mid-July 1863. A mob of fifty thousand, most immigrant Irish, burned down the draft office at Third Avenue and 46th Street, and then turned their anger on blacks around the city. Blacks were lynched and drowned and there were brutal beatings. Buildings were burned, including a church and an orphanage full of black children on the corner of 43rd Street and Fifth Avenue. Over four days, there were hundreds of dead and wounded, and a million and a half dollars in damage was done before the Army of the Potomac was dispatched to restore order. A headline in one Pennsylvania paper read: "Willing to fight for Uncle Sam but not for Uncle Sambo." What's in a name?

In the way that abusers become abusive, victims of racism become racists too, and the Irish, with an uninterrupted history of taking it, got good likewise at dishing it out.

"Prejudice," Muhammad Ali has said, "comes from being in the dark. Sunlight disinfects it."

ONE NIGHT IN August 1970, I went to the Mars Ballroom in Kilrush. It was packed with the local and visiting young, drinking and dancing as the young will do. A new face in a small place, I drew the scrutiny of the West Clare girls. Emboldened by two pints of porter, I asked a dark-haired beauty for a dance, and though I'm a clumsy waltzer and worse at rock and roll, she nonetheless remained my partner for the night. The band played American country music and Beatles tunes, lights reflected off a large disco ball hung by wires from the ceiling. We drank and talked and walked up the town for fresh cod at a late-night chipper. We went back to the Mars and danced some more. When the night finished with the playing of the national anthem, all of us standing there in the smoky dance hall singing to Dev, she rose on her tiptoes and kissed me. I kissed her back, then she disappeared, arm in arm with her giggling friends. "Call to me tomorrow," she had told me. "I'll be waiting for ye."

Back in Moveen, Tommy had taken himself to bed. He'd been all day drawing turf from the bog in Lisheen. But Nora, ever vigilant, was up and waiting by the fire. She made tea and commenced her interrogations.

"Were there a fair few there?" "Had ye drink taken?" "How were the band?" "Did ye meet anyone?"

I told her that I had fallen in love, was likely going to be staying in Ireland, marrying a Clare woman and raising a family.

"Wooo! . . ." said Nora. "Now for ye! And who's the lucky lady I wonder?"

"Sheila Delaney from Kilrush."

Nora's eyes narrowed and she straightened up, rummaging through the inventory of names and particulars she knew.

"Never mind that lady," she said in a low, cautionary tone, "Delaney's a tinker."

"But Nora. . . ."

"Never mind that lady, boy. She's a dead loss," Nora continued.

"From the terraces," she said, referring to the public housing estates built by the County Council. "What would you want with one of that crowd?"

There was in Nora's preachments on this theme none of the usual lilt in the words. The volume was lowered and the tone was flat, unambiguous, and intense.

I KNEW WHAT tinkers were. In 1970, you'd still see their red-and-green-painted wagons encamped outside of the larger towns—on the outskirts of Ennis and Galway and Kilrush. And there'd been a wagon down in Goleen, a little inlet of the ocean where Moveen edged up against the sea. And I remember a woman and her daughter coming to Nora and Tommy's door with a variety of secondhand household goods for sale. Nora sat her in by the fire and called her "missus" deferentially and bought a bit of carpet from her and gave her whiskey and her daughter pennies and sent her on her way with thanks and blessings.

There was about the encounter this vast ambivalence—Nora was glad for the visit and liked talking with the woman, questioning her on what she'd seen in her travels, but clearly thought of her as "the other." She was a tinker, a traveling person, a member of a class of people known for their music and horses and tin-smithing—from whence the name—and feared for their separate lives, separate language, separate lifestyle, separate laws.

And a tinker gone into the terraces was worse, to hear Nora tell it—like American Indians on the rez—the noble savage tied down to the dole.

The status of traveling people in Ireland is much like the status of "others" everywhere. Whether the otherness proceeds from

racial, ethnic, religious, economic, sexual, or behavioral variations,
the human response to otherness seems the same. We are attracted
to it and frightened by it. Suspicious and covetous, begrudging and
enamored—we find "the different" compelling and repellent. We
are divided by our loves and hates.

ON THE FIRST anniversary of September 11, I am back in New
York at the City University for a conference on the question of
"What Have We Learned Since 9–11 About Death and Grief and
Bereavement?" I've given my keynote speech the night before.
Once again I find myself walking downtown, to see the "remains"
surrounded by flags and flowers and eulogists.

The year gone by seems like a long national wake or shivah. We
have behaved like a large, closely knit, and occasionally dysfunc-
tional family, quibbling over blame and money and the proper
memorials. Twenty-five thousand people a day have stood in line
to pay their respects. The worst of the ravages have been removed:
the nearly twenty-thousand body parts, the fewer than three hundred bodies, the horrid mountain of disaster.

At Ground Zero, while the litany of the dead and gone was read,
achieving the cadence of lamentations, a wind blew through that
open space, filling the air with dust and flowers. And all I could
hear were the lines of a poem written years ago by a friend in the
midst of a sickness—a mortal peril that threatened his son, his
household, his family's future.

MERCILESS BEAUTY
Look to the blue above the neighborhood,
and nothing there gives any help at all.

We have seen the fuchsia, and it doesn't work.
Time flows away. The mystery it fills
with our undoing moves aside awhile
and brings a new reality into play,
apparently—and here is the main idea:
the wind of time appears to blow through here,
the periwinkle and the mayapple
trembling in wind that is of their own kind,
a gorgeous color of a clarity
that fills our eyes with brightness to see through,
for all the good it does us, and to tell
the morning glory from the glory of God.
           —from *Love's Answer: Poems by Michael Heffernan,*
               University of Iowa Press, 1994

The blue above the neighborhood was quiet. The wind of time
indeed blew through the place. The politicians said their pieces.
The pipers from the Emerald Society, having marched thirteen
miles to the place, piped "America the Beautiful." There was nothing in the weather or the music or the words that offered any clue
as to what we had learned in the year just spent among the ruins
and the dead. The "gorgeous color of a clarity," by which I might
have seen something new to tell "the morning glory from the glory
of God," was nowhere.

The smaller the world gets, the greater the hatreds seem. April
this year is full of unseasonable weather. The Jews are celebrating
Passover; the Christians, Easter. The Shiite Muslims in Iran and
Iraq are making their pilgrimage to Karbala by the hundreds of
thousands. They are going to the tomb of Hussein, the founder of

their sect and grandson of the Prophet Muhammad, who was murdered by Sunnis 1,400 years ago, the way Christians say Christ was, by Romans and Jews. For twenty-five years it was forbidden, under the rule of Saddam Hussein, for Shiite Muslims to make this pilgrimage, to observe the holy days of atonement, self-flagellation, chest thumping, and ritual sacrifices of lambs in commemoration of an event equivalent to the Crucifixion of Christ for Christians. The Shiites are thanking God for the end of Saddam Hussein and calling for the infidel Americans to leave. The clerics are jockeying for position.

In Ireland they are marking the fifth anniversary of the Good Friday Agreement by which, in 1998, all of the hateful parties to the "Troubles" gathered in a room to sort out how to organize their hates into a manageable government. As a friend of mine, born in Fermanagh, living in London with her husband and children, said, "Peace has broken out in my country!"

Maybe this is what the president's speech writer meant when he wrote that Ireland gives us hope for Iraq—that while we have no choice about our hateful natures, we can sit great hatreds down in the one room and organize a peace. We can seize this from the other possibilities. The themes of slavery and liberation, death and resurrection, oppression and freedom, sacrifice and miracle, new life, old grudges, pilgrimage and exodus, rage and tolerance are an important study. The world's grim history of apartheid and ethnic cleansing, holocaust and resettling, *jihad* and forced migration is a blight upon our human nature. What Oliver Cromwell did to the Irish in the seventeenth century—the ethnic cleansing—required him to see the slaughter of Irish peasants and their forced resettlement in the barren West as "the judgement of God on these bar-

barous wretches." Our species has not evolved much past such evil.

In 1953, James Watson and Francis Crick proposed the double-helix molecular structure of DNA. In 1990, the Human Genome Project took up its ambition to map the DNA structure of human beings. It turns out that we are, each and every one of us, one of a kind and all the same. Mother Teresa and Adolf Hitler have much in common. George Custer and Catherine of Siena, Mandela and Milosevic are genetically much the same. We all trace our mitochondrial roots to an Eve in Tanzania 150,000 years ago. The Mother of All Humans adrift in the world.

AND HERE I AM, now, a traveler. I look into Lorraine's large blue eyes and wonder if she can see me squinting. She is a traveling person too. We are both standing by for a flight to Detroit. I'm looking at my fellow pilgrims in this little room. We are each one and only and one and the same. When we cut each other, each of us bleeds. To any stranger, we all look the same. That I am Irish or American, a Clareman or Michigander, whether home in Milford or Moveen, the truth of my humanity is that I am none other than my species mates around the globe. We hunger, thirst, sleep, and long for peace. We all want to get home through the storm. The plane we are trying to get on is United.

The Sisters Godhelpus

MY SISTER BRIGID's yellow Lab bitch Baxter was put to death last Monday. What can be said of such proceedings? That every dog has its day? The following from my sister's partner, Kathy, tells the tale.

> It is with a heavy heart that I write this e-mail to notify family of the death of Baxter Bailey (11 1/2 years old) on Monday, July 14th. Kidney failure. She was buried in a deserved spot, at Mullett Lake. She is survived by her sister, Bogey Bear (who is a little lost as to what has transpired) and her mother/best friend/companion—Brigid. A brief ceremony will be held the weekend of the 25th on Mullett Lake.
>
> Whether you loved her, feared her or were entertained by her, she will never be forgotten. Long live her memory.
>
> Kathy

In receipt of which I replied:

> Dear Kathy and B,
>
> Thanks for the sad and tidy news. I will not pretend to
> have admired the deceased. She was, however, a walking
> (more lately hobbled) example of the power of love. She
> was not bright, not lovely, less communicative than most
> mum plants, and drugged into a stupor for most of her
> life. But here is the mystery—the glorious mystery—that
> a woman as bright and lovely, articulate and sober as our
> B loved her, loved her unambiguously. For a man of my
> own limitations (and they are legion) the love B showed
> to Baxter was a reminder of the lovability of all God's
> creatures—even me. In that sense she was a constant
> beacon of faith and hope and love. If this is what they
> call the Dog's Life, I say more of it is the thing we need.
>
> You and B will be in my prayers for a brief if deserved
> bereavement.
>
> Love & Blessings,
> T
>
> PS: Pat and I will get the stone and willn't stint.

It was a hasty but heartfelt sentiment, managed between the usual
mélange of mortuary, literary, and family duties. I meant only
comfort by it. And though we get the headstones at wholesale, the
gesture was genuine.

PART OF THE comeuppance for calling our small chain of
funeral homes Lynch & Sons is that the daughters—our sisters—

control the purse. Three of my father's six sons, I among them, went off to mortuary school and got licensed, years ago, to embalm the dead and guide the living through the funerary maze. Before our father died, we bought the enterprise from him. His three daughters—ever his favorites—went to university and business schools and were installed in various key positions. Mary is the bookkeeper and paymistress. Julie Ann is her factotum. Brigid handles trusts and insurance and pre-need finance and is the de facto comptroller at my brother Pat's funeral home. We call them "The Three Furies," and they travel between my establishment and Pat's, bringing light and joy and accountability.

When I see them together—Mary, Julie, and Brigid—I often think of the headlands on the Dingle Peninsula called "The Three Sisters," which rise in a triad of sweeping, greeny peaks to protect the Irish countryside from the ravages of the North Atlantic. Like those features in the West Kerry topography, they are strikingly beautiful, immovable, and possessed of powers we know nothing of. They are, it is well known, Irish in origin—the powers, the sisters. The source of all that is holy and hazardous about them is a matrilineage that finds its way back to a kitchen and cauldron in a boggy parish in the old country where only marginally post-Celtic mystics bedded with poor farmers who never knew what they were getting into. It is a lineage of women who emigrated on their own, in numbers equal to or greater than men, enduring steerage and indignity, years of indenture, to better themselves and their American children.

The sisters come by their powers honestly. They are their late mother's daughters and have inherited that sainted woman's charms and spells, blue eyes and Parian complexion, intellect and idolatries. They are, as she was, devotees of the votive and vigil, rosary and novena, perpetual adorations, lives of the saints, imitations of Christ, statues of the Blessed Virgin Mary and Sacred Heart, Stations of the Cross, relics, waters, ribbons and badges, prayerbooks and scapulars—all of which make them morally superior and spiritually dangerous. The arsenal of their godly wraths and blessed tempers would, in the best of circumstances, be turned on their spouses, to their betterments. But as each has partnered and consorted with the most amiable soulmate, they've only to train their tantrums upon their older brothers, whose puny potvaliances, collective and individual, are no match for The Furies. It makes them, I suppose, easier women to come home to.

Wednesdays Mary and Julie come to my funeral home in Milford for payroll and accounts—receivable and payable. Brigid remains at my brother's office but calls to consult with her sisters three or four times on the day.

Last Wednesday, when Mary and Julie read my sympathy note, they rolled their eyes and smote me with their disapproval. "How could you say such an awful thing about Baxter to your grieving sister?"

"What awful thing?" I asked, "a beacon of faith and hope and love?"

"This bit about the mum plant and stupor. . . . Couldn't you have just said something nice? Something about her loyalty?"

They did not see that stating the obvious about Baxter's life and times was central to the art of condolence and, a fortiori, the construction of the note's kindlier sentiment.

Truth told, the dog was a disaster, which had worn out her welcome by eleven years with everyone except, of course, my sister

Brigid. A female assigned a fashionably suburban, chicly Anglo-Irish, but still oddly mannish name, "Baxter Bailey" never seemed to know whether she was coming or going, whether to hump or be humped, whether she ought to lift a leg or squat. When she had just achieved adult size and indoor continence, she bit my sister—quite literally the hand that was feeding her—thereby missing the only requisite point of Dog 101, to wit: Don't bite the humans. B had her neutered. Later she growled and snapped at B's infant and toddling nieces and nephews as they approached to pet her. On the strength of these misdemeanors and distempers, I once had B talked into putting her down, citing the liability presented by a dog that might attack neighbors or their pets or children, houseguests or passersby. I reminded her of the One-Bite Rule, with roots in the Book of Exodus, near where the ordinances on the seduction of virgins are recorded (alas, the emergent patriarchy!), which held that an owner would be called to account for the second infraction of a domestic animal. I'd gone so far as to set an appointment with the vet for the euthanasia and had Baxter leashed and loaded in the backseat and B agreeably disposed to the good sense of it all. But when she got there, she waffled in her resolve. She asked the vet, instead, for medication, something, she pleaded, "to calm her down"—Baxter, not Brigid. The cocktail of pharmaceuticals thus prescribed amounted to the nonsurgical equivalent of lobotomy. She was given phenobarbital to control her seizures, Lasix as a diuretic, something for her stomach disorders and insomnia, and a giant daily dose of canine Thorazine—enough I daresay to dull an orangutan—to quiet her demons, real and imagined. Baxter remained more or less on the edge of a coma for the rest of her life. Like some of those old lads you'd see in the pubs, the tooth gone out of them, supping up their daily sedation. She never snapped at anyone or anything again. She roamed about, bumping into the landscape and geography and furniture, like an outsize, spongy orb in a game of pinball or bumper-pool. At the lake, Mullett Lake—where we've recreated *en famille* for years and ruined the property values—she would sometimes walk into the water, as if some distant memory of her breed still flickered in her. Brigid would have to wade in and lead her ashore. People would toss Frisbees and tennis balls in her direction, hoping to engage her in the usual play. They would bounce off her snout and hindquarters, causing not so much as a flicker in Baxter's glassy eyes. The customary commands—"Sit," "Fetch," "Heel," "Come"—meant no more to Baxter than a recitation from the *Tain* or the *Annals of the Four Masters*. To the voice of her mistress or any human directive, Baxter was uniformly nonresponsive. The only trick she ever performed was, "Breathe, Baxter! Breathe."

"Where there's life there's hope," Brigid would say, ever the loyal human, as if the dog's damage were reversible. It was a sad thing to witness, this zombified miscreant working her way through a decade and then some of meaningless days. Her end was a mercy to all and sundry.

But what my sisters Mary and Julie seemed to be saying was that no empathy or fellow feeling could be tendered that did not include the ruse that Baxter was Rin Tin Tin done up in drag, or Lassie or Old Yeller—a great dog to be greatly grieved and greatly missed—a loyal, loving, exceptional specimen of Man's (read Woman's too) Best Friend. When I protested that Baxter would not want to be placed on a pedestal, or to be loved for other than the amalgam of distress and misfortune that she was, that authentic feeling could not be based upon a vast denial of reality, they both rolled their eyes in counterclockwise turns and said, one to the other, "He just doesn't get it."

That I just don't "get it" is the conventional wisdom and the conversation's end with the several women in my life. Though I am the son of a good woman, now deceased and lamented, and sibling of three of them; though I am the father, friend, and spouse of females, like most of the men of my generation, and almost all of the men of my extraction, I just don't get it and maybe never will. A library of literature currently exists on the whys and whatnots about Irish men—with the notable exceptions of Bono and Liam Neeson—which render them denser than other specimens when it comes to "getting it" so far as women are concerned. The Irish-American male is similarly disposed, unless there is a remedial dose of Italian, Mexican, or Russian in his genealogy, in which case not getting it gives way to not giving a rap.

FIVE MORNINGS OUT of every seven, the woman across the street in the gingerbready Queen Anne with the Martha Stewart garden emerges with her two snow-white toy poodles to attend to what Victorians called "the duties of their [the dogs'] toilet." Each is the size of a bowling ball and their tiny feces like wee, green, cat-eyed marbles—about which more, alas, anon. These daft and dainty little sexless things are named for their mistress's favorite libations, "Chardonnay" and "Champagne," which are shortened in the diminutive to "Chardy" and "Champy," as she is heard to call out when they go bouncing about the neighborhood in search of somewhere to take their tiny designer shits. Most mornings the entourage looks a little dazed, as if they all might've gotten into the vodka-and-tonic late. But who am I to say?

She doesn't like me—the woman across the street. The list and variety of our quarrels and quibbles on civic, cultural, and neighborhood issues is a long and exhaustive one. I'm sure she thinks I just don't get it. Truth told, I'm not that gone on her. Except for the occasional wave or sidelong glance and nod, we make no effort at neighborliness. We knew from the get-go we would not be friends. And though I admire her refusal to maintain any pretense or decorum, it is better to do so from afar. Maybe we remind each other of each other's former spouses.

Still, I uphold her right to her ways as she upholds my right to mine. This is America, after all. Though we hold forth from opposite sides of the street, the name of the street is Liberty. So the insipid little dogs, the fellow she's married to (who must on the weekends attend to Chardy and Champy's morning office), the overgrowth of garden—these are situations I accept like variations on the theme of weather. It could be worse, is what I tell myself. In the same way, she tolerates me and mine: the overflow parking from the funeral home, the mysterious vans arriving at all hours, the bright *Impatiens* we plant every year among the uninspired juniper and yews and, the Dear knows, my manifest personal foibles. Like me, she has much to tolerate.

It's only when she brings Chardy and Champy over to the funeral home to sniff about in search of a proper shitting ground that I take especial umbrage. To give her and her poodles their due, she always comes armed with a plastic bag and a rubber glove—the latter effecting the transfer of the turdlettes from my greensward into the former. She is, in keeping with local and regional custom, fastidious about the fecal matters. I think she uses them with her prized delphinium. But for some reason I cannot shake the sense that I and my real estate have been shat upon, and that there is a kind of message hidden in the act, that there is some intelligence she intends for me to "get" by the witness of it. Nor can I shake the temptation, so far resisted, to mosey on over and shit on hers. There's liberty in it, and a kind of truth.

AFTER MY FIRST wife and I divorced, I was the custodial parent of a daughter and three sons from the time they were ten, nine, six, and four—until I was married again, some seven years later, to the Woman of My Dreams. It's when I most wanted to be a feminist. The divisions of labor and money, power and parental duties—those good-for-the-goose-and-gander concerns of the third-wave feminism of the day—were themes I found the most intriguing. I read de Beauvoir and Friedan, Brownmiller and Millett, Germaine Greer and Gloria Steinem. I read Robin Morgan's man-hating rhetoricals on "cock privilege" and castration and Doris Lessing's *Golden Notebook* and Andrea Dworkin's sad and incomprehensible screed and wondered if there were miseries out of which such people could really never be put. I was a card-carrying, contributing member of NOW. I vetted my personal lexicon for sexist terms. *Postman* became *mail carrier, chairman* became *chairperson, ladies* became *women.* I never said "girl." I made my sons wash dishes and my daughter take out the trash and filed for child support from my former spouse, in keeping with the equal-rights amends I was trying to make. I was encouraged by the caseworker from the Friend of the Court's office—a fetching woman with green eyes and a by-the-bookish style—who said the children should get fifty percent of their noncustodial parent's income. This, she assured, was a gender-indifferent directive. The state-prescribed formula called for twenty percent for the first child and ten percent for every one after that. "It's what you'd be paying," she said matter-of-factly, "if the shoe were on the other foot." I figured I could save it for their higher educations.

The judge, however, overruled the caseworker's recommendation. Her honor conceded that while in theory our sons and daughter deserved the benefits of both of their parents' gainful labors, she could not bring herself to order a mother to pay child support, even one who saw her children but every other weekend. It was enough that the erstwhile missus was making her own way in a difficult world. Supplemental payments for the support of her children were more of an indenture than the judge was prepared to order. During the brief hearing, I was advised by her pinstriped counsel to leave well enough alone. I just didn't get it after all.

In Ireland at the time, they had no ex-wives and more than once I thought, "How very civilized." There was no shortage of domestic misery, of course, no shortage of abuse, just no divorce. It wasn't allowed. So people moved apart and lived their lives as, more or less, ex-spousal equivalents. There was a Divorce Referendum in 1986, but the priests all preached against it in the country places. It failed by a convincing margin. Still men and women wanted civil disunions and lobbied for them until the measure passed just as convincingly in 1992. Now gay men and lesbians want to get married, and who could blame them, what with the bliss, for lobbying for the blessings and paperwork?

Back in those days, I kept a lovely cur, free of any registered pedigree or jittery habits. She had a small head, a large body, and an agreeable temperament. We called her Heidi. When she was a puppy, I walked her 'round our little city lot at the corner of Liberty and East Streets and the half-block next door occupied by the funeral home and its parking lot and told her that she could come and go as she pleased but that if she showed up at home, more nights than not, she'd be fed and petted and sheltered well; she'd be loved and cuddled, bathed and brushed. In short, if she would do her part, we'd do ours. Such was the nature of our covenant.

And though Heidi traveled widely, she never strayed. She would follow the mail carriers on their rounds, forfending them from more vicious dogs. She'd find her way to the corner butcher shop and beg for bones and to the bakery on Main Street to beg for day-old donuts. She was particularly fond of custard-filleds. She would stare balefully into the doorway of the delicatessen for hours until someone proffered some Polish ham or Havarti cheese or some other succulent or delicacy. Later in the day, she would make her way to the schoolyard to accompany my younger sons home from their day's studies. Evenings she'd position her repose in the drive-way of the funeral-home parking lot, acting the speed bump and sentinel whilst the children practiced their skateboarding or Frisbee or whiffle-ball. On weekends she'd be in Central Park, fishing with my oldest son or accompanying my daughter and her friends on their rounds through town, field-testing their ever-changing figures and fashions. She died old and fat and happy and was buried under the mock-orange bush where she used to shade herself against the summer heat. Near two decades since, she is still remembered with reverence; her exploits and loyalties are legendary.

Which is all I ever wanted out of love and husbanding, family and parenting—to be fondly regarded by the ones I loved; to be known for how I came home at night, minded the borders, kept an eye out for impending dangers, paid the piper, did my job, loved them all fiercely to the end. It was the dream I inherited from my mother and father for whom a division of labor did not mean a disproportion of power.

I WAS, IN those times, a casualty of the gender wars waged by the men and women of my generation over duties and identities. It was, I suppose, a necessary battle, which we did not choose and were powerless to avoid—damned if we did and if we didn't fight. We all took too seriously the carping and dyspepsia of a generation for whom sexism was a sin only men could commit, and only and always against women. Power and money were zero-sum games. Sex and love were often trophies. Women of the day kept their litany of injustices—the glass ceilings, the hostile work environments, the sixty-three-cents-on-the-dollar deal, the who-does-the-most-work-in-the-house debate. The little tally of inconsistencies I maintained kept driving me crazier and crazier. That the courts gave reproductive options to women but not to men was a bother. There was no clinic to which men could repair to terminate their impending paternity. If "choice" were such a fine thing, it occurred to me, oughtn't one and all, not one and half of the population have it? That my daughter might "choose" a career in the military but only my sons had to register for the draft struck me as odd. No less the victim-chic status of the feminist intelligentsia who were always ranting about "women and other minorities" while quietly ignoring the fact that women had been the majority for years. The planet was fifty-two percent female. That women not only outnumbered men, they outlived them—by years, not months, in

every culture—seemed a thing that ought to be, at least, looked
into. Never mind the incessant sloganeering, or the militia of
women who blamed Ted Hughes for Sylvia Plath's suicide or who
blamed their husbands for the history of the world or who turned
men into the tackling dummies for their chronic discontents.
Maybe it was all that "every intercourse is an act of rape" hysteria,
or "a woman needs a man like a fish needs a bicycle," or the way
they joked about the man who had his penis cut off by his angry
wife. I used to wonder what late-night talk-show host would survive any less-than-reverential comment about a woman's genitalia
if the damage had been reversed.

Violence against women was quite rightly abhorred whilst violence against men was generally ignored. Nothing in the literature
rang more true to me than something I had overheard in a conversation between pathologists who were autopsying a fatal domestic
case: "A man will kill his wife, then kill himself," one said grimly; "a
woman kills her husband, then does her nails." Whatever else I did
not "get", I got that one loud and clear: the higher ground of entitle-
ment that victims, self-proclaimed, could occupy. I'm certain there
were additional grievances, like so much else, I've forgotten now.

In ways that were not so for my parents' generation and, please
God, will not be so for my sons' and daughter's, the men and
women of my generation suffered a kind of disconnect that left
them each wary of the other's intentions, each ignorant of the
other's changing, each speaking a dialect the other could not
cipher, each wondering why the other just didn't get it. Such are
the accidents of history and hers—that we make aliens of our inti-
mates, enemies of friends, strange bedfellows entirely that crave
the common ground but rarely really find it.

So it is with nations and neighbors, parents and children, brothers and sisters, family and friends—the list we keep of grievances keeps us perpetually at odds with each other, alone in a world that is growing smaller, more distant from each other, more estranged.

The sisters, Godhelpus, are praying for peace and reconciliation and forgiveness. They are praying to be vessels of God's love and mercy. They say it will take a miracle and that the world changes one heart at a time. They have unleashed the hounds of their Hibernian faith—the rubrics of which involve candles, moonlight, chrisms, icons, incense and every manner of mystic unguents, passions, immersions, aromatics, and possibly herbs, the recipes for which were no doubt published in the Gnostic Gospels, found in those jars.

I STILL DON'T get it. And I've quit trying to. Years of living with and among women have convinced me I'm as well off with no dog in that fight. My daughter, my sisters, my beloved wife (in the associative, not possessive sense), and no few women that I count as lifelong friends, the memory of my mother, aunts, and grandmothers—they've all been and remain powerful and courageous and selfless humans, gifted with a dignity and calm that has made me wish I knew them better and all the more wary of their mysterious medicines. Most days I recite a litany of gratitudes for the pleasures of their company, the beauty and beatitudes of their intellections. I'm resolved to say nice things about their dogs. It keeps me, so far, safe from the hounds.

Young neighbor couples and their designer dogs go walking with leashes now on weekend mornings. Their puppies and their babies are all pedigreed. Everyone is better trained and behaved. At every corner there are dangers and warnings; at every intersection, flashing lights and signs. The lesson, of course, is to mind the traffic. They learn to speak and heel and fetch and to return. The men, as is their custom, bark out wisdoms. They pose and sniff, they howl and growl and whine. Their wives and pets grow weary of listening. Some things only the dogs hear, some the women.

I ORDERED A mum plant for Baxter's obsequies scheduled for later this month at Mullett Lake. I asked the florist to write, "Sorry," on the card.

I hope they get it.

Odds & Ends

From the Clare Journal, 1888

28 May

FIVE PEOPLE DROWNED ON THE CLARE COAST

Five persons were drowned on Saturday morning by a tidal wave on the Clare coast near Goleen Bay, half way between Kilkee and Carrigaholt. The unfortunate people were collecting seaweed when the wave suddenly overtook them and carried them out to sea. They were Michael Lynch, his son and daughter, and Michael O'Dea and his son, both men being farmers. Their bodies have not been recovered.

31 May

Further particulars of the sad drowning fatality near Kilkee on Friday, by which five poor people lost their lives, being swept to sea by a tidal wave, as briefly reported in our last, have come to hand. It appears that O'Dea and his son, and

Lynch, his daughter and son, were descending the cliff at the western side of Dunlicky Castle by an almost inaccessible passage. They reached to the water's edge, their objective being to cut seaweed. A long flat rock extends from the base of the castle to the sea, and at the terminations of this rock the water is about 30 feet deep. They had their work almost completed when the tide began to flow, but as the day was fine and the sea calm, they took no great precautions for their safety. A big wave, however, came up the slanting rock, and carried away young O'Dea; his father went to his rescue. Back went the others to render assistance, only to be carried away down the slope into the deep water. Two, however, escaped—a son of O'Dea's, 14 years, by holding on to the roots of some seaweed, saved his mother, bringing her up the rocks; but were it not for a boy named Burns, who sometime afterwards, passed by on the cliffs overhead looking for sheep, heard their pitiable lamentations, and assisted them up the steep incline, they too would have drowned. The body of the girl Mary Lynch was found on Sunday evening, and the coastguards, with their lifeboat, are busily engaged every day searching amongst the rocks and seaweed between the cliff and Healy's Island for the other bodies.

7 June

THE LATE DROWNING ACCIDENT NEAR LOOP HEAD

Up to Saturday last none of the remaining four bodies drowned in Goleen Bay, between Kilkee and Loop Head, has been found. On the day Miss Lynch's body was extricated from a reef of rock in depth of 36 feet of water, two other bodies were seen a short distance apart, but beyond the power of the people to reach them, owing to a depth of 150 feet of water. The water there is always very rough because of the large swells of the Atlantic breaking against the rocks. There were eight persons cutting seaweed on this steep ledge of rock which runs into the sea, a distance of 200 feet, on the day of this sad event, five of whom perished. A centenarian says he never heard from any of his predecessors, nor within his own knowledge or recollection, that any person ever cut seaweed on these rocks.

A Freak Wave

In September 1979, Dualco De Dona and I went out to fish for mackerel at Dunlicky. The great cliff out past the ruined castle provided ledge rocks on which to stand and cast the ribbons and sinkers out and let them sink into the evening's rising tide. The mackerel, if they were there at all, were always there in plenty. Dualco sat back under the overhang of rocks and watched me go about the labor—the long heave, the rising and reeling to make the ribbons move through the water and attract the silver fish. First one would hit, I'd set the hook, then wait to feel another and another. I'd set the hook again, the greater weight signaling the frenzy of fish below. Then I'd reel the whole wriggly business up the cliff—a hundred and fifty feet, or two hundred—the sinker bouncing off the rocks, everything from the rod to the reel to my body aching with these fish removed from their natural gravity. We were getting bagfuls and the day was fine, when a great roar came up from the rocks behind and a wave knocked me flat out with the weight of water, holding onto my rig, looking over the edge.

Dualco said it was like the hand of God, from where he was sitting, sheltered in the stones—the great curling hand of God that smote me flat out, face down at the edge.

We walked back to Moveen then. I was sopped through and through. That night we called with Nora to the Carmodys'. They lived in the house on the ridge above the sea near where we'd been fishing earlier. Mrs. Carmody had been another Nora Lynch before she'd married Patrick Carmody, and her Uncle John, known as Kant Lynch thereabouts, was living there with them in his old age. When we told the story of the day's adventures, old Kant looked up and spoke into the hush that suddenly had occupied the room.

"Mind yourself there, boy," the old man said, the milky cataract of his blind eye boring into me, his good eye gone watery and red, "the sea's ever hungry for Lynches there."

The Irish Times—*December 2000*

Wave Sweeps Boy Out to Sea
A search continued last night for the body of a five-year-old boy who was swept out to sea by a freak wave at Doolin, Co. Clare, yesterday. Tragedy struck when the wave knocked over the boy, his mother, four-year-old sister and their two-year-old friend as they walked along a rocky shoreline near Doolin pier, before sweeping the boy out to sea. The alarm was raised almost immediately. Efforts to locate the boy failed when rough seas prevented the local Marine Rescue Unit launching its lifeboat. According to the Gardai, the boy was from the north Clare village of Kilshanny, five miles inland from Doolin.

The Clare Champion

A headline in the *Clare Champion* has lived rent-free in my brain since the morning some years ago I first beheld it.

"Missing Man Found Dead in Pub Toilet," it reads, and shakes me the way no other thing has ever shaken me in seven words. The article that follows this horrendous declaration details the sad case of a local pensioner from Killaloe who went missing for three days before he was discovered "in the gents toilet of 'Molly's Bar' last Friday morning by a member of the cleaning staff." The publican, Mr. Horgan, assisted Gardai in their investigation. His explanation of what he calls "the whole sad saga," set forth in the penultimate and ultimate paragraphs of the story, are worthy of quotation here:

> "On the Sunday night before Mr. [name withheld with respects, etc.] died, one of the water cisterns in the toilet was vandalized. We placed an out of order sign on the door and it was locked using the childlock mechanism you see on a lot of toilet doors.
>
> "We can only surmise that John must have been taken short, and when the other cubicle was occupied he opened the one that was locked. Sadly, he must have died when he was in there. As the toilet was out of order and the door was locked we did not think to check it out," he [Mr. Horgan] explained.

Every time I read this I am chilled. Killed in a loo in Killaloe—Bejaysus if it doesn't prove Himself is an almighty Joker after all. But what about your man the publican, with that little item—"taken short." What does that mean to the North American ear?

Does it cover a host of contingencies from poor bladder control to porter poisoning to something chronic and acute? A diabetic coma, myocardial infarction, a hemorrhage?

How does one prevent being "taken short," ending up in the wrong stall of the gents' room in a pub in Killaloe, dead for three days and undiscovered? Is there a regimen one ought follow? The Dear only knows.

In my own drinking days—an epoch that ran uninterrupted from August 1963, just prior to the assassination of JFK, until the last Sunday in April 1989—I'd often find myself, I daresay, taken short. I fell off a building once and cracked some bones. I'd made the usual fool of myself with puke and words and near-disasters. And many's the time I'd crawl into the gents, squinting to read the bluey name of Armitage Shanks on the porcelain pisser. Like getting the eyes checked—so long as I could read the writing on the stall, I'd be good for another. Many's the time I came up short. And many's the time I went too long and many's the miracle that got me home to Moveen or Milford safe and sound.

No sense can be made of it, but the chill is good, and I'm sober now with years and better for it.

Wakes

Once you put a dead guy in the room, you can talk about anything. This verity was part of a tiny e-mail correspondence that I kept with Alan Ball, the creator of *Six Feet Under*—the HBO TV show about a family mortuary near Hollywood. Every episode has its hapless cadaver floating through the hour's narratives, along with Ball's free-ranging agenda—love in all its flavors, sex at all its ages, the ordinary angst of living in the world. He wrote, "You funeral types have always understood. Once you put a dead guy in the room you can talk about anything."

And it is so: once the existential ante has been upped, everyone can play for keeps and the constraints of social order are relaxed. Anything, to quote the well-worn bromide, goes.

It was the Irish who invented this. There's nothing like a corpse on the premises to loosen the old tongue, quicken the conversation, free the miser from the miserlies, set the blood to riot, and put folks on their knees for a variety of reasons—rosaries, rage, and excess among them. They sorted this out eons ago—during a cattle raid or warp spasm. It was Maeve or Cuchulain first noticed it, I think.

Anyway, in Ireland they've never had a shortage of corpses nor any compunctions about putting them to work. And when one sees the ability of the Irish to rise to such an occasion, with civility and community and charity, it makes one wish for wakes that went on forever. There's an appetite for sadness seasoned with beauty that is essential to the Irish table. Hence a man got dead in a ditch, a woman taken with a tumor, a hero killed at his heroics become props in a well-known community theatre. The news of death throws them into action. Someone is out getting clean linens for the bed. A coffin and shroud are ordered. The candlesticks and crucifix are polished up. Ham and cheese sandwiches are made in dozens. Loaves of soda bread, buckets of tea, biscuits and short-bread, bags of sweets. The house is quickly whitewashed and the street is swept, fresh wallpaper hung in the spare bedroom. Bottles of lager and porter appear. The neighbor lads go off to dig the grave with whiskey proffered by the next of kin. "Oh no, you needn't," the chief grave digger protests, with one mitt on the bottle's neck, the other on the spade. The priest turns kindly in anticipation of the stipends and honoraria. He ratchets up the homiletic gears to manage their full existential load. "The Lord," he will say, "has given. And the Lord has taken away." Amen.

Ah, God, it is a study in efficiency and humanity. There's a cheerfulness about it that belies the loss. "Sorry for your trouble," people say.

You don't so much *direct* an Irish funeral, my late great father used to say, as you *referee* it. For any event that can be counted on to bring the best out of people can be just as certainly counted on to bring out the worst. If the wake is grand for excesses of love and fellow feeling, it is no less able to bring out the black rage and odiousities, the foul temper and fighting soul that's in us. Bereavement and begrudgery are kissing and hitting cousins.

The dead mother or father is no sooner breathless than all the surviving sons and daughters start jockeying for the favored position—as if there were a sign to be given that "I Was Her Favorite," or "He Loved Me Best." Often this is connected to some bit of property—a field or a favorite chair or a portfolio of mutual funds. When everything is up for grabs, well, grabbing's what we do. Or we hug. You see a fair bit of hugging at these obsequies, too. And the slapping of backs and nodding of heads in mum consensus as to the mystery of it all.

If there's an opposite to the Irish funeral, it is the English one. Oh, they have their corpses, plenty of them, but they are, it would appear, embarrassed by them—it makes the empire that every Englishman has in him seem, well, vincible. Except for the Royals, who are still stuck in their Victorian habits and therefore must still go through the motions if not the emotions of a funeral, the English like their bodies disappeared and the untidy sentiments kept corked. The stiff upper lip is easier to manage when there is, shall we say, no stiff. The Mitfordian invention of the memorial service (fashionably renamed of late a "celebration of life") is most notable for what is missing—the dead guy. The finger food is plentiful, the talk determinedly uplifting, the music transcendent, the secular or religious witness heavy on Edwardian poetry, and all of the flowers "home grown." After which everyone seeks an orderly exit. The dead, of course, have been burned or buried on the sly without witness or rubric, and now occupy their urn or grave or columbarium, quiet as a hall closet full of outworn shoes.

These bodiless affairs lack an essential manifest. There's nothing "wrong" with them and nothing "right." Think of Disney World without the Mouse. They leave you with a sense of something missing. Whereas the English like such quiet, calm affairs, the Irish expect some weeping or retching on the dead's behalf, either from laughter or intemperance, before the living or the dead are given rest. They like the whiff of corruptibility that only rises off a corpse, after plentiful remembrance and reverie.

Keenly aware that when the worst has already happened, the best is somehow more possible, the Irish see their wakes as occasions for comfort and betterment.

I remember one Friday taking the sad news of a local death to a neighbor who lived without a phone and put down a fair amount of stout most Thursdays after he'd taken up the pension check. "Patsy's died in the night," I said, and readied myself for the old man's grief.

"Fair play to Patsy," your man said, steadying himself in the cabin door, "he's that tough job behind him, so."

Once at a wake in West Clare I heard a widow tell her parish priest, in answer to his queries on the cause of death, "Gonorrhea, Father—it has poor Jamesy swept, Godkeephim."

The churchman, blushing as churchmen use't, said, "The Lord spare us, Mary, there was never a man in all of the parish that died of gonorrhea; leastwise, I never heard of such a thing before. It must have been that time he went up north, the cratur, and maybe fell in with the wrong crowd. Ah, God, there do be temptations in the foreign place."

"Yes, yes, Father, the foreign place," Mary nodded, and caught her breath and wiped away a tear.

"What harm," said the priest, "aren't we all but human? We'll have Mass in the morning and no more about the other." He walked away shaking his bald head, which shone with the sweat of it.

I was still in earshot when the dead man's daughter came around to scold her mother over what she'd heard—whispering furiously. "Good Christ, Mammy! Why did you ever tell the priest Da died of gonorrhea? There was no gonorrhea in that man at all. It was *dia*rrhea took him!"

"Hush, my lovely," the widowed woman said, holding her daughter's face in her hands. "I'd rather your father be remembered for the great lover he never was than the big shit he always seemed to be."

Sunbeams shone through the windows during Mass. The children's choir sang. His bearers bore him proudly to the grave.

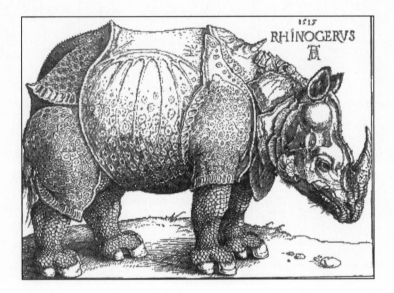

On Some Verses by Irish & Other Poets

I was in the "Deux Magots" in Paris one time and an American that I was introduced to asked me if I had known James Joyce. I said that I hadn't that honour, but I told him my mother had often served a meal to W. B. Yeats in Maud Gonne's house on Stephen's Green, and that the poet turned up his nose to the parsnips. "He didn't like parsnips?" said the American reaching for his notebook. "You're sure that is factual?"

"It is to be hoped," I replied, "that you've not called my mother a liar?"

"No, no, of course not," he said, "but she might have been mistaken—it might have been carrots," he added hastily.

"You must think I'm a right fool to have a mother that can't tell a carrot from a parsnip," I said nastily.

"No, no, of course—I mean I'm sure she could but it is very important. . . ." He wrote in the book: Parsnip—attitude of Yeats to.

—Brendan Behan, in *Brendan Behan's
Island: An Irish Sketchbook*

I'VE THIS IMAGE of the poet hammering lobster on the flag-stone floor.

They've been to the fishmonger's in Carrigaholt, bargained for a pair of behemoths, brought them back to Moveen to be boiled and now, bottles uncorked, spuds ready, butter drawn, the small room blurry with steam and hunger, they find that they've no utensil sufficient to liberate the sweet meat from its hard shell cas-ing. Thus the hammer, the "flaggy floor," and the "sense of a feast that had been fought for," the poet sends word in a note: "Great debris and great delight."

It's all metaphor—the lobster, the hammer, the flagstones, the feast—one meaning carried by another, as if "to bridge" (if we trace the word back to its Greek) the gap between what is and what *really* is.

I stole that thing about the bridge from another poet, who read it somewhere or stole it from another one or made it up. It's what we do: rent to own, borrow, steal—make things up and metaphor. Sometimes nouns are transformed into verbs. You may try this at home.

Poets can't help themselves. Every one of them—stone mad for double meanings, second helpings, things that are more than they seem. Or less. "All the world's a stage," writes Shakespeare. We bow to the audience that isn't there. Adjust our costume. Memorize our lines. Imagine "all the world's" watching, waiting, listening. They never show.

IT WAS A poet who told me to go to Ireland. And poems that first made me want to go. And poetry that keeps the lights on now, in the house that Nora Lynch bequeathed to me.

The first living poet of my acquaintance was teaching at Oakland University in Rochester, Michigan, in the fall of 1967. I took Professor Michael Heffernan's class in American Authors—Emerson, Melville, Thoreau, and Poe. Because he was young and apostate, Irish and American, a variously lapsed and observant Catholic, we became fast friends and drinking buddies. At his rented house on Brown Road, fifteen minutes from the campus, we studied Yeats and a variety of domestic and imported whiskeys and the Boston Symphony under Charles Munch. In this house I heard my first Mahler, drank my first Irish, and saw for the first time poems in the making. Each left me breathless and wanting more.

KENNEDY

One late afternoon I hitched from Galway down to Kinvara on the edge of the Burren, one of those long midsummer days when the sun labors at last out of all-day rain and sets very late in the evening. In dark pubs all up and down the street, the townsmen hunched to their pints, silent and tentative as monks at supper. Thinking to take my daily Guinness, I stopped, and Kennedy was there, his picture on the mantel behind the bar.

A black-headed citizen half in his cups sidled over and smiled. Ah Kennedy Kennedy, a lovely man, he said and bought me a Guinness. Ah yes, a lovely man, I said, and thank you very much. Yes Kennedy, and they slaughtered him in his youth the filthy communists, he said, and will you want another. Yes, slaughtered him in his youth, I said and thanked him very much.

All night till closing time we drank to Kennedy and cursed the communists—all night, pint after pint of sour black lovely stout.

And when it came Time, I and my skin and the soul inside my
skin, all sour and lovely, strode where the sun still washed the
evening, and the fields lay roundabout, and Kinvara slept in the
sunlight, and Holy Ireland, all all asleep, while the grand brave
light of day held darkness back like the whole Atlantic.

Heffernan's "Kennedy," drafted, corrected, revised, and retyped over the space of several months that autumn and winter, was elegant to me, bearing as it did the beauty of homemade words on the page. He called it a prose-poem and said he had an interest in the form. The idea that any day in any bar anywhere in Ireland could produce such a text produced in me the grand illusion that any parish in Holy Ireland was more inspiring than any place in suburban Michigan. Old monkish men, the ocean and light, Kinvara and Galway, talk of Kennedy and sour, black, lovely stout all seemed impossibly distant to me, and wonderful.

And poetry. The idea that an ordinary life in southern Michigan could produce a share of extraordinary words I owe to Michael Heffernan, because he was the first I'd ever seen—the first living poet with a Buick and a business suit and designs on a life that included an eventual marriage, a mortgage, and a full-time job, instead of the apparently requisite style of poets then—driving off into the late-sixties sunset in a rusted VW bus in bell-bottomed jeans, old sandals, and more hair than I would ever have. Here were poems that stung the heart about wanting women and the way that light shone on things, figures of plain force, myth, and history—and I knew that Ireland figured into it. What was more, though the moment that produced "Kennedy" could be traced to a bar in a small town in the golden, open West of Ireland, the work that produced it had been done in a bungalow on Brown Road near Pontiac, Michigan, in the shadow of auto factories and the interstate. One could come and go, traveling light in the portable universe of words, counting on images for transport.

In the course of the next couple of years, I introduced Heffernan to his first wife. He introduced me to Roethke, Berryman, Frost, and Bishop. He and his missus moved off to southeastern Kansas with a U-Haul to live in a big house and teach in a small college. He started publishing his poems in the quarterlies and journals. She grew more and more discontent. In February of 1970, I left for Ireland.

The book I took with me was *The Collected Poems of W. B. Yeats.* It was a hardbound blue book with the author's monogram embossed in gold on the front cover. I had a few of the poems or portions of them off by heart.

When you are old and gray and full of sleep
And nodding by the fire, take down this book

This seemed so excellent to me, warming my shins to the sods in Moveen that first winter I spent there decades ago. And Tommy Lynch, my cousin and namesake, his Wellingtons still wet from mucking about after milking his cows for the evening, would sit there at seventy, smoking his Woodbines, listening to my recitations.

"By cripes that man's a great one for the words—that William Butler Yeats, sure faith he is." And when I'd pass the book to him, he'd read it out with the precision he'd learned from the Moveen National School on the Carrigaholt road when he was a boy.

"Now for you, Tommy!" Nora would say, busy with the

evening's tea. "You'll have it by heart like a shot! Sure faith."

We were an odd trio—the old bachelor, his spinster sister, the blow-in Yank with his poetry and pocket watch—the room full of longings and imaginings, futures and pasts, the godawful winter lashing out of doors.

The notion that a book, a book of poems, could speak to one's beloved in her age, and say things that the poet meant to say but never could; and maybe quicken in her the caught breath, the look, "the soft look," Yeats called it, "your eyes had once, and of their shadows deep"—this had a powerful appeal to Tommy and to Nora and to me. It was, in my twenties, the sure faith that time, distance, and life's imbroglios could not trump love. Most days in my fifties I still believe it and I believe that in their seventies Tommy and Nora did too.

Beyond all of which there was the sound—the iambics and the rhymes—the acoustic infrastructure that made the saying of it such a pleasure. The ten-syllable line with its five thumps—this pentameter—echoed my own internal meter. I could walk its walk and talk its talk—*daDum, daDum, daDum, daDum, daDum: when You are Old and Gray and Full of Sleep.*

Of course, I made the requisite Yeatsian pilgrimage, hitching to Kilrush and Ennis, thence north to Gort, then on to Coole Park to see the swans and the tree with the great man's initials in it and on to Ballylee where the ancient tower stands, albeit not in the ruins he predicted, with its bridge and river, the broad green pasture, the hum of the motorway out of earshot, jackdaws diving from tree to tree. And carved on a stone there by his instructions, the inventory of "old mill boards and sea green slates/and smithy work from the Gort forge," with which he had "restored this tower for my wife

George"—the briefer line, the solid rhymes, the declarative confidence, like the music country people danced to. Lucky enough, I thought, to marry a woman named George—if only to rhyme her eventually with "Gort forge."

I slept in Galway that night. Then on to Sligo, where, following the poet's instructions, under bare Ben Bulben's head, I found Drumcliff churchyard and the grave upon which I cast as cold an eye as I could muster, said my thanks, and went away. I walked around the Lake Isle of Innisfree, located the waterfall at Glencar and the rock at Dooney where the fiddler played.

I was young. Poets were my heroes. Where they'd been is where I wanted most to be.

So I wandered around Ireland as long as I could, night-portering in Killarney, learning to milk cows and manage dung in Moveen, reading Yeats and dreaming of the future, wondering what my true love's name would turn out to rhyme with.

For most of the next two years, I vacillated among travels in Europe, the job at my father's funeral home, and an undirected course of study at the university.

In August 1971, I was in Venice with my friend Dualco De Dona, who had moved back to his family home in the Dolomites. We'd done the Grand Tour—Greece and Vienna, London and West Clare—back and forth and ended up at breakfast on the Grand Canal, in the salon of the Hotel San Cassiano, variously aching, as the young do, for art and love, some direction to life, and a future that included poetry.

Restless, broke, and mildly hungover, unable to articulate any of life's purposes, I rose from the table like a man of parts, settled my accounts, took the *vaporetto* from Accademia to the train station, where I rented a car, drove to Milan, boarded a plane for London and Detroit, and by that evening was dining at my local Coney Island talking about the Detroit Tigers with my brother. It was a shock to move so rapidly among the worlds.

Within six months I was married. Within a year I was enrolled in mortuary school. Soon after, the first of my sons was born. We moved to Milford when the family bought the funeral home there. It was June 13, 1974. My life was now rooted and full of purpose—family and funerals, taxes and accountants. It had direction—a wife, a job, another baby on the way, a future.

Poetry seemed a distant music.

In 1975 our daughter was born, in 1978 a second son. The business had grown from a hundred calls a year to a hundred and fifty. I was the president of the Rotary Club and the Chamber of Commerce. We bought a house next door to the funeral home and moved in with a mortgage and the dog. I was working and breeding and building as the young must do—networks, mergers and acquisitions.

By September 1979, my wife was pregnant with our fourth child. The funeral home was humming along. I bought a ticket and flew to Ireland for ten days because the ache inside me for Moveen had grown intolerable. It had been seven years since we'd gone there on our honeymoon. Nora had been to America, and we'd kept in regular contact. But I felt too distant from the place itself and the life that seemed important there.

Nora, now going seventy-seven, was holding her own against age and the weather and the powers that be. We drove up the Clare coast to Galway and bought books at Kenny's—anthologies and literary magazines—*Cyphers* and *Poetry Ireland*. We had nights by the fire with neighbors and friends—talk and songs and stories. The Carmody sisters, schoolgirls then, brought their tin whistles. The Murray girls would come and sing. Nora Carmody brought news of the world. The dear Collins sisters, Bridey and Mae, J. J. McMahon, the Curtins and Keanes—each brought a party piece. When my turn came round—"now Tom," J. J.'d insist, "now Tom, some Yeats"—I'd give out with it: "A Deep Sworn Vow," or "He Wishes for the Cloths of Heaven," or, if drink had been taken, "Broken Dreams." One night I read from *Death of a Naturalist*, by the northern poet Seamus Heaney, and watched as those small farmers tuned their attention to the poems' mention of "Toner's bog, good turf, flax-dam, townland," and an account of "when I first saw kittens drown, 'the scraggy wee shits'" tossed into a bucket, "a frail metal sound." This was a language they understood, full of things they were familiar with—hay barns and butter churns and "Turkeys Observed," a "Cow in Calf," an illegal bull— turned out in ways we'd never heard before.

"Good man for you, Tom," J. J.'d say. "Fair play to you."

There were love poems, family histories, a dark indictment of the neighborly racism behind the Famine, and one about the poet's youthful fascination with open spring wells like the one in Nora's lower field or across the road at Carmodys' and about the self-consciousness the older man endures.

> Now, to pry into roots, to finger slime,
> To stare, big-eyed Narcissus, into some spring
> Is beneath all adult dignity. I rhyme
> To see myself, to set the darkness echoing.

It was all metaphor for the examined life of deep and hidden things—lineage, history, habitat, and language—that give life meaning, purpose, and resolve. The act of writing poems becomes the grown man's mirror, looking into the wellspring of the self, the rhymes "set the darkness echoing." This was, like Yeats, a collaboration of form and sound and sense—the deft balance of self-reference, examination, and manifesto; the willingness to use what is handy to order the world and make one's own reflections relevant. And the evident faith in the language to make its own way, to shape its own course and fluency, like water—that close to nature—it made me feel alive to read it.

IN DECEMBER THAT year, up the street in the postman's bag with the catalogues and Christmas cards came Michael Heffernan's first slim book of poems, *The Cry of Oliver Hardy*. It was green and white and hardbound by the University of Georgia Press. It was sixty-one pages. It had his name on the front, his picture on the back, and inside he'd signed it, in broad blue ink strokes, on the title page. "Kennedy" was in it, and "The Plight of the Old Apostle," "St. Ambrose and the Bees," and some dozens more.

These poems that I'd seen years before, on his desk in his office in the house on Brown Road, had become a book for perfect strangers to pull from a shelf in a library or bookstore and read for themselves. The making public of this work he'd done in private— this *publication* made me wish that I had written some.

How, then, do you find it? In practice, you hear it coming from somebody else, you hear something in another writer's sounds that flows in through your ear and enters the echo-

chamber of your head and delights your whole nervous system in such a way that your reaction will be, 'Ah, I wish I had
said that, in that particular way.'
—from "Feeling into Words," in *Preoccupations*

Heaney's essay offered license, if not to steal, at least to borrow—poetic license—to sing along until the sound of my own
voice emerged from what I heard ring true in others.

> Finding a voice means that you can get your own feeling into
> your own words and that your words have the feel of you
> about them; and I believe that it may not even be a
> metaphor, for poetic voice is probably very intimately con-
> nected with the poet's natural voice, the voice that he hears
> as the ideal speaker of the lines he is making up.
> —from "Feeling into Words"

By now I was listening for the ideal speaker and had begun to
think in syllables and lines, to construct them, to hear the tumblers
of the language click into a fit of sound and image and utterance
that unlocked my meanings and their own.

And I was "borrowing" with impunity, lip-synching the poets I
most admired, plugging my own words into older forms—sestinas
and villanelles—to see if I could make them "fit." The rules, however arbitrary, made the rummage for the "right" word wider. For
every right word gotten, there were dozens, maybe hundreds, handled, held up, considered, and rejected. It was necessarily messy
work. The jettisoned words, scraps of phrases they fit into and later
revised away, whole poems or parts of poems, freshly minted in
late-night frenzy that would not, alas, survive the morning's

scrutiny, littered the workspace. The finished article, the thing well made, was a tiny diamond of a thing, extracted from the universe of words. There was about the enterprise, as the man hammering lobster would say years later, great debris and great delight, indeed.

ON HEFFERNAN'S instructions, I sent two poems off to John Frederick Nims at *POETRY* in Chicago. Yeats and Eliot and Wallace Stevens, Bishop and Berryman and St. Vincent Millay had published in *POETRY*. I figured a rejection from the best was better than from the least. But Nims took them. It was more encouragement than I needed. Then he took some more—one about our old dog, another about my grandmothers, a piece about man caught between competing instincts and cross purposes, immobilized by warring gravities.

I returned to Ireland, rented a typewriter from a shop in Ennis, and went to work on manuscripts in Moveen. Nora called it "the poetry business" and gave me a portion of her table on which to do it. I took the bike to Carrigaholt one day and posted off a manuscript to Eilean Ni Chuilleanain, an editor at *Cyphers*. I'd read and admired her work and the work of the consortium of Dublin writers—Pearse Hutchinson, Macdara Woods, and Leland Bardwell—who edited the magazine with her. Eilean took two poems. I was internationally unknown.

I was trying to organize a life balanced between the requisite and compelling work that paid the bills and the elective work of the imagination, between the rooted life in Milford and the life rooted in the magical language in Moveen, between a life organized around deaths and burials and a life that required what Heaney called "digging"—and what I thought of as disinterment.

And while the everyday enterprise of the local businessman, husband and father, and citizen-at-large in a small midwestern place was one that suited me, the rich life of language, drawn from the idiomatic wellsprings of Moveen and its American cousins, informed by memory and imagination, was a constant preoccupation. Often these lives competed for time and attention. Time spent on one was subtracted from the other. Other times, each seemed bound to the other—the aching humanity, beautiful and sad, that populated the funeral home, often spoke in private, primal tongues.

When the father of a young girl who had died horribly began his daughter's brief eulogy with "The thing you fear the most will hunt you down," the grim pentameter of it stung my ears—da *thing* da *fear* da *most* da *hunt* da *down*—the awful iambs coded to his beaten, broken heart.

Sometimes I would see in my children's eyes the knowledge that I was paying only a portion of the attention due their questions and curiosities, while carrying on an invisible word game with myself. The poem I was working on was called "Learning Gravity" and had to do with keeping balance.

THOSE EARLY PUBLICATIONS had occasioned an invitation from poets alive and thriving in Ann Arbor—Alice Fulton, Richard Tillinghast, Keith Taylor, and others—to join their monthly workshop. Since Heffernan, it was the first society of poets I'd known. It made me a better reader and writer and required me to contribute something every month. Most of those poets have become friends for life.

Early in the 1980s, Heffernan and I began corresponding in

sonnets. We'd noticed that a three-by-five postcard held a title in caps and fourteen lines of text and could be mailed for fourteen cents. It seemed as though the Postal Service was imitating art. We conspired to carry on accordingly. He'd been divorced and remarried and had become a father by now. My marriage, unbeknownst to me, was on the brink of breaking. Heffernan would write:

MIDSUMMER LIGHT AS THE SOUL'S HABITAT
It wasn't the turning of appearances
nor any of their exactions from the air
that made me think the afternoon was bees
or gangs of bears in rowdy robes of fur.
I hadn't thought of this for any reason
and this wasn't anyplace but my backyard.
Here was the flavor of an illusion
that stuck to my tongue like a hummingbird
beating its wings into a blur of hunger—
one of those tones from the soul's undergrowth
where animals devoid of any anger,
lifting up bits of landscape in their teeth,
would turn to look around them where they were,
loosening their faces into shreds of fire.

In receipt of which I would return:

MARRIAGE
He wanted a dry mouth, whiskey and warm flesh
and for all his bothersome senses to be still.
He let his eyeballs roll back in their sockets until

there was only darkness. He grew unmindful
of the spray of moonwash that hung in the curtains,
the dry breath of the furnace, parts of a tune
he'd hummed to himself all day. Any noise
that kept him from his own voice hushed.
He wanted to approximate the effort of snowdrift,
to gain that sweet position over her repose
that always signaled to her he meant business,
that turned them into endless lapping dunes.
He wanted her mouth to fill like a bowl with vowels,
prime and whole and indivisible, O . . . O . . . O . . . .

Heffernan's part of that year's correspondence became a fair portion of his second book, *To the Wreakers of Havoc,* in 1984.

For my part, the sonnets were inklings of the storm that would become my family's life in 1984 and end, in early 1985, with the dissolution of that marriage. I retained the house, the kids, the cat and dog, my day job and preoccupations. "Learning Gravity," a longish poem, got published in halves—ninety-some lines in Boston and a hundred lines in Dublin—all in the same month of that awful year. It was, like everything then, divided. I tried to imagine the unlikely traveler who might, by coming upon *The Agni Review* in, say, the Grolier Book Shop in Cambridge, and taking the plane out of Logan Airport for Dublin and finding *Cyphers* in, maybe, Books Upstairs in College Green outside of Trinity, reconnect the dismembered portions of the poem, as I had, working back and forth between Moveen and Milford, between Ireland and America.

It was Heffernan, in the late summer that year, who gave me a list of editors and publishers and instructions to send them a book-length manuscript. To each I sent a sample—half a dozen poems—and a cover letter saying I could send them more. The first to respond was Gordon Lish, then an editor at Alfred A. Knopf, who requisitioned the whole collection. Within the week, I had a contract and a small advance. With the money, I planned a trip to Ireland.

In Dublin I'd arranged a visit with Eilean Ni Chuilleanain and her husband, Macdara Woods, who lived in Selskar Terrace, Ranelagh. I wanted to thank them for publishing my work. Their rooms were full of books and manuscripts—the toil of words was everywhere. Both of them were editing *Cyphers* and she was lecturing at Trinity and they had a three-year-old son named Niall. All of us had new books due out that year. After a night's hospitality, Macdara walked me to the taxi stand. We spoke about Irish and American poets, about the ocean between them, about the interest on each side in the poetry of the other. Across the road a pub—the Richard Crosbie—was turning out the last of its late-night drinkers. It appeared in the title poem of Macdara's book:

STOPPING THE LIGHTS, RANELAGH 1986
2.
It takes some time to make an epic
or see things for the epic that they are
an eighteenth century balloonist
when Mars was in the Sun set out for Wales from here
trailing sparks ascended through the clouds
and sank to earth near Howth
while dancing masters in the Pleasure Gardens

played musical glasses in the undergrowth—
they have used the story to rename a pub
to make a Richard Crosbie of the Chariot

Here, as in life, the epic makes way for the ordinary, the monumental becomes mundane. In the end—this is the good news and the bad—they might rename a pub for you.

WHEN IT ARRIVED, in January 1987, with a cover the color of the Ordnance Survey map, sixty pages, perfect bound, the creamy paper and crisp print, it seemed a thing quite separate from myself, a finished thing that could assume its thin place on the shelf where it might eventually explain to my sons and daughter what I was doing all those times that I appeared distracted. But *Skating with Heather Grace* became a kind of passport.

In the spring of 1988, The Frost Place in New Hampshire gave me a fellowship to Annaghmakerrig—The Tyrone Guthrie Centre for the Arts in Newbliss, County Monaghan. The woman I would soon marry, Mary Tata, moved in with my children so I could go. Guthrie's old mansion housed, in monthlong residencies, a corps of working artists, writers, filmmakers and musicians. I met Conleth O'Connor there, a poet who would die in a few short years of drink—a sadness foreshadowed in his last book, *A Corpse Auditions its Mourners*. He took a copy of my book to his friend Philip Casey, the Dublin poet and fictionist, who showed it to his friend Matthew Sweeney, a poet from Donegal living in London. Sweeney showed the book to his editor, Robin Robertson, then at Secker & Warburg in London. They both showed up the following year to a reading I did at Bewley's Oriental Café in Grafton Street.

I was paid sixty punts, the going rate for visiting poets then, and sold some books to Books Upstairs. The next morning, I did an interview on the radio and read out poems all over the island. Macdara took me to Gerard Manley Hopkins's grave at Glasnevin Cemetery in the Jesuit plot, then hosted with Eilean that night a party of poets in Selskar Terrace. It was three in the morning when Macdara drove Pearse Hutchinson to his digs and me to mine. We were the last of the night's revelers. Our talk, somehow, got on to fly-fishing. Pearse cleared his throat in the backseat, then began.

"There is a grand story told on the subject of fishing by one of—may I say—your countrymen, from Clare, who reports the way the locals there use a goose for bait."

"For shark?" I said, incredulous, the willing straight man.

"No, no. Actually for trout," says Pearse in elegant deadpan.

The small coupe paused at the light. We waited for the punch line. When none seemed forthcoming, the car eased forth.

"Well," I said, "that was one massive trout or one midget of a goose."

"I suppose," said Pearse and cleared his throat again, the don among the ignoranti, "but, of course, your man did not elaborate."

I flew home grinning and determined to find the ancient text from which the poet had exhumed his story of the trout and the goose.

Macdara Woods followed my return to America, his first trip there, to do a series I'd arranged around the Midwest. When we met, in 1986, he'd been off the drink for four years. I'd seen him in his own local bar at home, The Hill in Ranelagh, where he gave up nothing of the society but refused the booze in favor of temperate drink. I'd been in trouble with alcohol for a while by then—

especially in the year since my divorce. It had turned on me and I wanted to stop. In late April of 1989, at a party to welcome Macdara Woods to Michigan, I sat in my study with Richard Tillinghast and Keith Taylor, quoting poems to each other and quietly killing a bottle of duty-free Black Bush I'd brought from Shannon two weeks before. The mix of Irish and whiskey and poetry and sociability had seemed an impossible alchemy to undo, but I knew that the whiskey was undoing me. It was Macdara Woods, a sober, sociable Irish poet, who modeled the possibility. The bottle of Black Bush we were after drinking was the last of the boozing I would have to do.

THE COLD
After the all hours drinking bout,
and the punchless acrimony,
he set off for the sea, on foot,
a good mile in the wind,
past zigzag lines of parked cars
and the disco din, past streetlights,
though if he'd needed light
the stars would have done—
down to the beach he wobbled,
a beercan in both pockets,
to sit on a rock and drink,
and think of his marriage,
and when both cans were empty
he removed his shoes
to walk unsteadily into the sea
and make for Iceland,

> *but the Atlantic sent him home again,*
> *not a corpse, not a ghost,*
> *to waken his wife*
> *and complain of the cold.*

"The Cold" is the first poem in Matthew Sweeney's *Blue Shoes*—a book he'd launched in Dublin the night before we met. After my reading at Bewley's, we traded books. Apart from the poem's icy precision—its exercise in Ulster understatement—it includes two venues important to Sweeney's work: the northern Atlantic coast of his Donegal upbringing and the ever-perilous domestic interior where men and women work out their lives. The poet-husbands of Sweeney's work are ever on the brink of complete rejection, ever the architects of their own disasters.

Though full of fantasies ("Pink Milk") and morbid curiosities ("The Coffin Shop") and his famous hypochondria ("A Diary of Symptoms"), the poems of Matthew Sweeney that always return to me are those in which the poet is the passive, sometimes absent witness to his own domestic unraveling. Like the Irish epic anti-hero who is turned into a bird and must roam the ancient woods, this modern Sweeney is willing to watch his own imagined betrayals from a branch of an oak tree in the backyard.

It was at Matthew Sweeney's invitation that I flew to London in late 1991 for a round of readings he'd arranged around the country. On a train ride to Evesham, he showed me the manuscript for his new collection called *Cacti*. In the title poem, a deserted man turns his house into a desert in hopes his woman will return. The text is edgy, like minimalist theatre, the space occupied by silence and wariness, the page dominated by white space. The poet

arranges the furniture and lets his characters work away. Something
fatal or fantastic seems always on the brink of happening.

I read in Evesham with Sean O'Brien, in Bristol and Loughbor-
ough on my own, and made an off-season pilgrimage to Iona by
train to pay homage to the Irish bardic poet St. Columba. I
returned to London to meet up with my new wife, Mary, and to
read at the Poetry Library with the Scots poet Jackie Kay in the
South Bank Centre. From our room in the Charing Cross Hotel,
we walked over the Thames on the Hungerford Bridge—the great
city of the language and its river seemed full of poems and friends
who wrote them.

Robin Robertson came to the reading and, in the bar of the
South Bank Centre afterward, made known his interest in publishing my work. Years later, Christopher Reid of Faber & Faber, at a
dinner at Robertson's home, would comment on my finding an
"English editor." Our host corrected him: "He has a Scots editor
with an office in London."

EARLY IN 1992, my father died. Nora fell ill soon after and I
found myself in Dublin early in March to do some legal work.
Macdara and Eilean, as always, had a room and a roast dinner
waiting, and a welcome. Eilean was scheduled to read that night
in the Abbey Theatre in honor of International Women's Day.
The director of *Poetry Ireland*, Theo Dorgan, had arranged for
several of Ireland's finest poets to read, with the country's new
president, Mary Robinson, there to welcome them. Eavan Boland
and Eithne Strong and Mary O'Donnell and Mary O'Malley and
Julie O'Callaghan and Eilean—it was the first time I ever heard
her read.

THE REAL THING
The book of Exits, miraculously copied
Here in this convent by an angel's hand,
Stands open on a lectern, grooved
Like the breast of a martyred deacon.

The bishop has ordered the windows bricked up on this side
Facing the fields beyond the city.
Lit by the glow from the cloister yard at noon
On Palm Sunday, Sister Custos
Exposes her major relic, the longest
Known fragment of the Brazen Serpent.

True stories wind and hang like this
Shuddering loop wreathed on the lapis lazuli
Frame. She says, this is the real thing,
She veils it again and locks up.
On the shelves behind her the treasures are lined.
The episcopal seal repeats every coil,
Stamped on all the closures of each reliquary
Where the labels read: Bones
Of Different Saints. Unknown.

Her history is a blank sheet,
Her vows a folded paper locked like a well.
The torn end of the serpent
Tilts the lace edge of the veil.
The real thing, the one free foot kicking
Under the white sheet of history.

This poetry of icon and idol, of womanly priesthood and invention, made me think of Nora Lynch, in extremis on the other side of Ireland that night, and the powerful medicine she was said to have—the spiritual muscle to bless and curse, to divine out of the ordinary, the real thing.

It was always the business of Irish poets, making their way from barony to barony, parish to parish, to bless and curse with powerful words, the way Moses was said to have cured those bitten by vipers with a serpent of brass hung on a pole and exposed to the people of Israel.

And that line—"Bones/Of Different Saints. Unknown."—put me in mind of the family reliquary, the great vault in Moyarta, with its gabled end and dark interior "lit by the glow from the cloister yard" when there'd been a death in the family; where Nora soon would be, with the bones of our common ancestors, Pat and Honora, dead a century, and her infant twin and her father. And my father and mother too recently dead, together in Holy Sepulchre, going to bone in the boxes I had put them in. These were the real things to me that night in the Abbey—these losses and pending losses among the last of my elders. Nora Lynch was dying in Moveen. Her history was "a blank sheet,/her vows a folded paper locked like a well." Her only hope, and mine—language, poems, words—"The real thing, the one free foot kicking/Under the white sheet of history."

When Nora died toward the end of that month, Macdara drove down from Achill Island in Mayo to be with us when we buried her. It was the done thing and a kindness.

In 1994, when a book was brought out by my Scots editor with an office in London, I was invited to readings in the United Kingdom and Ireland.

It was in Aldeburgh in East Anglia at a poetry festival that I first got a whiff of rare celebrity. The airfare paid for by my publisher, the car and driver waiting at the train station, the posters with my photo and name in bold Garamond, the banner over the High Street proclaiming the long weekend's literary events, the welcome from the festival committee, and the chummy greetings of the other luminaries—each added a measure to the gathering sense of self-importance.

We all had put on our public faces. There was Paula Meehan from Dublin, Deryn Rees-Jones, a young and comely Liverpudlian, Charles Boyle, then a junior editor at Faber & Faber. I was the American with Irish connections whose day job as a funeral director struck folks as sufficiently odd to merit mention in the local press. We were all poets of the book or two-book sort, on the edge of greater or lesser obscurity, to whom the keys to this North Sea-side city had been given in the first week of November 1995 for the Seventh Annual Aldeburgh International Poetry Festival. The tide of good fortune to which minute celebrities become accustomed was rising as we strolled the esplanade, Ms. Meehan and I, talking of friends we shared in Ireland and America, the rush of the off-season surf noising in the shingle, the lights coming on in tall windows of the Victorian seafront lodges. At one corner, a pair of local spinsters standing in their doorway called us in to tea and talk of literary matters. They had prepared an elegant spread of pastries and relevant questions about contemporary poetry and the bookish arts in general. We were, Paula and I, asked for what was reckoned expert testimony on verse and verse makers—the long deceased and the more recently published.

Then there were the panels and interviews, recorded for the local radio stations, and readings held in the Jubilee Hall, a vast brick warehouse that had been turned into a performance space by the installation of amphitheatric seating and microphones and stage lighting. The house was packed for every event, the sale of books was brisk, the lines at the signing tables long and kindly. They were so glad to meet us, so pleased to be a part of such a "magical event." The air was thick with superlative and serendipity, hyperbole and Ciceronian praise. The dull advance of the darkening year toward its chill end had been momentously if only momentarily slowed by the "glow" of our performances. And after every event the poets—me among them—were invited to a makeshift canteen across the street above the city's cinema. Teas and coffees, soups and sandwiches, domestic and imported lagers, local cheeses and continental wines were put out for the hardworking and presumably ever-hungry and thirsty poets who, for their part, seemed fashionably beleaguered and grateful for the afterglow among organizers and groupies. We were like down-market rock-and-roll stars on tour, clasping our thin volumes and sheaves of new work like the instruments of our especial trade, basking in the unabashed approval of these locals and out-of-towners. It was all very heady and generous.

A poet far removed from his own country, I felt at last the properly appreciated prophet. For every word there seemed an audience eager to open their hearts and minds. Strangeness and distance made every utterance precious. For while the Irish and Welsh and Scots were very well treated, and the English writers held their own, I was an ocean and a fair portion of continent from home and made to feel accordingly exotic and, for the first time in my life, almost *cool*.

Home in Michigan, a mortician who wrote poems was the social equivalent of a dentist who did karaoke: a painful case made more so by the dash of dullness. But here in England, I was not an oddity but a celebrity, being "minded" by a team of local literarians, smart and shapely women—one tendering a medley of local farm cheeses, another pouring a cup full of tea, another offering homemade scones, still another—the pretty wife of the parish priest—taking notes as I held forth in conversation with another poet on the metabolics of iambic pentameter and the "last time I saw Heaney" or "Les Murray" or some greater fixture in the firmament. And though I'd been, by then, abstemious for years, the star treatment was an intoxicant. The center of such undivided attention, I became chatty and fashionably manic, conversationally nimble, intellectually vibrant, generous and expansive in every way, dizzy and dazzling to all and every in earshot, myself included.

So it was when I espied, in the doorway of this salon, a handsome man I recognized as someone I had seen before, I assumed he must be from Michigan, since this was my first time ever in these parts. His dress was more pressed and precise than any writerly type—more American—a memorable face with a forgettable name, possibly a Milfordian on holiday or a fellow Rotarian, or a funeral director whom I'd met at a national convention who, having read about my appearance in one of the English dailies, had paused in his tour to make his pilgrimage to Aldeburgh to hear me read. It was the only explanation. My memory of him, though incomplete, was unmistakable: I knew this pilgrim and not from here.

I excused myself from the discourse with the churchman's wife and made my way across the room to what I was sure would be his eager salutations. But he seemed to look right past me, as if he'd come for something or someone else. Perhaps, I thought, he did not recognize me out of my familiar surroundings and funereal garb. The closer I got, the more certain I was that he and I shared an American connection. I rummaged through my memory for a bit of a name, or a place or time on which to fix the details of our acquaintance.

"How good to see you!" I said, "And so far from home!"

Fully fed on the rich fare of self-importance, I was expansive, generous, utterly sociable.

I took his hand and shook it manfully. He looked at me with genteel puzzlement.

"I know I know you but I can't say from where. . . ," I said, certain that he would fill in the details . . . the friend we had in common, the event, the circumstances of his being here.

"Tom Lynch," I smiled, "from Michigan," and then, in case our connection was mortuary, "from Lynch & Sons, in Milford."

"How nice to meet you, Mr. Lynch. Fines . . . Ray Fines. . . ." His voice was hesitant, velvety, trained; a clergyman, I thought. They were always doing these "exchanges" whereby one rector traded duties and homes for a season with another, the better to see the world on a cleric's stipend. Or a TV reporter, the UK correspondent for CNN, maybe wanting an interview with the visiting American poet?

"Are you here on holidays?" I asked him.

"No, no, just visiting friends." He kept looking around the room as if I wasn't the reason for his being here.

"And where did we first meet? I just can't place it," I said.

"I am certain I don't know," he said, and then almost shyly, "perhaps you have seen me in a movie."

"Movie?"

"Yes, well, maybe," he said. "I act."

It was one of those moments when we see the light or debouch from the fog into the focused fact of the matter. I had, of course, first seen him in America, in Michigan, in the Milford Cinema, where he'd been the brutal Nazi Amon Goeth, who shoots Jews for sport in *Schindler's List,* and more recently in *Quiz Show,* where he'd played the brainy if misguided golden boy of the American poet Mark Van Doren. He was not Ray Fines at all. He was *Ralph Fiennes.* His face was everywhere—the globalized image of mannish beauty in its prime, and dark thespian sensibility, privately desired by women on several continents and in many languages, whilst here I was, slam-dunked in the hoop-game of celebrity before I'd even had a chance to shine. Across the room I could see the rector's wife, watching my encounter with the heartthrob. She was wide-eyed and blushing and expecting, I supposed, an introduction.

A contortionist of my acquaintance, whose name would not be recognized were I to use it, though he has accumulated some regional fame for something he does with thumbs, once theorized that if the lower lip could be stretched over one's head, and one could quickly swallow, one could disappear. Never had I a greater urge to test the theory than that moment in Aldeburgh. I felt my lower lip begin to quiver and tried to calculate its elasticity, but all I could manage was an idiot grin. Mr. Fiennes, apparently a well-bred man, said nothing further and smiled kindly. I affected a hasty retreat, as if to make final edits and further fine-tunings to the reading I would be giving, alas, anon.

Eventually I read my poems to the many dozens assembled in Aldeburgh, and their applause, such as it was, was a delight and surprise. To have the work one has done in private considered by strangers in far places remains for me an unexpected gift. To hear new poems said out loud in the voice of their makers has kept the language alive for me.

I've read with Paula Meehan in England and Ireland and Michigan and heard the hush that widens in the room when she begins:

> Little has come down to me of hers,
> a sewing machine, a wedding band,
> a clutch of photos, the sting of her hand
> across my face in one of our wars
>
> when we had grown bitter and apart.
> Some say that's the fate of the eldest daughter.

. . . and heard the breath go out of those that hear it, when seven or eight minutes later, Paula brings "The Pattern" to its close—peace made, love told to the ghost of a mother who died too young.

And I've read with Dennis O'Driscoll, surely one of Europe's great men of letters. A civil servant for more than thirty years, he works for Irish Customs in Dublin. Apart from being among the most widely respected and widely published Irish critics of poetry, he is the author of seven collections of poetry, a volume of prose, and dozens of uncollected reviews, profiles, bits of literary biography. His poems are refreshingly liberated from the mythic-pastoral tributaries of his countrymen. His work is immediate, urbane, free of adornment, and uniquely citified as in this piece from *Weather Permitting*:

THE CELTIC TIGER
Ireland's boom is in full swing.
Rows of numbers, set in a cloudless blue
computer background, prove the point.

Executives lop miles off journeys
since the ring-roads opened, one hand
free to dial a client on the mobile.

Outside new antique pubs, young consultants
—well-toned women, gel-slick men—
drain long-necked bottles of imported beer.

Lip-glossed cigarettes are poised
at coy angles, a black bra strap
slides strategically from a Rocha top.

Talk of tax-exempted town-house lettings
is muffled by rap music blasted
from a passing four-wheel drive.

The old live on, wait out their stay
of execution in small granny flats,
thrifty thin-lipped men, grim pious wives. . . .

Sudden as an impulse holiday, the wind
has changed direction, strewing a whiff
of barbecue fuel across summer lawns.

Tonight, the babe on short-term
contract from the German parent
will partner you at the sponsor's concert.

Time now, however, for the lunch-break
orders to be faxed. Make yours hummus
on black olive bread. An Evian.

For someone who has been dropping into Ireland for three decades now, such a poem is indispensable—capturing as it does the full sweep of changes in the Irish mindset and economy in nine brief stanzas, twenty-seven lines. Better than any social or cultural study, "The Celtic Tiger" charts the distance from the meat-and-potatoes culture of the past century to the "hummus on black olive bread" and designer-water culture at the turn of the second millennium. It comes from a man who came of age when a civil-service job meant security. To work for the government or a bank, to teach or join the reverend clergy—these were the best and brightest future jobs in the 1960s and 1970s and the ones most manifestly left behind in the IT, EU, Irish Boom of the 1990s. O'Driscoll, born in 1954, in Thurles, County Tipperary, began working in 1970 for the Estates Division, collecting death duties before rising to his current assistant principal rank with the International Customs Branch.

His colleagues, no more interested in his poetry "than another fellow's greyhounds," nonetheless take notice when RTE sends a cab to bring O'Driscoll to and from the lunchtime Arts Show on the radio where his commentaries on books and writers are broadcast around the country. The man who was the Irish Customs delegate to the EU in 1996 was the editor for *POETRY Magazine's* Irish Poetry Issue in 1998. When we read together for the Lannan

Foundation in Santa Fe in the spring of 2001, he allowed as how we should call it "Death & Taxes," in observance of our day jobs.

The army of poets who make poems in English never falls short of volunteers. And though there is some sniping in the ranks, some friendly fire and begrudgery, at the end of the day they all bed down with words still ringing in their ears.

In the years since I began writing poems, there have been wars and upheavals, disasters and deaths, drunks and recoveries, marriages and children. Presidents and prime ministers have come and gone. There are peace accords and suicide bombers, more terror and technology. The news of the day most days repeats itself. It seems the same war, the same outrage, the same sadness. The fresh word that is poetry remains. In the best and worst of times, it has been the work of poets that sees us through.

I'VE OPENED the house to writerly friends. They stay for days or weeks or months on end. I've lost count of the projects finished there, or started. Early on, I tried to say that everything from Moveen West back to the Loop belonged to me—the flora and fauna and history, the stories and the people and geographies. "You can have anything out the kitchen window east," I'd tell them. "The rest is mine." Writers are such amiable thieves, they'd go off with anything and call it their own. I didn't want some visiting writer taking the things I'd staked out years ago—Dunlicky, the Bridges of Ross, the story of lovers at Loop Head, the underground river that divides Moveen West from East, the characters there both living and dead. But then, what was I if not a visiting writer, stealing the images and stories I'd heard, telling them over and over in my own voice? So I gave up. The only rent they'd owe me would be words.

I had the Kennys up in Galway make a book—a largish binding of blank pages, with *Lynch—Moveen West* on the cover—and wrote the lease agreement on the first page inside.

Rentals Ledger
Des Kenny up in Galway made this book
of pages fit for ink and acid free
and sewn into a leather binding. He
put Lynch—Moveen West *on the cover. Look,*
there's whitespace left for the likes of you
so if you're a writer the rent is do.
Pay Breda Roche coin of the realm for coal
and turf, fresh linens, clean towels. The phone's
on the honor system. Pay as you go.
But leave this absentee landlord poems,
paragraphs, sentences, phrases well turned
out of your own word horde and what you've learned
here in these ancient remedial stones
where Nora Lynch held forth for ninety years,
the last two decades of them on her own.
Alone by the fire in the silence she
recited the everyday mysteries
of wind and rain and darkness and the light
and sang her evening songs and sat up nights
full of wonder and reminiscences.
If you hear voices here the voice is hers.
She speaks to me still. If she speaks to you,
ready your best nib. Write what she tells you to.

There are bits of stories by fictionists from Glasgow and Dublin and Amsterdam. There are verses by Irish and other poets, from the U.K. and the Continent, the Americas and the Antipodes. Philip Casey left his funeral instructions.

THE WINDFALL OAK
On Webster's isle find a windfall oak
and hollow it to my measurements.
Make sure I go in my casual clothes.
No fancy lining, just wood and bark,
the rough-cut halves secured with rope.
Seal it if you must with wax,
then form a circle around my tree
to celebrate my love and laughs,
my fountain pen, my pain, my hope
in well-wrought verse and song, and ceilidh.
Then plant this sapling in the earth.

Linda Gregerson left "Cranes on the Seashore" to let me know how it was for her:

  I.
  Today, Tom, I followed the tractor ruts north
        along
        the edge of Damien's pasture. I missed all the

  dung slicks but one. The calves did not judge me
        or, comely
        darlings, judged me benign. The ditches

and the token bits of barbed wired weren't, I like
   to think,
  intended to halt my trespass much more than they

did. The hedge-crowned chassis might have been one
   of my father's
  own. And then the rise, Tom, the promised

North Atlantic, and I'm fixed.

The poem plays out, in three more sections, the activities of the poet's two young daughters who have hiked with her up Sonny Carmody's field across the road, to the ridge overlooking the ocean that bounds Moveen. Megan is trying to draw the cliffs. Emma is enchanted by Damien Carmody's Holstein calves, the smallest of which, slow to the bucket of feed, she reckons at first is "simply less greedy." The images of motherly understanding and daughterly innocence are calming and sweet. But in between these ruminations, the poet retells the awful story she has read in the section of that week's *Clare Champion* called, "Turning the Clock Back," which reprints every week something from the archives of fifty and a hundred and one hundred twenty-five years ago. It is the story of two girls at a nearby beach on a June evening in 1874, "washing skeins of new spun wool." They are, the paper reports, mistaken for cranes by a young Mr. Dowling who, from some distance, takes aim with his gun and shoots them both. It is a horrible miscalculation.

  Of Mr. Dowling's youth and upright family
   the writer

> *cannot say enough (his obvious*
>
> *promise, their moneyed remorse);*

Is it the landlord's son who has shot the local girls "both in the employ of the Leadmore farm"? Who else would have a rifle and "moneyed remorse"? The disaster seems entirely too natural, set as it is in the pastoral of seaside, field and farm. Once out, the awful facts must multiply. Innocence is lost. The holiday is over. It is time to go. The rent, as always, must be paid.

> *God*
>
> > *keep us from the gun sight. Here is*
> > > *one*
> > *for the landlord and one (we're almost*
>
> *gone) for the road.*

Breda Roche leaves the key under the mat and a fire down, fresh milk in the fridge, some eggs and scones. She leaves the big book on the table to collect the rents.

The house that was left to me is full of ghosts and their good voices. The talk is circular and intertwined. Everyone's connected. Each party piece inspires others.

IF LIFE IS linear, our brief histories stretched between baptisms and burials, and the larger history tied to events that happen in a line: and then, and then, and then, and then . . . poetry is the thing that twists history and geography and memory free of such plodding. Everything is tributary, every image and experience capable of turning on itself a hundred different ways.

It's all a metaphor: the house with its voices, the book of rents, the poet hammering lobster on the flagstone floor. The Heaneys and Reids are dining on fresh catch in Moveen. "What I remember is the problem of cracking the backs of the lobsters . . ." the Nobel laureate writes. "The Reids were in residence in the cottage and had acquired the creatures wherever: mighty movers, a match for Dürer's rhino any day." And we *are* moved and mightily—to see the armor cladding and the claws, like cloven pincers, and the hungry dinner guests' dilemma.

But Dürer never saw a rhino and made his famous woodcut out of words found in a letter that came from Lisbon to Nuremberg with a hasty scribble of the awful ungulate—the four-footed beastie, as it was called—an alien species from another world, a gift from the king of Cambodia to the king of Portugal for the Royal Zoo, *Rhinoceros unicornis*, which would, as history has it, some years hence be lost at sea with all hands on board, en route to the care and keeping of His Holiness in Rome. None of which matters. They are only facts. What is remembered is the image wrought from words, the oddly lovely heavy-breathing thing. Five hundred years later, it is still, for all its errors, for all its flaws, the thing we see when we hear "rhino." We see best what we say in words. "Fast, jolly and cunning," Dürer wrote, describing the creature in his border notes.

It's all a metaphor: the poet, like a rhino, on all fours, "beyond all adult dignity," "fast, jolly and cunning," banging at the boiled lobster with a hammer on the stone floor, like hammering for diamonds in coal, gold in rock, the pearl in the oyster, the precious bit among the many pieces. "Did we splatter the shells? I think we may have."

It's all a metaphor: the sense, he reports, of "a feast that had been fought for," whereby the lobster is linked to all hard-won feeds—the fish hauled from the ocean, the plucked hen, the things we grow and gather in, the hunted, slaughtered, butchered things we cook and eat—all metaphor for what we need: the feast, the common meal, the open table and celebration—all metaphor for life's work in words, for life's work, for life, for the images and talk among us all, living and dead, "great debris and great delight."

"POETRY," THE POET Heaney says the poet Auden said, "is what we do to break bread with the dead." Is it anything, I wonder, like hammering lobster? "Rhyme and meter," Heaney adds, "are the table manners."

He's reading at the University of Michigan.

Auden taught here in Ann Arbor briefly, after moving to the United States the year that Yeats died in France, the year Heaney was born in the North of Ireland. And Heaney's friend, the great Russian poet Joseph Brodsky, taught here when he was exiled from Russia in 1972. He died on the same day Yeats died—January 28— almost sixty years later.

Some months before Yeats died, he gave, in "Under Ben Bulben," directions to his countrymen:

> *Irish poets, learn your trade,*
> *Sing whatever is well made,*
> *Scorn the sort now growing up*
> *All out of shape from toe to top.*

When Auden got word about Yeats's death, he wrote his famous elegy, "In Memory of W. B. Yeats," in which he gives his own directive, borrowing the dead man's "table manners":

Earth, receive an honoured guest:
William Yeats is laid to rest.
Let the Irish vessel lie
Emptied of its poetry.

When Brodsky died, too young, too soon, in 1996, Heaney borrowed for "Audenesque" the rhyme and meter that Auden had borrowed from Yeats, and Yeats from Blake, and Blake from, maybe, a children's rhyme.

Joseph, yes, you knew the beat
Wystan Auden's metric feet,
Danced to it unstressed and stressed
Laying William Yeats to rest.

And here it is April, some years since. Heaney will read in Sligo this year at the Yeats International Summer School. The Belfast that Joseph Brodsky saw when he wrote "Belfast Tune" ("Here is a girl from a dangerous town/she crops her dark hair short/so that less of her has to frown/when someone gets hurt") is blooming with daffodils and a kind of peace. Auden's poem "September 1, 1939," written at the start of World War II, has become suddenly famous since the horrors of September 2001. One commentator in the *Times Literary Supplement* writes, "Auden's words are everywhere." ("I and the public know/what all schoolchildren learn,/those to whom evil is done/do evil in return.") After sixty-five years, it still rings true.

Heaney turns sixty-five this month. This June will mark the hundredth Bloomsday and Kavanaugh's Centenary is on this year.

The language gives us much to celebrate. So I install the ancient meter in my ear—*What an undertaking Tom/Tump-ti tump-ti tump-ti tum*—and go out for a walk, to hear what happens.

> *Once a school boy in West Clare,*
> *Stood to ask me when and where*
> *I got my "poet's license"?*
> *"Hush," the teacher seethed. "Silence!"*
>
> *The laughing class went quiet.*
> *The silence echoed. "Try it,"*
> *I whispered, to embolden.*
> *"We're born with it," I told him.*
>
> *Next day in the morning mail:*
> *Mister, do I pass or fail?*
> *'Tweedle dum and tweedle dee*
> *Had to go out for a pee!'*
>
> *Pass, I wrote, Good man for you!*
> *Reckoning good p's and q's*
> *Dumb fellows who'll never rhyme*
> *Whilst dee and pee'll tweedle fine.*

That boy's face, in a classroom in Cross Village, between Carrigaholt and Loop Head, the look of play and portent in his eyes, of mischief and hidden meanings, the sure sense he had that words were gifts and a way with them was powerful medicine put

me in mind of what I first found in Ireland at the fire in Moveen
where Nora strove among her home and kitchenwares and her
brother Tommy with his cattle and the land, at a life that seemed a
series of feasts worth fighting for.

> *Great debris, delight indeed:*
> *So it is with this life. We*
> *Hammer at the moment till*
> *All that's left is memorable.*

Epilogue

Fair Una MacMahon, the yellow-haired bride
Of the Lord of Dunlica, sits lone by the tide;
The red eye is quench'd in the blue, sullen main,
And the night-mist hangs pale over stormy Moveen.
The waves, in a war-dance, are shouting below,
And tossing about their tiaras of snow,
Besieging the bounds of that cliff-guarded shore,
Which may challenge their might for five thousand years more.
But why sits fair Una alone on the verge
Of that desolate rock, by the roar of the surge?
The wave-spray is silvering the silk of her hair,
The darkness grows 'round her, and still she is there!
The sea-birds are shrieking, like ghosts, 'round the cliffs,
And the fishers have steer'd to the brown bay their skiffs,
For they know by the low dingy scud of the South,

That the fiend of the tempest to-night will be out.
And Una has watch'd, from the dusk to the dark,
For the breeze-swollen wings of her Ocean-Chief's bark,
Which has gone in pursuit of some maritime prey,
Since morning put on the sun-splendors of day.
—from "The Pirate of Dunlica—A Legend of Corcovaskin," in *Lays and Legends of Thomond*, by Michael Hogan, the Bard of Thomond

After Words

28 August 1982

Late Tea

Fine light now, the best evening ever. Nora is preparing the mackerel I caught this afternoon at Dunlicky. Dualco is out front preparing the plaster to repair the damage to the wall the plumbing did. The whole room is full of white sunlight slanting in wide shafts through the west window. (Nora just doused Dualco with the water from the fish cleaning when she opened the door and gave it a heave—even with a sink indoors, nothing changes too quickly.) We'd a good three jars at Pierce Fennells Dolphin after fishing and have put the minimum of gas in the Ford to make it to Shannon in the morning. Dualco leaves at 10:15 for Milan and I go at 2 P.M. and those are the facts that underscore the evening and produce a kind of frenzy in us all—each trying to avoid confronting that.

This morning from the window the whole expanse of Dingle to the west was visible, out over the Shannon, the Slieve Mish mountains, Mount Eagle, huge Brandon, and two little dim alps in the farthermost—Blaskets or Skelligs. The light was just right, and the clouds, so that every edge was articulated.

Two nights of American Wakes now: Thursday the Moveen crowd—Sam and Mary Ellen Curtin, J. J. McMahon, Sonny Carmody and his singing daughters, Ann and Lourda, with their tin whistles, Michael and Mary Murray from the cliff road, and my Carmody cousins, Nora (nee Lynch) and Patrick, from above on the hill, more of my relations here, and Patrick Collins and May, who always come. Then last night the Shannons from Cross came by for tea at 10 P.M. So we made for Pierce Fennells for the *ceili* music and a few jars. Back at 1:30. As always, Dualco and Nora stayed up talking things into the last coals, politics, religion, the way of the world—Dualco because after a few pints, after midnight, he gets his other wind and Nora because, at eighty this year, she has learned to waste no time on sleep that might be better spent in meaningless society with others.

All day yesterday was spent on bringing the water into the house—no mean progress when I consider that water here has always been a quarter-mile down the land, brimming up from a spring well and only available in single bucketfuls, lugged back uphill in every weather. But now, thanks to Dualco, we have a stainless-steel sink top set to an old five-bob table that years ago was built to the appropriate size. We've buried the water here from the road and drainpipe to the ditch out back lined with stone tiles beneath the whitethorn hedge that hides the eastern flanks of the estate. A small hole was chiseled through the slate stone wall—

three feet thick—and nothing fell. As Nora said when the thing was finished, it's a miracle. Further, she was correct to say, the composing of it (the buying of parts and pieces) was harder than the playing it all together. "The best when the rest are out," she says. I always wonder if such improvements here improve anything at all. The last vestige of preindustrial country life—the huge open hearth with the fire on the floor is only saved because the cast-iron stove that Nora is keen on cost five hundred pounds at Brew's.

I don't know. I'm stung by half a dozen images of Ireland this time—a vision of a young woman wrapped in old spinster clothes, a shawl around her, nubile and hidden, senile and full of life. This time we seemed to go nowhere. Two weeks staring in the fire, or tilting pints, or listening to the wind blow. Primal, meditative things, bringing the water in, making our water in the old way, under stars.

About Nora I've no particular worries. She seems vibrant and alert, lacking only youth's eyesight but not its visions.

Off the Atlantic, a bank of clouds is moving overland, scattering the light beams, moving great shadows through the room. My children, to whom I owe the aching sore in my heart that has reddened for some days now, promise to meet me at the airport. Tomorrow, in the evening, thanks be to God.

(Dublin is the fastest-growing city in Europe—RTE says so, ending the news.)

Acknowledgments

The idea for this book belongs to my agent, Richard McDonough, who has championed my work for most of a decade. Robin Robertson and Jill Bialosky, my editors and friends, have been unfailing in their support for this work and have guided this book into being. I am ever grateful.

My colleagues at Lynch & Sons in Milford are a gift to me and to the communities we serve.

To Michael Heffernan, Matthew Sweeney, Richard Tillinghast, Keith Taylor, Seamus Heaney, Dennis O'Driscoll, Philip Casey, Peter Stine, Macdara Woods, Eilean Ni Chuilleanain, David Crumm, Bob Root, John O'Donohue, and Martina Scanlan, whose voices and sound counsel added to this text, I am always indebted. Likewise I'm grateful to Julie Young, Pat Lynch, Mary Callaghan, Marilyn and Mike Kinna for their contributions. Especial thanks to George Martin for his careful reading, comments, and corrections.

Portions of this book were broadcast on BBC Radio in the series *Colloquies,* produced by Kate McAll, with whom I've worked for a decade now. She is an ideal listener, a deft writer and editor, and friend for life.

Excerpts from this book have appeared, often in slightly different form, in *Image, The Cresset, The Christian Century,* the *New York Times, The Bastard on the Couch,* the *Times of London,* the *Irish Times, The U.S. Catholic,* and the *Los Angeles Times,* to whose editors I am grateful.

Thanks too to Gerry Collison, editor of the *Clare Champion,* and his staff of reporters and photographers for delivering to my home in Milford every week word from my home in West Clare.

To P. J., Breda, and Louise Roche; Sonny and Maura Carmody and family; the Murray sisters, Anne, Katherine, Maureen, and Theresa; Patrick and Nora Carmody; James and Maureen Carmody; J. J. McMahon; Martin Roche; Fr. Patrick Culligan, P. P.; Fr. James Walsh, P.P.; Mr. Michael P. Houlihan, Esq.; Mr. Geroid Williams, Esq.; Dr. Paddy Waldron, Jr., and Mr. Patrick Waldron, Esq.; Mary Ann Radscheid; and Maureen O'Dea Mundy—each of whom has shared his or her virtuosity at seeing things for how they are—I am indebted.

There is no reckoning my debt to Mary Tata, who has abided both my absences and presences for twenty years, thanks be to God.

Notes on Frontispieces

The author wishes to thank Michael Lynch for assistance in the selection, preparation, and presentation of the images in this book, many of which have been rescued from a careless archivist. Likewise, the work of Joe Vaughn has added substantially to this project.

Fit & Start

Coast Road, Moveen

The Ethnography of Everyday Life

Bedroom window, Moveen, 1979

The Brother

Gravestones, Moyarta

The Same but Different
Image from the *Illustrated London News,* Moveen, 1849

Inheritance
Property detail

Death Comes for the Young Curate
First Solemn High Mass

Bits & Pieces
Nora Lynch on the Moveen Road

Great Hatred, Little Room
Back of cottage, Moveen, 1970

The Sisters Godhelpus
The Sisters

Odds & Ends
Funeral, Moveen

On Some Verses by Irish & Other Poets
Dürer's *Rhinocerus*

Epilogue
Grave marker, Moyarta

After Words
Fresh mackerel, Dunlicky (Joe Vaughn)

Selected Bibliography

It is impossible to credit all the sources that have contributed to these essays. The following books provided rich material. In addition to the titles listed here, I am deeply indebted to the Online Publications of the Clare County Library, Ennis, and to the work of CLASP—The Clare Local Areas Studies Project.

Ardagh, John, *Ireland and the Irish, Portrait of a Changing Society*. London: Hamish Hamilton, 1994.

Arensberg, Conrad M., and Solon T. Kimball, *Family and Community in Ireland*. Ennis: CLASP Press, 2001.

Auden, W. H., *Collected Poems*. Ed. by Edward Mendelson. New York: Vintage International, 1991.

Brodsky, Joseph, *Collected Poems in English*. New York: Farrar Straus and Giroux, 2002.

Cahill, Thomas, *How the Irish Saved Civilization*. New York: Bantam Doubleday Dell, 1995.

Chuilleanain, Eilean Ni, *The Brazen Serpent*. Winston-Salem, NC: Wake Forest University Press, 1995.

Clune, Rev. G., *The Little Ark*. Published by the Church of Moneen, Kilbaha, Co., Clare, Ireland, 1990.

Coogan, Tim Pat, *Wherever Green Is Worn—The Story of the Irish Diaspora*. London: Hutchinson, 2000.

Cozzen, Donald B., *The Changing Face of the Priesthood: A Reflection of the Priest's Crisis of Soul*. Collegeville, MN: Liturgical Press, 2000.

Craig, Patricia, ed., *The Oxford Book of Ireland*. Oxford: Oxford University Press, 1998.

Crealey, Aidan H., *An Irish Almanac*. Cork and Dublin: Mercier Press, 1993.

Danaher, Kevin, *The Hearth and Stool and All! Irish Rural Households*. Cork and Dublin: Mercier Press, 1985.

Dinan, Brian, *Clare and Its People: A Concise History*. Cork and Dublin: Mercier Press, 1987.

Dutton, Hely, *Statistical Survey of the County of Clare*. Ennis: Online Publication of CLASP Press, 2001.

FitzGerald, M. Ashe, *Thomas Johnson Westropp (1860–1922): An Irish Antiquary*. Department of Archaeology, University College Dublin, 2000.

Foster, R. F., *Modern Ireland 1600–1972*. London: Penguin Books, 1989.

———, *W. B. Yeats—A Life: Vol. II, The Arch-Poet*. Oxford: Oxford University Press, 2003.

Gregerson, Linda, *Waterborne*. New York: Houghton Mifflin Company, 2002.

Harrison, Robert Pogue, *The Dominion of the Dead*. Chicago: The University of Chicago Press, 2003.

Harvey, John, *Dublin*. London: B. T. Batsford Ltd., 1949.

Hayden, Tom, ed., *Irish Hunger*. Dublin: Wolfhound Press, 1997.

Heaney, Seamus, *Electric Light*. New York: Farrar Straus and Giroux, 2001.

————, *Finders Keepers: Selected Prose 1971–2001*. London: Faber and Faber, 2002.

————, *Poems, 1965–1975*. New York: Farrar Straus and Giroux, 1980.

————, *Preoccupations: Selected Prose 1968–1978*. New York: Farrar Straus and Giroux, 1980.

Heffernan, Michael, *Love's Answer*. Iowa City: University of Iowa Press, 1994.

————, *The Cry of Oliver Hardy*. Athens: University of Georgia Press, 1979.

————, *To the Wreakers of Havoc*. Athens: University of Georgia Press, 1984.

Hogan, Michael, *The Lays and Legends of Thomond*. Limerick: City Printing, 1924.

Kenny, Mary, *Goodbye to Catholic Ireland*. London: Sinclair-Stevenson, 1997.

Killen, John, ed., *The Famine Decade: Contemporary Accounts 1841–1851*, Belfast: Blackstaff Press, 1995.

Kissane, Noel, *The Irish Famine—A Documentary History*. Dublin: The National Library of Ireland, 1995.

Knott, Mary John, *Two Months at Kilkee—Co. Clare, 1836*. Ennis: CLASP Press, 1997.

Laxton, Edward, *The Famine Ships—The Irish Exodus to America 1846–1851*. London: Bloomsbury, 1996.

Lloyd, John, *Lloyd's Tour of Clare, 1780*. Whitegate, Co. Clare, Ireland: Ballinakella Press.

Long, Thomas G., *Witness of Preaching*. Westminster: John Knox Press, 1990.

Lopate, Philip, *The Art of the Personal Essay: An Anthology from the Classical Era to the Present*. New York: Anchor, 1997.

Meehan, Paula, *Pillow Talk*. Dublin: Gallery Press, 1999.

Miller, Kerby, and Patricia Mulholland Miller, *Journey of Hope: The Story of*

Irish Immigration to America. San Francisco: Chronicle Books, 2001.

Millman, Lawrence, *Our Like Will Not Be There Again—Notes from the West of Ireland*. Fredonia, N.Y.: White Pine Press, 1997.

Moloney, Mick, *Far From the Shamrock Shore*. Cork: The Collins Press, 2002.

Mulqueen, Noel J., *The Vandeleur Evictions in Kilrush, 1888, The Plan of Campaign*, Ennis: The Clare Champion Ltd., 1988.

Murphy, Ignatius, *A People Starved: Life and Death in West Clare 1845–1851*. Blackrock, Co. Dublin: Irish Academic Press, 1996.

———, *Before the Famine Struck: Life in West Clare 1834–1845*. Blackrock, Co. Dublin: Irish Academic Press, 1996.

Murphy, Paul, *Do You Think You'll Like the Wind?* Cork: The Collins Press, 1995.

O'Brien, Flann, *Myles Away from Dublin*. London: Flamingo, 1993.

O Dalaigh, Brian, ed., *The Strangers Gaze—Travels in County Clare 1534–1950*. Ennis: CLASP Press, 1998.

O'Donnell, Edward T., *1001 Things Everyone Should Know About Irish American History*. New York: Broadway Books, 2002.

O'Donohue, John, *Anam Cara: A Book of Celtic Wisdom*. New York: Cliff Street Books, 1997.

O'Donovan, John, Eugene Curry, *The Antiquities of County Clare: Ordnance Survey Letters 1839*. Ennis: CLASP Press, 1997.

O'Driscoll, Dennis, *Weather Permitting*. London: Anvil Press, 2000.

O'Flaherty, Liam, *A Tourist's Guide to Ireland*. London: The Mandrake Press, 1930.

O'Muircheartaigh, Joe, *Chronicle of Clare 1900–2000*. Ennis: Fag an Bealach, 2000.

O Murchandha, Ciaran, ed., *County Clare Studies*. Ennis: The Clare Archaeological and Historical Society, 2000.

O Suilleabhain, Sean, *Irish Wake Amusements*. Cork and Dublin: Mercier Press, 1997.

Poirteir, Catl, ed., *The Great Irish Famine*. Dublin: RTE/Mercier Press, 1995.

Poverty Before the Famine, County Clare 1835. Ennis: CLASP Press, 1996.

Power, Samantha, *"A Problem from Hell": America and the Age of Genocide*. New York: Perennial, 2003.

Ruckenstein, Lelia, and James A. O'Malley, eds., *Everything Irish*. New York: Ballantine Books, 2003.

Spellissy, Sean, *A History of County Clare*. Dublin: Gill & Macmillan, 2003.

Sweeney, Matthew, *Blue Shoes*. London: Secker & Warburg, 1989.

Toibin, Colm, and Diarmaid Ferriter, *The Irish Famine: A Documentary*. London: Profile Books, 1999.

Westropp, T. J., *Folklore of Clare*. Ennis: CLASP Press, 2000.

White, Anna MacBride, and A. Norman Jeffares, eds., *The Gonne–Yeats Letters 1893–1938 Always your friend*. London: Pimlico, 1993.

Woodham-Smith, Cecil, *The Great Hunger: Ireland 1845–1849*. London: Hamish Hamilton, 1962, Penguin Books Edition, 1991.

Woods, MacDora, *Stopping the Lights at Ranelagh*. Dublin: Dedalus Press, 1997.

Yeats, William Butler, *The Collected Works of W. B. Yeats Volume I: The Poems: Revised Second Edition*. New York: Scribner, 1996.

Permissions